A SEMANTIC STUDY OF TRANSITIVITY RELATIONS IN CHINESE

A SEMANTIC STUDY OF TRANSITIVITY
RELATIONS IN CHINESE

BY

SHOU-HSIN TENG

254

UNIVERSITY OF CALIFORNIA PRESS

BERKELEY • LOS ANGELES • LONDON

UNIVERSITY OF CALIFORNIA PUBLICATIONS IN LINGUISTICS

Volume 80
Approved for publication May 17, 1974

Issued August 1, 1975

University of California Press
Berkeley and Los Angeles
California

University of California Press, Ltd.
London, England

ISBN: 0-520-09520-0

Library of Congress Catalog Card Number: 74-620100

CONTENTS

CONTENTS (Cont'd)

ABBREVIATIONS

AN   — auxiliary noun, classifier, or measure (ge, ben, etc.)

asp   — perfective or inchoative aspect (le)

exp   — experiential aspect (guo)

g.p.   — genitive particle (de)

i.p.   — inchoative particle (qilai)

l.v.   — locative verb (zai)

m.p.   — modificational particle (de)

Neg   — negation (bu or mei)

part   — particle (ma, ne, etc.)

p.p.   — passive particle (bei, jiao, etc.)

p.t.   — pre-transitive (ba)

p.s.   — progressive suffix (zhe)

p.v.   — progressive verb (zai)

Pro-V.   — pro-verb (nong)

s.p.   — successful particle (zhao or dao)

X   — reduplication

Author's note: Romanization of Chinese sentences is in the Pin Yin system.

PREFACE

This work studies the semantic roles of nominal elements occurring in a sentence. These roles are dichotomized into Transitivity and Circumstantial relations, the criteria for which are fully developed, and only the former type of relations constitutes the scope of this study.

A set of Transitivity relations, namely, Agent, Patient, Range, Goal, and Causer, is established to account for the various semantic ranges of the traditional designation of subject and object. Their semantic and syntactic characteristics are given.

These relations are developed within a semantic framework in which verb-centrality is postulated, and the inadequacies of the noun-centrality theory are discussed. The inter-relationship of verbs and nouns is discussed within this framework, and classification of verbs in terms of these relations is also presented.

I would like to express my gratitude to my dissertation advisers; Professor Wallace Chafe, chairman, for his enlightening instruction as well as careful and untiring guidance throughout the entire dissertation, the influence of whose teaching is explicit in every page; Professor Kun Chang, for both his detailed and penetrating examination of the entire work and his constant suggestions, encouragement, and concern; Professor William Wang, whose pioneering works on Chinese transformational grammar initiated my interest in the field, for discussing the organization and for his encouragement and confidence in me when this work was being undertaken.

Professor Chao Yuen Ren read the theoretical foundations of this work, and I benefited from his valuable suggestions and comments. Without his monumental work on Chinese grammar, I would certainly have been drowned in the deep sea of collected material.

My deep appreciation is due to Janet Hamilton Teng, my wife, not only for typing my near unintelligible manuscript, but also for acting as my English informant and for constructing innumerable starred sentences in English to illustrate the point in Chinese.

I would also like to thank Samuel Cheung for being my constant Chinese informant and audience and Arax Kizirian, of POLA, for typing the dissertation.

CHAPTER 1

Introduction to Three Grammatical Theories

In this chapter, three grammatical theories — Fillmore's case grammar, Halliday's systemic grammar, and Chafe's grammar — will be briefly introduced. Only the bare outline and the mechanical apparatus of each grammar are presented in this chapter. General properties which differentiate one theory from the other will be presented in Chapter 2. The scope of discussion is limited to the organization of the underlying structures. How various underlying structures in each theory are transformationally realized in the surface structure will not concern us.

1. The Case Grammar

The significance of the case grammar, as presented in Fillmore (1968), is best illustrated against the perspective of the current syntactic theory, as presented in Chomsky (1965). In Chomsky's framework, the functions of nouns are wholly definable by and thus derivative from the configurations which hold among different grammatical categories (such as S, NP, and VP). Thus, e.g. the following definitions are possible

subject-of = [NP,S] — i.e. NP which is immediately dominated by S
direct-object-of = [NP,VP] — i.e. NP which is immediately dominated by VP

In this way, the functions, e.g. subject and object, are defined by relations and are not necessary notions in the specification of sentences. This type of specification Fillmore refers to as "pure relations" (1968:16).

Fillmore (1970) has demonstrated that the "pure relations" grammar imposes too much structuring on the grammatical categories in the underlying structure so that certain generalizations are missed. For example, in the following sentences

(1) a. The door opened.
    b. John opened the door.
    c. The key opened the door.

'the door' in (a), 'John' in (b) and 'the key' in (c) are specified with the relation [NP,S] and are thus "subject," but it is obvious that 'John' is an actor in the way that 'the door' and 'the key' are not. The subject of the verb receives three, in our example, different semantic interpretations. Consequently, three different verbs, all realized as 'open,' have to be established to accommodate different selectional restriction; one, an intransitive verb, takes an inanimate subject, another, transitive, takes an animate subject, and the third, transitive also, takes an inanimate subject. That is, these verbs have different specifications in the lexicon, as below,

(2) a. − [−NP] , + [−animate] − #
    b. + [−NP] , + [+animate] − [−animate]
    c. + [−NP] , + [−animate] − [−animate]

The second inadequacy of this grammar is that it cannot capture the fact that 'the door' in all these sentences is understood to undergo the same type of process, i.e. the role is constant in all three cases, but it is a subject in (a) but object in (b) and (c). The relatedness of the verbs and of the nouns in question cannot be captured in this "subject-object" grammar.

Fillmore thus proposes to assign constant values to nouns which apparently play the same role in different environments; 'the door' is Objective in all three cases and 'John,' as Agentive, and 'the key,' as Instrumental, enter the construction as optional roles. In this way, we need only to postulate one verb with the specification [–Objective (Agentive) (Instrumental)]. A consequence of this postulation is that the underlying structure is no longer structured so as to define the grammatical functions such as subject and object. Instead, the different roles, i.e. cases, are unordered in the underlying structure, and a set of transformations distributes nouns into their appropriate positions. "Subject" and "Object" are then surface structure notions. In contrast to "pure relations," as in Chomsky's framework, Fillmore's relations between nouns are "labelled."

Fillmore's case categories are given below (see 1968:25 for definitions of these cases).

Agentive (A): e.g. *He* cried.
Instrumental (I): e.g. He cut the rope *with a knife.*
Dative (D): e.g. *He* is tall. / He killed *a bird.*
Factitive (F): e.g. He sang *a song.*
Locative (L): e.g. He is *in the house.*
Objective (O): e.g. He bought *a book.*
Benefactive (B): e.g. He sang a song *for Mary.*
Essive (E): e.g. He is *a student.*
Comitative (C): e.g. He sang a song *with Mary.*

Cases are generated into a sentence in the following manner. A sentence consists of two major constituents, Modality (M) and Proposition (P), i.e.

$S \rightarrow M + P$

The Modality component includes such elements as negation, tense, mood, and aspect. Proposition is then expanded into a verb and one or more cases (C), i.e.

$P \rightarrow V + C_1 + C_2 \ldots C_n$

Each case then expands into a case-marker (K) and an NP, i.e.

$C \rightarrow K + NP.$

The resulting phrase structure is as in figure 1.

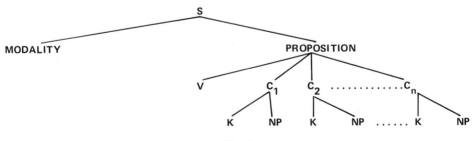

Fig. 1

2. The Systemic Grammar

Central to the Systemic Grammar as presented in Halliday (1967a, 1967b, 1968) are two components, experiential and discoursal or informational. The experiential component defines "the linguistic expression of the speaker's experience of the external world." It provides "a conceptual framework for the encoding of experience in terms of processes, objects, persons, qualities, states, abstractions and relations" (1968:209). Within this component is defined "transitivity," which sets up the "content" organization within the sentence as its scope.

The informational component, on the other hand, defines "grammar above the sentence" (1968:210), within which the speaker relates one sentence to another. The notions "given" and "new" information are thus defined in this component and not in the experiential component.

Our concern in this thesis is the notional organization within a sentence, and we shall in this chapter focus our attention primarily on the experiential component. This component corresponds to the organization of case categories in the case grammar.

Transitivity refers to "a network of systems whose point of origin is the 'major' clause, the clause containing a predication" (1967a:38).

Three types of major clause (hereafter sentence) are postulated, as given in (1).

(1) a. Action sentences: Action here includes physical and abstract processes. It is not confined to activities alone, and not all these sentences are answerable to "what is X doing?" Thus sentences of this type may include the following verbs: wash, throw, sell, march, fall down, rain, and open. However, action sentences do define "events."

   b. Mental-process sentences: These consist of four sub-types: reaction (like, hate), perception (hear, see), cognition (believe, realize), and verbalization (say, promise).

   c. Relational sentences: These include two sub-types: ascriptive (be, look) in which an attribute (either an adjective or a substantive) is assigned to an attribuant, and equative (be, resemble) in which an identification is assigned to an identifier.

Action, mental-process, and relation are then the three types of processes underlying all sentences. The following categories are operative in these three types of sentences:

(2) a. In action sentences:
   Actor: Subject of a transitive (directed action) or intransitive (non-directed action) verb
               E.g. *She* washed the clothes.
               The prisoners marched.
   Goal: Object of a transitive verb.
               E.g. She washed *the clothes*.
   Range: Object of a non-directed action verb
               E.g. He ran *the race*.
   Initiator: Subject of an intransitive verb used transitively
               E.g. *He* marched the prisoners.
   Benefactive: Indirect object
               E.g. He gave *John* the book.

b.   In mental-process sentences:
    Processor: Subject of a mental-process verb
            E.g. *He* likes the play.
    Phenomenon: Object of a mental-process verb
            E.g. He likes *the play*.
            (also *The play* pleases me.)

c.   In relational sentences:
    Attribuant: Subject of an ascriptive verb
            E.g. *She* looks happy.
    Attribute: Complement of an ascriptive verb
            E.g. She looks *happy*.
            She is a *student*.

The following categories are developed to inter-relate these three types of sentences at the most abstract level,

(3) a.   Cause: Actor of a directed action verb and Initiator
    b.   Affected: Actor of a non-directed action verb, Goal of a directed action verb, Processor, and Attribuant
    c.   Range: Range of an action verb, Phenomenon, and Attribute

These three categories define the participation network of a sentence, and other categories such as Beneficiary, Instrument, Manner, Time and Place enter into relationship with, and not as the constituents of, the participation network.

The generation of sentences is as follows. A set of grammatical features of sentences are selected out of a network of options, e.g. effective (directed action) and descriptive (non-directed action) (see Halliday 1967a:47 and 1968:201-3). The combinations of these (grammatical) features determine the selection of types of sentences, types of verbs, and types of participation nouns. Thus a sentence such as

(4) Mary bought a car.

is specified as

Action: effective: operative: goal - transitive

which constitutes the grammatical description of the sentence. The feature "action" determines that the verb occurring in the sentence must be an action verb, as opposed to a mental-process verb, and the feature "effective" selects an action verb out of the sub-class of verbs which take "goal." In his framework, verbs are sub-classified into three classes:

Class O, e.g. seem, Class I, e.g. march, and Class II, e.g. wash.

Class O verbs occur in relational sentences, Class I verbs in descriptive sentences, and Class II verbs in effective sentences.

3.   The Chafian Grammar

The grammatical theory presented in Chafe (1970) states that every sentence is built around a predicative element. A predicative element is a necessary component of most types of utterance and can be referred to as verb. In most cases, a verb is accompanied by one or more arguments or nouns. The semantic roles which the accompanying nouns play in given sentences are not independently selected in the process of sentence generation as in the case grammar but are uniquely specified by verbs in question. In other words, once a type of verb is selected, a definite role is automatically assigned to the nouns which accompany the verb. Therefore this theory postulates the centrality of verbs.

In the generation of the semantic structure, verbs are selected by means of a set of selectional units. At the highest level, three such units are recognized, viz. Action, Process, and State. These units may co-occur, though subject to severe constraints. (In fact, only "process" and "action" may co-occur.) To satisfy the well-formedness of a semantic structure containing one (or two) such units, one (or two) participant nouns have to be specified. The well-formedness of various types of semantic structures are shown in Diagram A.

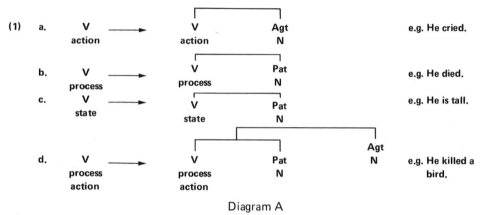

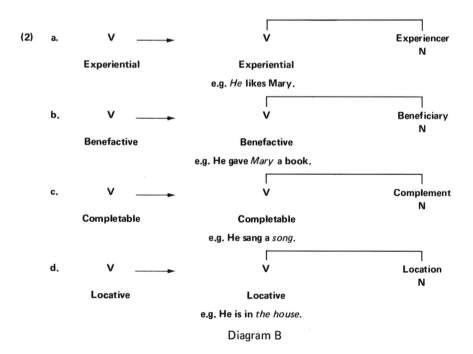

Diagram A

Chafe states, on the centrality of verbs, that "It is the verb which is the control center of a sentence, determining by its own internal specification what the rest of the sentence will contain" (1970:165).

Diagram B

Other selectional units which sub-categorize the primary three types of verbs are Experiential, Benefactive, Completable, and Locative. These features further dictate the presence of other participant nouns, as in Diagram B.

Another relation is Instrumental, which is different from the others "in not being associated with a particular selectional unit within the verb. There is nothing parallel to 'Benefactive' or 'Experiential' which requires the verb to have an accompanying instrument. What is necessary ... is that the verb be specified as an action-process" (1970:152). It can be introduced in the manner shown in Diagram C.

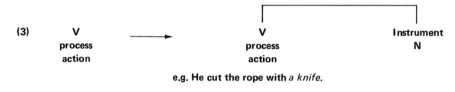

e.g. **He cut the rope with** *a knife.*

Diagram C

The above is a short sketch of the essential verb-noun relations postulated in the Chafian grammar. The features of the verbs, viz. Action, Process, and State are quite distinct from the roles Agent, Patient, Beneficiary etc., in the sense that the former group of features are selectional units, which impose classifications of verbs. Some verbs, for example, are intrinsically Action verbs and cannot in normal circumstances function as Process or State verbs. But in the area of nouns, no claim can possibly be made that certain nouns are intrinsically Agent, Patient, etc. These relations are only temporary roles assigned to nouns when they accompany certain verbs. At the most, it can be stated that certain types of nouns do not function in certain capacities. For example, no inanimate nouns can be Experiencers. This kind of constraint will be discussed in later chapters.

Both verbs and nouns may be inflected. Nominal inflections include number and definite, and verbal inflections include tense and aspect. However, while the former inflections modify nouns alone, the latter inflections modify the whole sentence. This treatment is in agreement with that of the case grammar, in which such inflections as tense and aspect are constituents of Modality, indicating that these inflections have the entire proposition as the scope of modification.

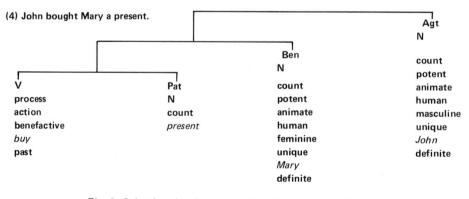

Fig. 2 Selectional units: occurring directly below V or N
Lexical units: those which are italicized
Inflectional units: those which occur below italics

There are then four types of features occurring with both verbs and nouns in the underlying structure. The highest in the hierarchy are the all-inclusive units, verb and noun. Selectional units, e.g. Action, State, Animate and Count, narrow down the choice of a particular type of verb or noun. These units sub-classify verbs and nouns. Inflectional units, e.g. tense or number, may occur with all types of verbs or nouns, but a set of constraints has to be obeyed. These constraints on inflectional units are directly statable in terms of selectional units. The fourth type is lexical units, e.g. 'sing' and 'tall,' which specify the information content of a sentence.

All these features are illustrated in the semantic structure of the sentence in figure 2.[1]

[1] In this thesis, 'flat' tree diagrams (or 'mobiles') (adopted from Chafe 1970) refer to underlying (semantic) structures, where linearity is of no theoretical consequence. Standard tree diagrams refer to a level of representation where linearization (Chafe 1967) has already taken place but before any transformation has applied. Thus the latter correspond to the conventional concept of deep structure as presented in Chomsky (1965).

CHAPTER 2

Some Aspects of a Relational Grammar

In this chapter, some general properties are discussed, with a view to comparing the three theories in the last chapter to see how they formulate these properties, and to see in what way they are adequate or inadequate in characterizing them. Finally, in each section a theoretical framework will be postulated which is modified and reformulated from these three theories and which will be adopted in this thesis for the description of Chinese.

1. Generation of Relational Structures

1.1. Generation in Three Theories

In the case grammar, the generation of relational structures (i.e. underlying structures) takes place in two different constituents, viz. Modality and Proposition. The constraints which hold between these two components will be discussed in Section 3, and our attention in this section will be paid to the component of proposition.

In Fillmore's framework, the structure of proposition is formed by generating various case categories. The configuration of various case categories forms the case frames (1968:26-27), which then determine the insertion of verbs. In Halliday's framework, various grammatical features of sentences are first generated (i.e. selected). These features then specifically determine both the types of participants and the types of verbs which may occur in a given sentence. In Chafe's framework, the semantic structure of a sentence is in a sense entirely determined by the selectional features of verbs. The verb features then uniquely specify the types of nominal roles. In other words, the verb features do not "select" types of nouns, but rather they "assign" certain roles to the nouns which occur with them. The selectional features of nouns are generated partly independently and partly in accordance with the verb features. For instance, the selection of the nominal features such as "feminine" and "unique" is in general independent of verbs[1] and the selection of "animate" or "human" is in general determined by verb features.

1.2. Noun-Centrality and Verb-Centrality

We see above that Fillmore postulates the centrality of nouns and Chafe, verbs. The consequences of each postulation will be examined below.

Fillmore states that "At least one case category must be chosen and no case category occurs more than once" (1968:24). The first constraint follows from the fact that the insertion of verbs is dependent on "case frames." If no case is selected, then no verb may be inserted. The result would be the absence of the entire proposition. This constraint, however, contradicts the following data, in which no verb-noun relation is observed.

---

[1] 'Feminine' in some cases is determined by verbs, so that 'piaoliang' – 'pretty' may not occur with masculine adults and 'shuai' occurs only with masculine adults.

(1) a. Zheli hao men.
here very stifling
(It's very stifling here.)

b. Wuzi-li hen an.
house-inside very dark
(It's very dark in the house.)

c. Dixiashi-li hen chaoshi.
basement-inside very damp
(It's very damp in the basement.)

These are usually called "subjectless" sentences. In English they may include meteorological sentences such as "It is raining," but their Chinese counterparts may not be analyzed in the same way.[2]

It may be argued that the locative phrases in (1) are in fact the Locative case category as postulated by Fillmore. Fillmore's Locative includes both spatial and temporal references. It is usually the case that subjectless sentences occur with locative and temporal references, but our issue here is whether these references constitute a case category in the proposition. Fillmore suggests that there may be two types of Locative, namely outer Locative and inner Locative (1968:26, Ft. 24), the former occurring in the Modality and the latter in Proposition. In this analysis, sentences in (1) may receive two

---

[2] For instance, the verb-noun sequences in

(i) a. Xia yu le.
down rain asp
(It started raining.)

b. Xia xue le.
down snow asp
(It started to snow.)

may not be postulated as unanalyzable units, corresponding to 'to rain' and 'to snow' in English, since we also observe

(ii) a. Yu xia da le.
rain down big asp
(The rain started to fall more heavily.)

b. Xue xia da le.
snow down big asp
(The snow started to fall more heavily.)

Moreover, compare the deletions below,

(iii) a. Ta zuotian yao; jintian bu yao le.
he yesterday want; today Neg want asp
(He wanted it yesterday; he doesn't want it today.)

b. Zuotian xia yu; jintian bu xia le.
yesterday down rain; today Neg down rain asp
(It rained yesterday; it is not raining today.)

The deletion of 'he' in (a) falls within the regular pattern of nominal anaphoricization, and the deletion of 'rain' in (b) should be similarly accounted for. There is no difference between 'he' and 'rain' in this regard. It will be postulated here then that meteoroligical sentences in Chinese in fact consist of Agent (natural force) and Action verb. That the Agent in these sentences usually occurs post-verbally is not unique. It is shared by many instances of non-anticipated occurrences of events, e.g.

(iv) a. Lai le yi-ge ren.
come asp one-AN person
(Someone's coming.)

b. Pao le yi-zhi tuzi.
run asp one-AN rabbit
(A rabbit got away.)

descriptions, but they are not ambiguous sentences. It is an arbitrary decision to choose one or the other, and thus such an analysis is inadequate. Pre-verbal locatives may be defined as outer Locative and post-verbal locatives as inner Locative in Chinese. Only inner Locative is subject to Locative-transportation, i.e., while inner Locative may be pre-posed to the pre-verbal position outer Locative may not be post-posed, e.g.,

(2)   a.   Ta zai fangzi-li xie zi.
             he l.v. house-inside write word
             (He is writing in the house.)
     b.   *Ta ba zi xie zai fangzi-li.
             he p.t. word write l.v. house-inside
     c.   Ta zai heiban-shang xie zi.
             he l.v. blackboard-top write word
             (He is writing (characters) on the blackboard.)
     d.   Ta ba zi xie zai heiban-shang.
             he p.t. word write l.v. blackboard-top

Using this criterion, we find that the Locative in (1) can not be post-posed, e.g.

(3)   a.   *Hen men zai zheli.
             very stifling l.v.
     b.   *Hen an zai wuzi-li.[3]
             very dark l.v. house-inside

Thus sentences in (1) contain only outer Locative. Furthermore, if we follow Lakoff (1968b) and analyze (outer) Locative as originating from a higher sentence, we observe that the lower S in (1) contain no nominal elements at all.

Verbs such as 'men' — 'stifling' and 'an' — 'dark' are referred to in Chafe (1970) as Ambient verbs. They require no participant nouns. This peculiar property of these verbs may be directly stated on the verbs themselves. That is, in the process of sentence generation, if the verb feature Ambient is selected, no accompanying nouns are required. This is one respect in which the case grammar fails, since nouns in the case grammar are given primary status and are to govern the insertion of verbs.

The second constraint, that no case category appears more than once, has to do with phrasal conjunction and comitative. Compare the following pair of sentences,

(4)   a.   Wo gen ta xiang mingtian yikuar chuqu.
             I and he think tomorrow together out-go
             (He and I would like to go out together tomorrow.)
     b.   Wo xiang mingtian gen ta yikuar chuqu.
             I think tomorrow with he together out-go
             (I would like to go out with him tomorrow.)

(a) is phrasal conjunction and (b) is a comitative sentence (cf. Lakoff and Peters 1969 and my paper "Comitative versus phrasal conjunction" 1970). Phrasal conjunction involves two nouns of identical case categories, while comitative is a separate category — which involves the notion of 'principality' (Teng 1970).

(5)   a.   Zhang San gen Li Si yikuar ba xiaotou zhau-zhu le.

---

[3] Prof. Y. R. Chao pointed out to me that these sentences can be grammatical if the Locative nouns are given as afterthought 'subject'. In this reading, there is usually a slight pause before the Locative.

Z.S. and L.S. together p.t. thief catch-firm asp

(Z.S. and L.S. caught the thief together.)

b. Zhang San gen Li Si yiqi bei xiaotou da-shang le.

Z.S. and L.S. together p.p. thief hit-injured asp

(Z.S. and L.S. were injured together by the thief.)

c. Zhang San ba shu gen bi yikuar diu le.

Z.S. p.t. book and pen together lose asp

(Z.S. lost his books and pens together.)

d. Wang Er gei Zhang Xiansheng gen Zhang Taitai mai-le

W.E. give Z. Mr. and Z. Mrs. buy-asp

yige liwu

one-AN present

(W.E. bought a present for Mr. and Mrs. Zhang.)

(a) is 'A+A', (b) 'D+D', (c) 'O+O', and (d) 'B+B'. For constraints on the double occurrence of other cases see Appendices 1 and 2 in my paper (1970).

The important issue here is the generation of the semantic structure of phrasal conjunction. There are two basic types of phrasal conjunction, viz. circumstantial and lexical (see Teng 1970), e.g.

(6) a. Xiao Ming gen Xiao Hua yikuar chu-qu le.

X.M. and X.H. together out-go asp

(X.M. and X.H. went out together.)

b. Xiao Ming gen Xiao Hua zai dajia.

X.M. and X.H. p.v. fight

(X.M. and X.H. are fighting.)

(a) is "circumstantial" and (b) "lexical."

Lexical phrasal (i.e. more than one occurrence of a given case) is uniquely determined by multiple-reference verbs such as 'dajia' — 'fight,' 'shangliang' — 'negotiate,' and 'taolun' — 'discuss.' To guarantee the well-formedness of the semantic structures containing these verbs and to differentiate this case from the circumstantial case, we have to mark multiple-reference as a selectional feature of verbs in question and not to depend on the case frame.

What we have seen in this section is that the generation of semantic structures has to be controlled by verbs. To determine verbs by means of nouns, as is possible in the case grammar, cannot account for sentences involving Ambient and multiple-reference verbs.

1.3. Inherent vs. Circumstantial and Sentential Features

In the last section we have seen cases of Ambient and Multiple-reference due to the intrinsic nature of verbs. These characteristics are marked as the lexical property of these verbs. But in the following sentences,

(7) a. Zhang San mai-le yi-liang xin che.

Z.S. buy-asp one-AN new car

(Z.S. bought a new car.)

b. Zhang San gei ta taitai mai-le yi-liang xin che.

Z.S. give he wife buy-asp one-AN new car

(Z.S. bought a new car for his wife.)

(8) a. Zhang San xie-le yishou shi.

Z.S. write-asp one-AN poem
(Z.S. wrote a poem.)
  b. Zhang San gei ta taitai xie-le yishou shi.
      Z.S. give he wife write-asp one-AN poem
      (Z.S. wrote a poem to his wife.)

we notice that the Benefactive phrase is optional in both (7) and (8), but there is a difference. In (7.a), though the Benefactive phrase is absent, we still understand that Z.S. himself is the Beneficiary noun (or Goal, see Chapter 7). The same cannot be said of (8.a). We can account for this difference by postulating verbs such as 'mai' — 'buy' as Benefactive verbs and verbs such as 'xie' — 'write' as not intrinsically Benefactive. There are two ways to account for sentences such as (8). We may either postulate 'xie' as taking up the feature Benefactive in this particular context or postulate Benefactive as a feature of the sentence as a whole. The former alternative is attractive for the reason that the Benefactive phrase can be generated in the semantic structure neatly by the feature Benefactive occurring with verb, similar to the intrinsic feature Ambient or Multiple-reference specifying no noun at all or two (or more) nouns. But this approach becomes unsatisfactory in the case of other features such as Instrumental and Volitional. When a verb such as 'xie' occurs in the sentences

(9) a. Zhang San xie-le yifeng xin.
         Z.S. write-asp one-AN letter
         (Z.S. wrote a letter.)
     b. Zhang San yong maobi xie-le yifeng xin.
         Z.S. use brush-pen write-asp one-AN letter
         (Z.S. wrote a letter with a brush-pen.)

can we say that 'xie' is an instrumental verb in (b) but not in (a)? And in the following sentences,

(10) a. Ta bu xiao-xin ba zhi men ti-le yige dong.
          he Neg careful p.t. paper door kick-asp one-AN hole
          (He carelessly kicked a hole in the paper door.)
      b. Ta sheng-qi-qi lai ba zhi men ti-le yige dong.
          he angry+i.p. p.t. paper door kick-asp one-AN hole
          (He angrily kicked a hole in the paper door.)

(a) is a non-volitional sentence and (b) volitional. Can we say that the same verb is volitional in (b) and non-volitional in (a)? It seems that intentionality has to do with Agents and not with the property of verbs.[4]

We shall postulate these optional features as "grammatical features" (Halliday 1967-8) of sentences. These grammatical features will be referred to as sentential features. In Chafe's framework, the optional occurrence of Benefactive and Instrumental is

---

[4] In some cases, the features 'happening' and 'doing' (cf. Halliday 1968:198ff) are directly determined by verbs. In other words, some verbs incorporate the feature 'happening', e.g.
  a. Ta tiao xia qu le. (doing)
      he jump down go asp
      (He jumped down.)
  b. Ta diao xia qu le. (happening)
      he fall down go asp
      (He fell down.)
Refer to section 4.2 of this chapter for more discussions of 'feature incorporation'.

introduced in the manner shown in Diagram D (refer to Section 5.3 of this chapter for an alternative analysis).

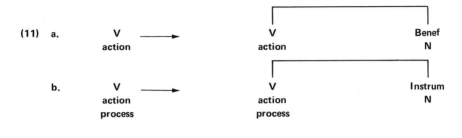

(11) a.

V		V	Benef
action	→	action	N

b.

V		V	Instrum
action	→	action	N
process		process	

Diagram D

I shall understand this generation mechanism to be the equivalent of postulating sentential features, which control the generation of these phrases, since the notion "optionality" has to do entirely with the "informational content" of a sentence and not with the "cognitive experience" of the speaker.

There is a clear difference between Benefactive and Instrumental on the one hand and Volitional and Happening on the other. Benefactive is a constituent which must be selected by Benefactive verbs but may be selected by other Action verbs. Instrumental is always optionally selected, subject to the selectional features of verbs. On the other hand, Volitional and Happening reflect how a sentence is reported by the speaker and how he evaluates the events in question. In Fillmore's framework, these features occur in the Modality constituent of a sentence. Volitionality may be specified in the manner shown in Diagram E.

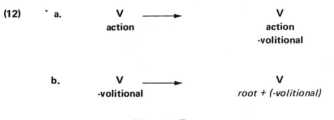

(12) a.

V		V
action	→	action
		-volitional

b.

V		V
-volitional	→	root + (-volitional)

Diagram E

That verbs may select 'non-volitional' and not 'volitional' reflects the fact that the unmarked reading of verbs is that of "volitional." (b) allows for the morphological realization of the feature (refer to Chapter 4, Section 3).

Another example of sentential features is Passive. Passive in Chinese cannot be analyzed as derived from the active counterpart through different topicalizations to do with the "discourse structure" (cf. Halliday 1968 and Chafe 1970, Chapter 15). Passive in Chinese conveys the feature "pejorative" in most cases (L. Wang 1944, Vol. 1:181). In the following pair of sentences,

(13) a.   Zhang San kan-jian Li Si.
      Z.S. look-see L.S.
      (Z.S. saw L.S.)

b.   Li Si bei Zhang San kan-jianle.
L.S. p.p. Z.S. look-see asp
(L.S. was seen by Z.S.)

Li Si in (a) can be treated as Phenomenon, in Halliday's sense, in that Li Si's role is only as the object of Zhang San's perception, but Li Si in (b) is not only the "topic" of the whole sentence but is also depicted as a kind of "sufferer." Apparently, the feature "pejorative" has nothing to do with the property of verbs in question.[5] It is derived from the speaker's subjective rendering of the event. It reflects how the role of Li Si is viewed by the speaker in this case. For this reason, Passive or Pejorative will be postulated as a sentential feature. Even here, it is not without problem if we want to postulate that the feature "pejorative" reflects how the surface subject, the "sufferer" as has been described, is viewed by the speaker, for in the following cases, such a description is highly inappropriate, e.g.

(14) a.   Fan bei gou chi-le.
rice p.p. dog eat-asp
(The rice was eaten by a dog.)
b.   Chezi bei ta chuang-huai-le.
car p.p. he bump-bad-asp
(The car was damaged by his bumping it into something.)

It is the whole event and not the subject that is viewed by the speaker as "unfortunate."

Even though the status of sentential features is different from that of verb features, there are constraints which hold between them. "Volitional" occurs only with Action verbs, "Happening" generally with Process verbs and "Pejorative" never with adjectives.

In conclusion, I shall simply quote Chafe's position about the generation of semantic structures. He states that "It is the verb which is the control center of a sentence, determining by its own internal specification what the rest of the sentence will contain — not completely, of course, but to a significant degree" (1970:165). The only qualification on this quotation which we have seen in Section 1.3 is that some features (i.e. sentential features) are not the internal specifications of certain verbs, but rather they reflect how an event occurs and how the speaker evaluates an event. Centrality of verbs will be one of the major grammatial concepts adopted in this thesis for the description and analysis of Chinese.

2.   Selectional Restrictions

In the syntactic theory presented in Chomsky (1965), selectional restrictions are stated in terms of a set of features such as "animate" and "human." The verb 'sha' — 'kill' in the sentences,

(1) a.   Ta sha-le yizhi ji.
he kill-asp one-AN chicken
(He killed a chicken.)
b.   *Ta sha-le yige qiu.
he kill-asp one-AN ball

---

[5] 'Pejorative' is postulated as a lexical property of verbs in C.Li (1969). It is beyond my understanding how verbs such as 'kan-jian' — 'see' (this is a verb compound and not a lexical verb) can be pejorative. The sense of 'pejorative', to me, is the meaning of the whole sentence, of how the event which is reported evaluated by the speaker.

(He killed a ball.)
- c. *Qiu sha-le yizhi ji.
ball kill-asp one-AN chicken
(The ball killed a chicken.)
- d. *Lang sha-le yizhi ji.
wolf kill-asp one-AN chicken
(The wolf killed a chicken.)

has the selectional specification

(2) 'sha' — 'kill': [+human] ____ [+animate]

This is a fact and has to be accounted for in any grammatical theory. In the case theory, 'sha' — 'kill' receives the case frame

(3) 'sha': [____ D + A]

This case specification achieves two tasks simultaneously; firstly it specifies the semantic roles the nouns play which are associated with 'sha,' and secondly it automatically specifies the animacy of both nouns involved by the definition of these case categories.

(4) a. Agentive → +Animate
    b. Dative   → +Animate

However, note that this case specification for stating selectional restrictions is adequate in this instance only for the data in English, since the translation of (1d) is grammatical in English. In Chinese, we need to specify the feature [human] instead of [animate] for the agent of 'sha.'

Again, the different case specifications in the following sentences account neatly for animateness,

(5) a. Neidong fangzi hen gao. [____ O]
        that-AN house very tall
        (That house is very tall.)
    b. Ta gege hen gao. [____ D]
        he elder-brother very tall
        (His elder brother is very tall.)

However, the question is, what is gained by attempting to capture the different roles of nouns by ignoring the relatedness of verbs? The different specifications in (5) obviously neglect the fact that there is only one verb 'gao' — 'tall' involved in both cases. How significant is the fact that the noun in (a) is inanimate and that in (b) is animate? It is more appropriate to postulate that animateness is a further specification of a semantic role shared by both nouns in (5). This is the approach in both Chafe (1970) and Halliday (1967-8), in the former Patient is postulated for both and in the latter, Affected.

The specification of animateness for verbs such as 'gao' — 'tall,' 'ganjing' — 'clean,' and 're' — 'hot' is circumstantial in the sense that either plus or minus animate may occur with them, whereas for verbs such as 'pang' — 'fat (human)' vs. 'fei' — 'fat (animals),' the specification has to be one or the other, i.e. not circumstantial but lexical. The first group, then, need not be marked as regards selectional restrictions. The difference in specifications is shown below,

(6) a. V_{state} : gao-'tall', ganjing-'clean', re-'hot'

b.   V
     state   : qiong-'poor', yan-'strict', heqi-'kind'
     human

c.   V
     state   : fei-'fat', xunfu-'tamed'
     animate
     -human

d.   V
     state   : lan-'lazy', ke-'thirsty', huopo-'lively'
     animate

The same mechanism can be applied to verbs with more than one accompanying noun, e.g.

(7) a.   V
     process
     action   : sha-'kill,' pian-'trick,' dai-'catch'
     human Agt
     animate Pat

b.   V
     process
     action   : guan-'close,' ba-'extract,' ban-'move'
     -animate Pat

It is not within the capacity of the present case grammar to specify these various kinds of selectional restrictions merely by means of the case frame, although it is not difficult to modify the case grammar such that information as seen in (6) and (7) can be incorporated into the specifications of case relations, so that, for instance, verbs in both (6.b) and (c) will receive identical case roles but with different specifications as regards selectional features. This is in fact the approach in Chafe (1970), as commented above.

3.   Occurrence Restrictions

Occurrence restrictions here will be loosely used to cover any constraints on the occurrence of an element, including the frequently talked about notion "co-occurrence restrictions."

3.1. Constraints on Verb Inflections

Recall that in the case grammar, a sentence is generated in two constituents, viz. Modality and Proposition, in the former are included "such modalities on the sentence-as-a-whole as negation, tense, mood and aspect" (Fillmore 1968:23), and in the latter are included verb and a set of case categories. We shall in this section concentrate on the aspectual inflections of verbs. Our concern here is how to state the constraints and not what the constraints are.

In Lakoff (1966), a set of syntactic characteristics is presented, which differentiate Active verbs and Stative verbs. Three of them are shown below,

(1) a.   Only Active verbs may occur in the imperative construction.
    b.   Only Active verbs may occur in the progressive aspect.
    c.   Only Active verbs may occur with manner adverbs.

E.g.

(2) a. Ni kan zijide shu!
you read self-g.p. book
(Read your own book!)

b. Ta zai kan shu.
he p.v. read book
(He is reading books.)

c. Ta xihuan jingjingde kan shu.
he like quietly read book
(He likes reading books quietly.)

(3) a. *Ni zhidao tade mingzi!
you know his name
(Know his name!)

b. *Ta zai zhidao wode mingzi.
he p.v. know my name
(*He is knowing my name.)

c. *Ta hen rexinde zhidao wode mingzi.
he very enthusiastically know my name
(*He knows my name enthusiastically.)

Lakoff's postulation, as stated in (1), is to state the constraints by means of verb features. Fillmore, on the other hand, takes another position. He comments that

"The question we need to ask is whether Lakoff's features are primitives in the lexical entries for verbs, or whether they permit reduction to concepts of the type I have been outlining (i.e. case frames)" (1968:31).

In other words, statements in (1) may be reformulated as in (4).

(4) a. Only Agentive may occur in the imperative construction.

b. Only verbs which take Agentive may occur in the progressive and perfective (see 5 below) aspects.

c. Only Agentive may occur with manner adverbs.

For our discussion of aspectual inflections, we need to add the perfective aspect, which does not occur with state verbs, e.g.

(5) a. Ta mei kan shu. [___ A]
he Neg+asp read book
(He didn't read books.)

b. *Ta mei zhidao wode mingzi. [___ D]
he Neg+asp know my name
(He didn't know my name.)

The ungrammaticality of sentences in (3) and (5b) follows from the fact that they contain Dative instead of Agentive. Thus in the case grammar, the constraint which holds between Modality and Proposition is that the progressive and perfective aspects may not occur in Modality if the case category Agentive is absent from Proposition.

However, in the following sentences

(6) a. Ta mei si. [___ D]
he Neg+asp die
(He didn't die.)

    b. Pingzi mei po. [___ O]
       bottle Neg+asp break
       (The bottle didn't break.)
    c. *Ta mei ben. [___ D]
       he Neg+asp stupid
       (He didn't become stupid.)

the perfective aspect occurs with Dative and Objective. The question is not so much whether it is factually correct to state that perfective occurs only with Agentive (obviously it is not), as how to state the restriction.

If the constraint is to be stated in terms of case categories, we find that perfective occurs with Agentive, a type of Dative (6a) and Objective, and does not occur with another type of Dative (6c). How do we differentiate these two types of Dative? Note that when the proposition constituents of (6a) and (c) are ideatical how can we state different constraints in their Modality constituents? It is clear the constraint has to be stated in terms of verb features, as proposed by Lakoff (1966). However, his single opposition "active vs. stative" is not adequate, since the problem of verbs such as 'si' – 'die' and 'po' – 'break' still remains. Note that Lakoff's discovery procedure would classify these verbs together with other stative verbs, e.g.

    (7) a. *Ni si! (Except as a curse.)
        you die!
      b. *Ta zai si.
        he p.v. die
        (He is dying.)
      c. *Ta hen yuanyide si-le.
        he very willingly die-asp
        (He died very willingly.)

These verbs are members of the third category of verbs in Chafe (1970), viz. Process. By recognizing this verb feature, we are able to make the following statements,

    (8) a. The progressive aspect may occur only with Action verbs.
      b. The perfective aspect may not occur with State verbs.

What we have seen is that constraints on inflections cannot be stated in terms of case categories. They have to be stated in terms of selectional features of verbs.

So far, we only discuss the independent inflection of individual verbs. We shall now look at cases in which the inflection of embedded verbs is governed by higher verbs. Detailed accounts can be seen in my "Verb inflection constraints in complementations" (1969) and Huddleston (1969, Section 6.5).

Observe that in the following sentences,

    (9) a. Wo zhidao ta hui qu shuijiao.
        I know he will go sleep
        (I know he will go to bed.)
      b. Wo zhidao ta shui-le jiao le.
        I know he sleep-asp nap asp
        (I know he has slept.)
      c. Wo zhidao ta zai shuijiao.
        I know he p.v. sleep
        (I know he is sleeping.)

the embedded verb occurs in plain form (i.e. no inflections), in perfective, and in progressive, respectively. This is a case where the higher verb imposes no constraints on the inflection of the embedded verb. Now, in the following sentences,

(10) a. Ta hen xiang qu shuijiao.
         he very think go sleep
         (He would very much like to go to bed.)
     b. *Ta hen xiang shui-le jiao le.
         he very think sleep-asp nap asp
         (He would very much like to have slept.)
     c. *Ta hen xiang zai shuijiao.
         he very think p.v. sleep
         (He would very much like to be sleeping.)

no inflection may take place in the embedded sentence. The embedded verb has to stand in "futurity" relation to the higher verb. Contrary to this, the embedded verb in the sentences,

(11) a. *Ta hen houhui qu mai shu.
         he very regret go buy book
         (He much regrets going to buy books.)
     b. Ta hen houhui mai-le shu.
         he very regret buy-asp book
         (He much regrets having bought the book.)
     c. *Ta hen houhui zai mai shu.
         he very regret p.v. buy book
         (He much regrets buying books.)

has to take perfective and stand in "anteriority" relation to the higher verb. In my paper (1969) verbs such as 'xiang' – 'think,like' are referred to as "imminent" verbs and verbs such as 'houhui' – 'regret' as "factual."

If we follow Fillmore's proposal to state this constraint, we find that the case categories observed in (9), (10), and (11) are identical; Dative in the higher sentence and Agentive in the embedded sentence. These three different types of dependency relations can not be stated. Again, we have to resort to verb features. The constraints can be stated as below,

(12) a. The embedded verb may not be inflected if it is governed by imminent verbs.
     b. The embedded verb must be in the perfective if it is governed by factual verbs.

3.2. Co-Occurrence of Case Relations

We may roughly classify those case categories as listed in Fillmore (1968) into two groups,

(13) a. Group A: Agentive, Dative, Objective, Factitive, Essive, (inner) Locative.
     b. Group B: Benefactive, Instrumental, (outer) Locative, Comitative.

This classification is according to whether there is co-occurrence restriction holding among case categories, that is, within Group A, the occurrence of, say, Objective in the presence of Agentive is entirely determined by the type of verb in question, whereas the occurrence of a case from Group B in the presence of a case from Group A is not. In this sense, co-occurrence restriction exists only between Group A and Group B. The status of Group B case categories is obvious; they are in general optional and more than one of them may occur simultaneously in a sentence.

Fillmore's abbreviatory device to indicate the possible range of environments a verb may occur in, e.g.

(14) 'kai': [___O (I)(A)]
    a.   Men kai le.
        door open asp
        (The door opened.)
    b.   Ta kai-le men.
        he open-asp door
        (He opened the door.)
    c.   Zhege men, zheba yaoshi buneng kai.
        this-AN door, this-AN key Neg-can open
        (This key cannot open this door.)
    d.   Ta yong zheba yaoshi kaide men.
        he use this-AN key open-m.p. door
        (He opened this door with this key.)

does not truly reflect the notion "optionality" Instrumental in (14) is optional, but Agentive is not optional, in that when it is absent the verb is a Process verb but the verb functions as a Process-Action verb when Agentive is present. The verb property has to remain constant when truly optional elements are absent or present. The shift of verb property is more conspicuous in the pair of verbs below,

(15) a.   Fan hen re.
        rice very hot
        (The rice is very hot.)
    b.   Ta zai re fan.
        he p.v. hot rice
        (He is heating the rice.)

Traditionally, 're' — 'hot' in (a) is analyzed as an adjective and 're' in (b) as a verb. On the other hand, no shift of verb property is observed in the following pair,

(16) a.   Ta mingtian yao lai.
        he tomorrow want come
        (He wants to come tomorrow.)
    b.   Ta mingtian yao gen Zhang Xiaojie lai.
        he tomorrow want with Zhang Miss come
        (Tomorrow he wants to come with Miss Zhang.)

Comitative in (16b) is a true optional constituent.
Now compare the following sentences,

(17) a.   Ta yong dao ba ji sha-sile.
        he use knife p.t. chicken kill-die asp
        (He killed the chicken with a knife.)
    b.   Ta yong shoujang zoulu.
        he use cane walk-road
        (He walks with a cane.)

    c.   *Ta yong hen duo dongxi hen zhong.
         he use very many thing very heavy
         (He is very heavy with many things.)
    d.   *Ta yong dao si le.
         he use knife die asp
         (He died with a knife.)

The co-occurrence restriction of Instrumental may be stated in either of the following two ways,

(18) a.   Instrumental may occur only with Agentive.
      b.   Instrumental may occur only with Action verbs.

It is adequate in this instance to state it in terms of either case categories or verb features.
    On the other hand, the restrictions of Benefactive (not Goal, cf. Chapter 7, Section 6) are more complex, e.g.

(19) a.   Wo gei ta mai-le yiben shu. (action)
         I give he buy-asp one-AN book
         (I bought a book for (=on behalf of) him.)
      b.   Wo zhen ti ni gaozing. (state)
         I true substitute you happy
         (I feel really happy for you.)
      c.   Ta wei zu-guo er si. (process)
         he for father-country thereby die
         (He died for his country.)

Fillmore states that "The occurrence of B expressions is dependent on the presence of an A" (1968:31). This statement contradicts data in Chinese (19.b and c) as well as in English.[6] The most that can be said is that the presence of an Agentive can in most cases freely select Benefactive, but Benefactive is not exclusively accompanying Agentive. In (19), it occurs with Agentive and Dative, but its occurrence with Dative is extremely irregular. The same problem remains with stating the restrictions by verb features. Most Process and State verbs do not occur with Benefactive, e.g.

(20) *Process verbs*:
      a.   *Ta gei wo xing le.
         he give I wake asp
         (He woke up for me.)
      b.   *Ta gei pengyou wang-le zhejian shi le.
         he give friend forget-asp this-AN thing asp
         (He forgot this thing for his friend.)

[6] E.g. a. John died for me.
       b. Please win the next prize for me.
And if Benefactive is to include also the traditional indirect object (cf. Halliday 1967), counter-examples increase significantly,
       c. I owe John ten dollars.
       d. I lost two dollars to John.
       e. I gained him two customers.

(21) *State verbs*:
  a.   *Wo gei ta ai Zhang Xiaojie.
       I give he love Zhang Miss
       (I love Miss Zhang for him.)
  b.   *Wo gei ta zhidao zhe-jian shi.
       I give he know this-AN thing
       (I know this thing for him.)

It seems that only exceptional cases of Process verbs and State verbs occur with Benefactive. How do we state this restriction?

In Lakoff (1965, 1966) the notion "markedness" is utilized to state exceptions in syntax. Using this notion, we may state that unmarked Action verbs (buy, write, mail) and marked non-action (die, happy, ashamed) verbs occur with Benefactive and unmarked non-action (fat, tall, kind) verbs as well as marked action verbs (learn, cry, walk) do not. Thus, in the process of generating semantic structures, the occurrence of Benefactive is specified in either of the two ways shown in Diagram F.

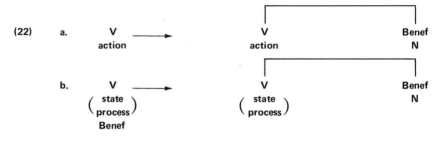

Diagram F

By (a) we define that Benefactive occurs with Action verbs unless marked otherwise on individual verbs, and by (b) we define that it does not occur with State or Process verbs unless individual verbs are marked otherwise.

4.   Deep Identity of Verbs

In Chomsky's theory, the verbs in the sentences,

(1) a.   Men kai le.
         door open asp
         (The door opened.)
    b.   Wo kai-le men.
         I open-asp door
         (I opened the door.)

receive entirely different specifications and have to be recognized as two verbs. By assigning constant case relations to the nouns in (1) and by postulating the notions "subject" and "object" as a surface notion, Fillmore is able to relate these two verbs in a significant way. (For a systematic argument on this point, see Fillmore 1970.) What we are interested in in this section is not verbs such as 'kai' which has the same phonetic form in different syntactic environments but cases where no surface relatedness is observed. This will be referred to as "lexical suppletion."

Generally speaking, lexical suppletion may result from the following phenomena (cf. Fillmore 1968:30-31)

(2) a. Subject selection: In terms of the case grammar framework, this is when different cases are chosen as the surface subject from identical case frames, e.g. 'mai' – 'buy' vs. 'mai' – 'sell.'

    b. Feature incorporation: This is a notion currently advocated by Abstract Syntacticists (see Chomsky 1970 and Lakoff 1970) which is broader than their "predicate-raising" and includes such features as causative, successful, honorific, etc. We shall differentiate this from the next case by restricting this to the presence or absence of the same feature, e.g. 'jiao' – 'ask' vs. 'qing' – 'ask', and 'san' – 'scattered' vs. 'sa' – 'scatter.'

    c. Variable reference: This is when different features such as direction and volition are incorporated, e.g. 'tiao' – 'jump' vs. 'diao' – 'fall.'

4.1 Subject Selection

In the pairs of sentences,

(3) a. Zhang San gen Li Si mǎi-le che le.
    Z.S. with L.S. buy-asp car asp
    (Z.S. bought the car from L.S.)

    b. Li Si ba che mài gei Zhang San le.
    L.S. p.t. car sell give Z.S. asp
    (L.S. sold the car to Z.S.)

    c. Zhang San jiao Li Si Yingwen.
    Z.S. teach L.S. English
    (Z.S. teaches L.S. English.)

    d. Zhang San gen Li Si xue Yingwen.
    Z.S. with L.S. learn English
    (Z.S. learns English with L.S.)

we may think of a transaction of a commodity or knowledge between two parties. Let us call the originating party "Source" and the terminating party "Goal." (For a more complete account of this, see Chapter 7.) The monetary transaction verb is realized as either 'mǎi' – 'buy' or 'mài' – 'sell,' depending on whether the Goal or the Source is selected to be the surface subject. The same is true for 'xue' – 'learn' and 'jiao' – 'teach.' We may ask, is this subject selection entirely free? That is, is the selection not controlled by other factors, and does everything remain constant in either realization? Note that in both (3a) and (b) Zhang San remains as Goal, and Li Si as Source, but viewed from a different angle, Zhang San is the Agent in (a) but the Agent in (b) is Li Si. Obviously, the assignment of Agent to either the Goal or the Source is different in either sentence. In

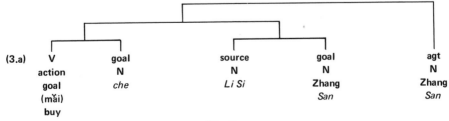

Fig. 3

this sense, subject selection is not free but controlled by the assignment of Agent. Their underlying structures are different, see figures 3 and 4.

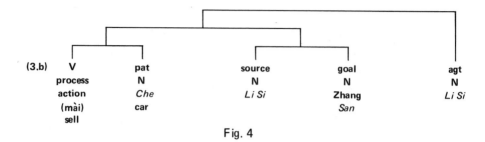

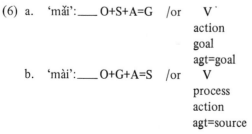

Fig. 4

Refer to Chapter 7, Section 3 for a discussion on the difference between Action-Goal and Process-Action verbs.

It may be the case that the active-passive opposition is the only case where we find different subject selections with constant verb-noun relations, so that all the case relations in (4) remain the same as in (3.b),

(4) Che bei Li Si mài gei Zhang San le.
    car p.p. L.S. sell give Z.S. asp
    (The car was sold to Z.S. by L.S.)

Different subject selections do not always exhibit lexical suppletion. Some examples are given below. It may be informative to compare them with English equivalents,

(5) a.   Fangke gen fangdong zu fangzi.
          tenant with landlord rent house
          (Tenants rent houses from landlords.)
    b.   Fangdong ba fangzi zu gei fangke.
          landlord p.t. house rent give tenant
          (Landlords let houses to tenants.)
    c.   Ta xihuan gen pengyou jie qian.
          he like with friend loan money
          (He likes to borrow money from friends.)
    d.   Tade pengyou xihuan ba qian jie gei ta.
          his friend like p.t. money loan give he.
          (His friends like lending him money.)

Instead of postulating two, though related, verbs such as 'mǎi' – 'buy' and 'mài' – 'sell' in the lexicon as below,

(6) a.   'mǎi':___O+S+A=G   /or   V
                                   action
                                   goal
                                   agt=goal
    b.   'mài':___O+G+A=S   /or   V
                                   process
                                   action
                                   agt=source

we only have to postulate one verb of monetary transaction, viz. [___O + S + G + A] and specify that the Agent of this verb has to be identified with either Source or Goal. This leaves us the possibility that not every verb which is associated with Source and Goal has to have the Agent identified with either one. This is seen below,

(7) a. Ta ba dongxi cong Zhang San jia ban-dao Li Si jia le.
        he p.t. thing from Z.S. house move-reach L.S. house asp
        (He moved the thing from Z.S.'s house to L.S.'s.)
    b. Ta ba qiu cong zhuo-shang tui-dao di-xia.
        he p.t. ball from table-top push-reach ground-under
        (He pushed the ball to the ground from the table.)

4.2. Feature Incorporation

This phenomenon will reveal cross-linguistic differences in the degree of incorporation. Just comparing Chinese with English, we notice that Chinese is more "analytic." Compare the difference of verbs used in the following sentences,

(8) a. Ta zai zhao shu.
        he p.v. look-for book
        (He is looking for a book.)
    b. Ta zhao-dao shu le.
        he look-for-reach book asp
        (He found the book.)

'Dao' which indicates "successful" or "accomplished" is morphologically manifest in the Chinese sentence but the corresponding semantic feature in English is incorporated in the verb 'find.' Lexical suppletion, in this case, is observed only in English and the different specifications may be formalized as

(9) a.   V   V
           action   →   action
           zhao + successful   *zhao + dao*
    b.   V   V
           action   →   action
           look(for) + successful   *find*

See Chafe (1970) Chapters 11 and 12 for discussions of derivational units such as 'successful.'

Without realizing this morpholigical derivation, many compound verbs in Chinese are forcedly postulated as polysyllabic verbs (as a result of the so-called polysyllabic inclination of modern Chinese), corresponding neatly to their English counterparts. As an example, in the sentences,

(10) a. Ta kan-yi-kan Zhang San.
         he look-one-look Z.S.
         (He looked at Z.S.)
     b. Ta kan-jian Zhang San.
         he look-see Z.S.
         (He saw Z.S.)

'Kan' is analyzed as a verb with the case frame [__O + A] and 'kanjian' also as a lexical verb with the case frame [__O + D] (cf. Y.C. Li 1971, Chapter 3.2). This approach neglects the fact that they are related by morphological derivation, similar to 'wide' and 'widen' in English. In fact, 'jian' also expresses "accomplished" or "successful," except that it modifies perception verbs only.

Compare the following,

(11)   a.   Ta zhao lai zhao qu cai zhao-dao shu.
              he look-for come look-for go only look-for-reach book.
              (He looked around and then he found the book.)
       b.   Ta kan lai kan qu cai **kan-jian** Zhang San.
              he look come look go only look-see Z.S.
              (He looked around and then he saw Z.S.)

Feature incorporation resulting in lexical suppletion is seen below,

(12)   a.   Women you guangdade xiaoyuan.
              we have large-m.p. campus
              (We have a large campus.)
       b.   Women lai kuoda xiaoyuan.
              we come enlarge campus
              (Let us enlarge the campus.)

The relation between 'guang' and 'kuo' is that of causation, i.e.

(13)   a.   V   V
           state   →   process
           guang   *guang + inchoative*
           large, vast
       b.   V   V
           process   →   process
           guang + inchoative   action
                             guang + inchoative + causative
       c.   *guang + inchoative + causative*   →   *kuo*
                                       enlarge, extend

Incorporation of "causative" is not available for some verbs, e.g.

(14)   a.   Pingzi po le.
              bottle break asp
              (The bottle broke.)
       b.   Ta ba pingzi nong-po le.
              he p.t. bottle make(pro-V)-break asp
              (He broke the bottle.)
       c.   *Ta po-le pingzi.
              he break-asp bottle
              (He broke the bottle.)

Note that in (b) the causative construction 'make – break' is analytic in Chinese but incorporated in English. Now consider that in the following sentences,

(15)   a.   Mao si le.
              cat die asp
              (The cat died.)
       b.   Ta ba mao sha-le.
              he p.t. cat kill-asp
              (He killed the cat.)

    c. Ta ba mao sha-si le.
        he p.t. cat kill-die asp
        (He killed the cat.)
    d. Ta ba mao nong-si le.
        he p.t. cat make(pro-V)-die asp
        (He killed the cat.)

both (c) and (d) are the causative counterpart of (a), and the difference is that 'nong-si' leaves Instrument unspecified whereas 'sha-si' specifies 'knife' as the Instrument. This is seen below by the fact that 'sha' is incompatible with other instruments,

(16) a. Ta yong dao ba mao sha-si le.
        he use knife p.t. cat kill-die asp
        (He killed the cat with a knife.)
    b. *Ta yong duyao ba mao sha-si le.
        he use poison p.t. cat kill-die asp
        (He killed the cat with some poison.)
    c. *Ta yong gunzi ba mao sha-si le.
        he use stick p.t. cat kill-die asp
        (He killed the cat with a stick.)

In this sense, 'sha' corresponds to English 'to knife.' Now let us look at the derivation of 'nong-si' — 'cause-die' and 'sha-si' — 'kill-die.' They are both the causative counterparts of 'si' — 'die' and can be derived from the underlying configuration as given in (17).

(17) a.   V   →   V
            process   process
            si   action
                             si + causative

    b. si + causative   → $\begin{cases} \text{nong-si / Instrument unspecified} \\ \text{sha-si / knife as Instrument} \end{cases}$

I shall not go into the currently controversial issue of whether the derivation should be "lexical" as seen in (17) or "transformational" as proposed in McCawley (1968). (Refer to Fodor 1970 for a discussion of this issue.)

    Note that there is no incorporation taking place in (17). On the other hand, we understand that there is no difference in meaning between (15.c) and (b), and if we follow the same analysis as in (17), we have to postulate that 'sha' alone is also a complex predicate, incorporating the process 'si' — 'die,' derived in the manner specified in (17.b). However, I shall argue below that this cannot be the case.

    In the first place, a similar verb, 'si' — 'tear,' is observed to behave like 'sha,' e.g.

(18) a. Ta ba xin si-le.
        he p.t. letter tear-asp
        (He tore up the letter.)
    b. Ta ba xin si-po le.
        he p.t. letter tear-break asp
        (He tore up the letter.)

Although both sentences mean that the letter was torn, we would not want to say that 'si' — 'tear' is the causative counterpart of 'po' — 'break' (cf. 14). What we can postulate is that 'si' — 'tear' is an intrinsic Process-Action verb, which implies the resultative state 'po'

— 'broken, torn' as part of its semantic property. Similarly, 'sha' — 'kill' implies 'si' — 'die.' Other verbs such as 'shao' — 'burn' may be associated with 'si' — 'die' but does not as part of its intrinsic meaning imply it, e.g.

> (19) a. Tamen ba niu shao-si le.
>   they p.t. cow burn-die asp
>   (They burned the cow to death.)
>   b. Tamen ba niu shao-le.
>   they p.t. cow burn-asp
>   (They burned the cow.)

(a) specifies the death of the cow as a result of burning, but (b) does not imply this process. The most likely reading of (b) is that the cow is already dead before they burned it.

Secondly, if 'sha' — 'kill' is a causative counterpart of 'si' — 'die,' sentences containing it should exhibit ambiguity as to whether it is the "action" aspect or the "result" aspect of 'sha' that is being referred to when adverbs such as 'cha-yidiar' — 'almost' are present, as suggested in McCawley (1968). This is not the case. In the following sentences, ('A' refers to action and 'R' to result)

> (20) a. Ta cha-yidiar ba mao nong-si.   (A or R)
>   he almost p.t. cat make-die
>   (He almost killed the cat.)
>   b. Ta ba mao cha-yidiar nong-si.   (R)
>   he p.t. cat almost make-die
>   (He almost killed the cat.)
>   c. Ta cha-yidiar ba mao sha-le.   (A)
>   he almost p.t. cat kill-asp
>   (He almost killed the cat.)
>   d. Ta ba mao cha-yidiar sha-le.   (A)
>   he p.t. cat almost kill-asp
>   (He almost killed the cat.)

(a) is the only ambiguous sentence, in which the action can be understood to be either performed or not. This ambiguity is explained when we adopt the derivation as given in (17.a), since the scope of the adverb can be assigned to either of the two "predicates" in the semantic structure. The non-ambiguity of (c) and (d) can only be explained by the fact that 'sha' — 'kill' is an "action" verb only; it does not incorporate the process 'si' — 'die,' though it implies it. In terms of Chafe's framework, it is an intrinsic Process-Action verb, not derived. In passing, I should mention that the compound 'sha-si' — 'kill-die' behaves like 'sha.'

The incorporation of the feature "honorific" is seen below,

> (21) a. Qing ni jiao ta chu-qu.
>   please you ask he out-go
>   (Please ask him to go out.)
>   b. Qing ni qing ta chu-qu.
>   please you invite he out-go
>   (Please ask him to go out.)

The syntactic environments of 'jiao' — 'ask' and 'qing' — 'ask, invite' are identical, and they need to be stated only once if they can be identified in the underlying structure, except for the feature "honorific."

4.3. Variable Reference

It may be argued that the pairs 'mǎi' — 'buy' vs. 'mài' — 'sell' and 'xue' — 'learn' vs. 'jiao' — 'teach' are not results of different subject selections but of incorporating different direction features, e.g. 'mǎi' — 'buy' incorporates "inward" and 'mài' — 'sell' "outward." Note that (3.a) and (b) refer to the same event from the point of view of different parties, whereas in

(22) a. Zhang San mǎi-le che le.
         Z.S. buy-asp car asp
         (Z.S. bought a car.)
     b. Zhang San mài-le che le.
         Z.S. sell-asp car asp
         (Z.S. sold the car.)

two unrelated events are involved. There is no point in talking about "subject selection" in totally unrelated events. A genuine case of variable reference is seen below,

(23) a. Zhang San ba che na-hui-lai le.
         Z.S. p.t. car fetch-return-come asp
         (Z.S. brought back the car.)
     b. Zhang San ba che na-hui-qu le.
         Z.S. p.t. car fetch-return-go asp
         (Z.S. took the car back.)

in which the same event is reported in two dimensions: either "inward" or "outward" as far as the speaker is concerned. Note that in English these two variables are incorporated into the verbs, 'bring' incorporates "inward" and 'take' "outward." Chinese remains "analytic" in this case.

In the following pair of sentences,

(24) a. Zhang San ba yizi yi la . . .
         Z.S. p.t. chair one pull
         (Z.S. gave the chair a pull.)
     b. Zhang San ba yizi yi tui . . .
         Z.S. p.t. chair one push
         (Z.S. gave the chair a push.)

'La' — 'pull' incorporates "inward" and 'tui' — 'push' "outward" direction and these verbs are in suppletive relation, so that

(25) a.   V
         process
         action   →   la-'pull'
         root + inward
     b.   V
         process
         action   →   tui-'push'
         root + outward

For an example of lexical suppletion due to volition, compare that in (26)

(26) a. Ta tiao-xia-qu le.
         he jump-down-go asp
         (He jumped down.)

b.   Ta diao-xia-qu le.
     he fall-down-go asp
     (He fell down.)

'Tiao' always refers to a volitional event and 'diao' always non-volitional. However, in most cases, intentionality is expressed by verbs without variable phonetic shapes, and consequently ambiguity results, e.g.

(27) a.   Ta (bu xiaoxin) ba pingzi da-po le.
          he (Neg careful) p.t. bottle hit-break asp
          (He broke the bottle carelessly.)
     b.   Ta (sheng-qi-qi-lai) ba pingzi da-po le.
          he (angry + i.p.) p.t. bottle hit-break asp
          (He angrily broke the bottle.)

What we have seen in this section is that the traditional notion "antonym" is more specifically and systematically defined. Antonyms which are discussed here are of two types. In one type, the occurrence of one event logically entails the other, so that if 'buying' takes place, someone must have sold something and if someone has borrowed something, someone must have lent something. This type of antonym is accounted for here by the process "subject selection." In the other there is no such logical entailment, so that if someone has pulled someone else, it doesn't follow that someone must have been pushed. Thus 'push' and 'pull,' related though they are to a significant degree, do not refer to the same event. This type of antonym is here accounted for by the process "variable reference."

5. Hierarchy of Verb-Noun Relations

Fillmore's base rules of the nature

(1) a. $S \rightarrow M + P$
    b. $P \rightarrow V + C_1 + C_2 \ldots C_n$

seem to introduce all case categories on equal status, although it is stated in his work (1968) that the introductions of certain categories such as B and I depends on other categories such as A. Evidence will be presented below which clearly indicates hierarchy among them.

5.1. Dependency Relations

This point has already been made in connection with co-occurrence restrictions (refer to Section 3.2) and will only be briefly recapitulated here. Recall that case categories can be divided into two groups,

(2) a.   Group A: Agentive, Dative, Objective, Factitive, Essive, (inner) Locative.
    b.   Group B: Benefactive, Instrumental, (outer) Locative, Comitative.

Dependency exists only between the selection of a case category from Group B and the occurrence of a category from Group A. In other words, Group B is dependent on Group A. What has been demonstrated before is that occurrence restrictions must be stated in terms of verb features rather than case categories. Even in this framework, the hierarchy is clear. The selection of Group B categories is dependent on verb features, but Group A categories are not selected but specified by verb features. This is the notion "well-formedness of semantic structures" discussed in Chafe (1970). Group A categories can define "well-formedness" but not Group B categories, since the latter are in most cases optional.

This means that verbs are adequately characterized by Group A categories alone, and these categories alone define case frames. In Chafe's framework, none of the categories in Group A is optional nor predictable and they have to be specified in the lexicon. To illustrate this, let us look at these two types of Locative, inner and outer. In the sentences below,

(3) a. Ta zai puzi-li mai dongxi.
      he l.v. shop-inside buy thing
      (He is buying things in the shop.)

   b. Ta zai jiaoshi-li xie zi.
      he l.v. classroom-inside write word
      (He is writing in the classroom.)

the outer Locative occurs freely. In fact, it may occur with all Action verbs. In this way, outer Locative does not impose sub-classifications of Action verbs. Now, in (4)

(4) a. *Ta ba dongxi mai zai zhuozi-shang.
      he p.t. thing buy l.v. table-top
      (He bought the thing (and put it) on the table.)

   b. Ta ba zi xie zai zhuozi-shang.
      he p.t. word write l.v. table-top
      (He wrote the word on the table.)

we observe that the inner Locative occurs with 'xie' but not 'mai.' Therefore, inner Locative divides all action verbs into Locative and non-Locative, i.e.

(5) a. Locative Action: 'xie' — 'write,' 'fang' — 'put,' 'gua' — 'hang,' 'tie' — 'paste,' and 'bai' — 'place.'

   b. Non-Locative Action: 'mai' — 'buy,' 'ba' — 'extract,' 'bu' — 'catch,' 'huan' — 'change,' and 'cha' — 'examine.'

The semantic structures which contain verbs in (5.a) also contain Locative phrases. This notion is formalized in Diagram G.

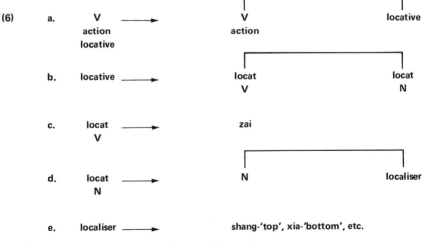

Diagram G

I shall borrow Halliday's terms "transitivity" and "circumstance" (1967a) to refer to Group A and Group B respectively. [I shall here take the liberty of interchanging the definitions of "transitivity" and "participation" as presented in his work. This is to avoid the terminological question of why all the nouns which participate in a sentence are not participant nouns. Therefore by "transitivity relations" in this thesis is meant "participant" nouns in Halliday's work.]

5.2. Transitivity Relations and Prepositions

In the case grammar, each case is expanded into the following constituents,

(7)   C   →   K + NP

K (i.e. Kasus) represents the prepositions of each case category. In Y.C. Li (1971), the following prepositions are recognized as case markers,

(8)   *Transitivity relations*:
     a.   Agentive: gei, bei, ai, shou, jiao, rang, you, zao, gui
     b.   Dative: gei
     c.   Objective: ba, jiang, guan
     d.   Factitive: ∅
     e.   Essive: ∅

(9)   *Circumstantial relations*:
     a.   Benefactive: wei, ti, gei
     b.   Instrumental: na, yong, shi
     c.   Comitative: gen, he, tong
     d.   Locative: zai, dao   (Li doesn't differentiate inner and outer Locative.)

However, I shall only discuss those which are productive. For example, among the so-called Agentive markers, 'bei' will be the representative, since it can replace 'gei,' 'ai,' 'shou,' 'jiao,' 'rang,' 'zao' almost without restriction. 'You' and 'gui' differ from the others in that they have additional semantic import, that of "allocation of responsibility." Among the objective markers, 'ba' alone will be considered, since 'jiang' rarely occurs, in speech at least, and 'guan' has extremely restricted environments (with 'jiao' – 'call' only). Thus the prepositions which merit careful scrutiny and which have to do with Transitivity relations are only three, viz. 'bei,' 'gei,' and 'ba.'

First of all, I would like to briefly re-examine the definition of Dative as presented in Fillmore (1968) and Y.C.Li (1971). In Fillmore (1968), Dative defines the following nouns,

(10)   a.   Animate subjects of state verbs.
       b.   Animate objects of action verbs.
       c.   Animate indirect objects.

The definition in (10.c) is disputable. Both Chafe (1970) and Halliday (1967-8) consider indirect objects as Benefactive. It seems to me that Fillmore postulates them as Dative primarily for the fact that many indirect objects are governed by the preposition 'to' (in English) when they occur in the adjunct position (e.g. He gave John the book → He gave the book to John). It is doubtful that there is a semantic justification. Moreover, he would like to say that the preposition for Benefactive is in general 'for.' Unfortunately, many indirect objects can be governed by 'for' as an adjunct (e.g. He sang Mary a song → He sang a song for Mary). The relationship between "indirect objects," 'to,' and 'for' is an extremely complex one and is not at all resolved by Fillmore's postulation. In fact, his analysis further entangles the whole issue. The only advantage, as far as I am aware, of this analysis is that it predicts the preposition 'to' in many cases (cf. "That is amusing to me").

Unfortunately, Y.C.Li (1971) adopts Fillmore's postulation into Chinese verbatim. Below are Chinese examples of (10)

(11) a. Ta ai Zhang Xiaojie.
         he love Zhang Miss
         (He loves Miss Zhang.)
     b. Ta sha-le Zhang Xiaojie.
         he kill-asp Zhang Miss
         (He killed Miss Zhang.)
     c. Ta song gei Zhang Xiaojie yi-duo hua.
         he give give Zhang Miss one-AN flower
         (He gave Miss Zhang a flower.)

Note that Li's postulation of 'gei' as the Dative preposition is based only on (10.c), one of the most questionable issues in Fillmore (1968). It is clear that Zhang Xiaojie in (11.c) plays the semantic role of Recipient, which is usually a definition of Benefactive. How is the difference between Dative and Benefactive accounted for in Fillmore's and Li's framework?

As will be explained later (Chapter 7), I postulate 'gei' phrases as seen in (11.c) as Goal. Excluding this type of 'gei' phrases from the consideration of Dative, we find that the preposition for Dative is in fact "zero." In Y.C.Li (1971:182), another marker 'shi' is postulated as Dative marker. His example is as below,

(12) Zhe-jian shi shi Wu Gang hen shangxin.
      this-AN thing cause Wu Gang very sad
      (This thing made Wu Gang very sad.)

'Shi,' one of many causative verbs, is postulated by Fillmore as taking the case frame [__ S + A] (Fillmore 1968:28). We shall disregard whether or not the subject is A (see Huddleston 1970) but accept the postulation of an embedded sentence. The question concerning Li's postulation is, how can a verb (which is assigned the case frame as above) also be a case marker? His analysis would amount to treating, e.g. 'sha' in (11.b), as a Dative marker. Furthermore, the subject of the embedded sentence of 'shi' is not always Dative, as Li has claimed, e.g.

(13) a. Zhe-jian shi shi ta da ku-qilai.
         this-AN thing cause he great cry-i.p.
         (This thing made him cry out.)
     b. Zhe-jian shi shi ta zheng ye shui-bu-zhao.
         this-AN thing cause he whole night sleep-Neg-s.p.
         (This thing made him unable to sleep all night.)

Next, we shall investigate the so-called Agentive marker 'bei.' It is reasonable to expect that if 'bei' always governs Agentive, sentences with 'bei' should contain only Action verbs. Compare the following sentences,

(14) a. Zhe-jian shi bei ta zhidao le.
         this-AN thing p.p. he know asp
         (This thing was discovered by him.)

    b.   Ta bei Xiao Zhang kan-jian le.
        he p.p. Xiao Zhang look-see asp
        (He was seen by Xiao Zhang.)
    c.   Ta bei zhe-jian shi nong hutu le.
        he p.p. this-AN thing Pro-V confused asp
        (He was confused by this thing.)
    d.   Zhe-jian shi gei ta wang-le.
        This-AN thing p.p. he forget-asp
        (This thing was forgotten by him.)

What 'bei' governs are Dative in (a) and (b) and "inanimate causer" in (c). These sentences are by no means exceptional cases, and since this is a fact, it is beyond understanding why 'bei' is chosen to represent Agentive alone. Even if it is chosen to render its English counterpart 'by,' we should still question whether such a postulation is in fact justified in English. Cases in which English 'by' governs other cases than Agentive are not difficult to find.[7] What is more difficult to explain in this postulation is the fact that not every Agentive can occur in 'bei' construction, e.g.

  (15) a.   Ta chang-le yi-shou ge.
         he sing-asp one-AN song
         (He sang a song.)
      b.   *Ge bei ta chang-le.
         song p.p. he sing-asp
         (The song was sung by him.)
      c.   Ta zhu-le guo tang.
         he cook-asp pot soup
         (He cooked a pot of soup.)
      d.   *Tang bei ta zhu-le.
         soup p.p. he cook-asp
         (The soup was cooked by him.)

Thus the relationship between Agent and 'bei' is extremely weak. For a more detailed account of "passive" in Chinese, refer to H. Wang (1959), Lü (1948), and C.Li (1969).

    'Bei' will here be tentatively postulated as transformationally introduced when "object" and "subject" are inverted. The factor which triggers this inversion is the semantic feature "pejorative" (L. Wang 1944 and C.Li 1969). As a consequence of this re-analysis of 'bei,' the preposition for Agentive is "zero" also.

---

[7] For instance,
a.   He is loved by everyone.
b.   He is admired by everyone.
c.   This is known by everyone.
d.   It was blown away by the wind.
Verbs in the first three sentences are not Action verbs. The verb in (d) is an Action verb, but according to Fillmore's analysis, 'the wind' is not Agentive but Instrumental. If nouns such as 'the wind' and 'the rain' can be conceived of as Agents, at least in the contexts of their inherent activities (e.g. 'blowing' of the wind and 'washing' of the rain), such sentences as (d) above no longer constitute counter-examples. However, for more discussions relating to this problem, refer to Huddleston (1970).

Now the function of 'ba' will be investigated. Y.C.Li postulates it as governing Objective. Note that Objective defines the following nouns,

(16) a. Inanimate subjects of state or process verbs, e.g.
Men huai-le.
door bad-asp
(The door broke.)

b. Inanimate objects of action verbs, e.g.
Ta mai-le yi-ben shu.
he buy-asp one-AN book
(He bought a book.)

c. Objects of state verbs, e.g.
Ta pa lei sheng.
he fear thunder noise
(He is afraid of thunder.)

Objectives in (b) and (c) are not governed by 'ba,' and moreover they cannot occur in 'ba' construction, i.e.

(17) a. *Ta ba yi-ben shu mai-le.
he p.t. one-AN book buy-asp
(He bought a book.)

b. *Ta ba lei sheng pa.
he p.t. thunder noise fear
(He is afraid of thunder.)

If the deletion of case markers is stated in terms of their position in a sentence, i.e. always deleted sentence-initially (see Fillmore 1968), the absence of 'ba' in (16.b) and (c) cannot be accounted for. If case markers are postulated in the underlying structure and are again deleted even when they occur in 'expected' positions, it is pointless to postulate them at all. If the occurrence of 'ba' is restricted to a certain class of verbs (Process-action verbs in C.Li 1969), and if it occurs only when Objective is preposed, e.g.

(18) a. Ta ba chezi mai-le.
he p.t. car sell-asp
(He sold the car.)

b. Ta ba shuiguan chai-le.
he p.t. water-pipe dismantle-asp
(He dismantled the water-pipe.)

then it is much more truthful to the situation to introduce it transformationally. Otherwise, we would have to regard the word order as seen in (18) as more basic than that in (16.b) and (c), which is counterfactual.

Furthermore, the strongest objection to treating 'ba' as Objective marker is the fact that it governs other cases than Objective, e.g.

(19) a. Ta ba fan-ren sha-si le. (Dative)
he p.t. crime-person kill-die asp
(He killed the criminal.)

      b.   Ta ba men shang-le suo. (Locative)[8]
           he p.t. door install-asp lock
           (He installed a lock on the door.)
      c.   Ta ba xiaotou gei pao le. (Agentive)
           he p.t. thief p.p. run asp
           (He let the thief get away.)

Y.C.Li remarks, on this situation, that

    "While O (Objective) may not be marked by anything other than Ba . . . it seems that Ba marking an NP . . . which is A (Agentive), is allowed, under the condition that (it) be animate, while the subject NP be inanimate!" (1971:158).

    What we see in (19) is that both the subject and the object in (19.a) are animate, contrary to what he claims. However, even if his statement were correct as far as data in Chinese are concerned, we would like to ask whether his constraint is based on a semantic notion (that is what the case grammar attempts to capture) or a transformational notion. As is obvious, his introduction of 'ba' to govern Agentive is utilizing only surface structure notions.

    What I have demonstrated is that the introduction of 'bei' and 'ba' has to be stated transformationally, utilizing the surface structure notions "linearity," "subject," and "object." They both govern a heterogeneous group of case categories. In permissive environments, 'bei' is introduced by an "inversion" transformation and 'ba' by a preposing transformation (distinct from various kinds of topicalization transformations).

    The purpose of this brief discussion is to show that if transitivity relations are introduced in the manner of (7), i.e. C → K + NP, we are faced with the rule

(20) K → ∅ / Agentive, Dative, Objective, Factitive, Essive

and it is meaningless to set up a category when it is not attested in the grammar. The conclusion is that judging from the introduction of prepositions, case categories may be divided into two major groups, one governed and the other not governed by prepositions. The dichotomy concluded from this criterion coincides with that concluded from dependency relationship. Therefore the generation procedure of Transitivity relations is different from that of Circumstantial relations. Transitivity relations cluster around (notionally not syntactically) the verbs and form the inner core of all semantic structures. Circumstantial relations, on the other hand, form the peripheral parts of sentences. They are selected, obligatorily (rare) or optionally, by the inner core.

---

[8] More examples of accusativized Locative are given below,
a.   Ta ba hua-ping dou cha-le hua.
     he p.t. vase all insert-asp flower
     (He filled all the vases with flowers.)
b.   Wo yijing ba tong zhuang-le shui.
     I already p.t. bucket load-asp water
     (I already filled the bucket with water.)
c.   Ta ba yizi tu-shang youqi le.
     he p.t. chair paint-on paint asp
     (He painted the chair with some paint.)
In a later chapter (Chapter 5, Section 4), however, I present more discussions of similar cases and favour the treatment of these accusativized Locatives as playing double-roles, not only as Locative but also as Patient. This new treatment would have the advantage of retaining the semantics of the so-called "ergative" construction in Chinese, that is, it takes nouns which undergo a certain kind of change. In this analysis, the Locative nouns above are not ergativized in the capacity of Locative but Patient. For an excellent explication of the ergative construction in Mandarin, consult H. Frei (1956).

5.3. The Status of Circumstantial Relations and Prepositions

The status of prepositions in Chinese is rather uncertain. This is primarily because many prepositions function also as main verbs, synchronically and even more so diachronically (see L. Wang 1958). It may be asked how the notion "preposition" is established in Chinese syntax in the first place if this category is indistinguishable from verbs. As can be realized, this is partly a Western innovation.

As far as the prepositions of Circumstantial relations are concerned, the Benefactive preposition is the verb which means 'to give,' the Instrumental preposition 'to use,' the Locative 'to exist, to be located,' and Comitative 'to follow.' All these prepositions occur preceding main verbs. However, these minor verbs are not the only verbs in this position. For example, in the pair of sentences,

(21) a. Ta xihuan yong maobi xie zi.
         he like use brush-pen write word
         (He likes to write with brush-pens.)
     b. Ta xihuan qi jiaotache shang xue.
         he like ride bicycle go school
         (He likes to go to school by bicycle.)

the phrases 'yong maobi' — 'use brush-pen' and 'qi jiaotache' — 'ride bicycle' cannot be differentiated on syntactic nor semantic grounds, since both function as a type of modifier of the main verb phrase (qualifying the manner of the action), but only the former is usually described as a prepositional phrase. The latter phrase is called the first VP in VP series (Chao 1968:325). In other words, (21.a) is conceived of as a simplex sentence and (21.b) as a complex sentence (i.e. embedding). No justification is given for the discrepancy.

In Lakoff (1968a and 1968b) it is proposed that Locative and Instrumental adverbs can be analyzed as derived from higher sentences, so that in the underlying structure, there is no need for such a category as adverb. This means that Circumstantial relations as such may be eliminated from the participant roles in the underlying structure co-occurring with Transitivity relations. Instead, they participate as Transitivity relations in their own right, in sentences which are connected to other sentences. For example, in the sentence

(22) Ta zai Zhongguo nian shu.
     he l.v. China read book
     (He is studying in China.)

we may think of two sentences 'Ta zai Zhongguo' and 'Ta nian shu' which are related in a particular way. The relationship may be either co-ordination or subordination. In Chafe (1970), subordination is suggested for Locative. Note that the verb 'zai' — 'l.v.' is a State verb (which may optionally take a Locative noun), so that we may analyze (22) as meaning "The event of his studying takes place in China." The action sentence 'Ta nian shu' as a whole is treated as a Patient noun, of a Locative verb. This is shown in figure 5.

The following observation in Chinese may reveal the minor "predicator" nature of these "circumstance" prepositions. First, almost all verbal predicates in Chinese may undergo the following transformation, if they involve the property "certainty" or "strong assertion."

(23) a. Ta yao lai.
         he want come

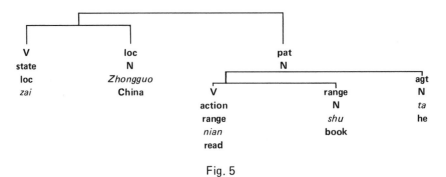

Fig. 5

(He wants to come.)
    b.   Ta shi yao lai de.
        he be want come particle
        (I am certain that he wants to come.)

The construction 'shi . . . de' has the semantic import of "certainty" not on the part of the subject but of the speaker. Many instances of Circumstantial relations may also occur in this construction, e.g.

(24) a.   Zhongguo ren yong kuaizi chi fan. (Instrumental)
          China person use chopsticks eat rice
          (Chinese people eat with chopsticks.)
     b.   Zhongguo ren chi fan shi yong kuaizi de.
          China person eat rice be use chopsticks
          (It is the case that Chinese people eat with chopsticks.)
     c.   Zhongguo zai 1945 nian dedao shengli. (Time)
          China l.v. 1945 year obtain victory
          (China obtained victory in 1945.)
     d.   Zhongguo dedau shengli shi zai 1945 nian (de).
          China obtain victory be l.v. 1945 year part
          (It is the case that China obtained victory in 1945.)
     e.   Ta gei mama mai zhe-jian yifu. (Benefactive)
          he give mother buy this-AN dress
          (He is buying this dress for his mother.)
     f.   Ta mai zhe-jian yifu shi gei mama de.
          he buy this-AN dress be give mother part
          (It is the case that he is buying this dress for his mother.)
     g.   Ta zuotian gen ta baba yikuar shang-jie. (Comitative)
          he yesterday with he father together go-street
          (Yesterday he went to town with his father.)
     h.   Ta zuotian shang-jie shi gen ta baba yikuar de.
          he yesterday go-street be with he father together part
          (It is the case that yesterday he went to town with his father.)

To state the context of the application of this transformation adequately, it is necessary not to differentiate prepositional phrases from verb phrases. It may be argued that the transformation above is but another version of the 'focus' transformation. In other words, the transformation may do two things; it may change the string

(25) a. X Y Z

into either of the following (supposing Y is the constituent to be focussed)

    b. X shi Y Z de
    c. X Z shi Y de

In this analysis, (24.b) and (d), for example, are derived from the following two sentences respectively,

(26) a. Zhongguo ren shi yong kuaizi chi fan de.
        China person be use chopsticks eat rice emphatic-part
    b. Zhongguo shi zai 1945 nian dedao shengli de.
        China be l.v. 1945 year obtain victory emphatic-part

However, we observe that other prepositional phrases and modifying VP's (i.e. first VP in VP series in Chao's analysis) do not undergo the transformation (25.c), e.g.

(27) a. Wo shi gen ta jie qian de.
        I be with he borrow money emphatic-part
        (I borrowed money from him.)
    b. *Wo jie qian shi gen ta de.
        I borrow money be with he emphatic-part
    c. Ta shi kai che chu-qu de.
        he be drive car out-go emphatic-part
        (He went out in his car.)
    d. *Ta chu-qu shi kai che de.
        he out-go he drive car emphatic-part
        (May mean: He went out to drive his car.)

If (25.c) is postulated, we have no way to prevent these ungrammatical sentences. This observation points to the fact that the prepositional phrases seen in (24) are different in nature from others. This difference suggests that sentences continuing Circumstantial prepositional phrases may be complex in the underlying structure.

    The underlying structure of Locative has already been suggested in figure 5 and the underlying structure of Comitative should involve phrasal conjunction (see Section 1.2 of this chapter). Those for Instrumental and Benefactive are suggested in figures 6 and 7 respectively.

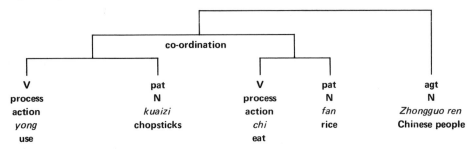

Fig. 6

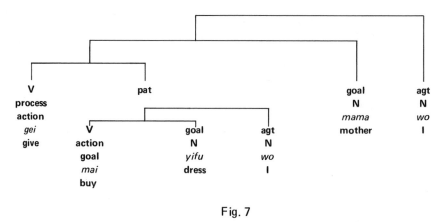

Fig. 7

Co-ordination instead of sub-ordination of VP's is postulated for Instrumental for the reason that in some instances 'qu' — 'go' may be inserted between the VP's, similar to other types of VP co-ordination where the first VP is not a prepositional phrase and where the second VP expresses the "purpose" of the first VP, e.g.

(28) a.   Ta shang jie mai shu.
           he go street buy book
           (He is going to town to buy books.)
      b.   Ta shang jie qu mai shu.
           he go street go buy book
           (He is going to town to buy books.)

Obviously, sentences here do not involve embedding. We can postulate the optional insertion of 'qu' only between VP's (or S's with identical subjects) which are co-ordinated. Sentences such as (27.c) above contain VP's with sub-ordination relationship and 'qu' is not allowed. We observe the occurrence of this 'qu' also in sentences containing Instrumental phrases, e.g.

(29) a.   Ni yong zhe-kuai bu zuo jian yifu.
           you use this-AN cloth make AN dress.
           (Make a dress with this cloth.)
      b.   Ni yong zhe-kuai bu qu zuo jian yifu.
           you use this-AN cloth go make AN dress
           (Make a dress with this cloth.)

The underlying structure of Benefactive as given in figure 7 is identical to that of (30.a),

(30) a.   Ni gei ta yi-kuai qian.
           you give he one-AN money
           (Give him a dollar.)
      b.   Ni gei yi-kuai qian gei ta.
           you give one-AN money give he
           (Give a dollar to him.)

except that the Patient in (30.a) is a single noun rather than a whole sentence. Furthermore, note that the relation Goal always introduces the preposition 'gei,' which will always be identical to the "highest" verb in Benefactive sentences. In the surface structure, haplology takes place between these two 'gei.' This postulation is supported by the contrast between (30.a) and (b); in the former, when the main verb 'gei' and the Goal preposition 'gei' occur together, one is deleted, and in the latter, if they are separated, both remain on the surface.

The proposals in this section concerning the underlying structures of Circumstantial relations are only tentative and are suggested as a possible direction for further study. The primary purpose in this section is to demonstrate that case categories as presented in Fillmore (1968) are not of equal status, either semantically or syntactically. They are classified in this thesis into Transitivity and Circumstantial relations. The former relations are postulated as defining the semantic structure of a simplex sentence, while the latter are suggested as originating from more complex semantic structures (i.e. with embedding or co-ordination). This means that Circumstantial relations as such can be eliminated from the general framework of verb-noun relations. They are definable in the underlying structure in terms of Transitivity relations themselves, so that the Locative preposition 'zai' is no different from the locative State verb 'zai', and the Instrumental and Benefactive prepositions 'yong' and 'gei' are not, in our framework, differentiated from the ordinary Process-Action verbs 'yong' and 'gei' respectively.

As far as the status of prepositions are concerned, we have eliminated the Transitivity prepositions in Section 5.2, and in 5.3 we have re-analyzed the Circumstantial prepositions as ordinary verbs. The category 'preposition' will be in this thesis restricted to relational verbs which are introduced under various relational categories such as Goal, Source, and inner Locative. These will be discussed separately in later chapters.

CHAPTER 3

Transitivity Relations

In this chapter an adequate set of transitivity relations will be presented for the description of Chinese sentences. Some are adopted from current theories (see Chapter 1), some are redefined to capture characteristics of Chinese, and some new ones are postulated. Detailed treatments are given in the subsequent chapters.

1. Introduction: Fillmore (1968), Halliday (1967-8), and Chafe (1970) Compared

The Transitivity relations in these three theories have already been given in Chapter 1. These are listed below again for easy reference.

(1) a. Fillmore: Agentive, Dative, Objective, Factive, Essive.
  b. Halliday: Causer, Affected, Range.
  c. Chafe: Agent, Patient, Complement, Experiencer, Beneficiary.

No straightforward one-to-one correspondence is observed to hold among these theories. Let us examine how they each conceive of these relations by looking at a representative set of sentences.

(2) a. Zhang San Zai ku.
    Z.S. p.v. cry
    (Z.S. is crying.)
  b. Zhang San hen gao.
    Z.S. very tall
    (Z.S. is very tall.)
  c. Zhang San si le.
    Z.S. die asp
    (Z.S. died.)
  d. Zhang San sha-le yi-ge ren
    Z.S. kill-asp one-AN person
    (Z.S. killed someone.)
  e. Zhang San mai-le chezi le.
    Z.S. sell-asp car asp
    (Z.S. sold the car.)
  f. Zhang San chang-le yi-shou ge.
    Z.S. sing-asp one-AN song
    (Z.S. sang a song.)
  g. Zhang San hen xihuan Li Si.
    Z.S. very like L.S.
    (Z.S. likes L.S.)
  h. Zhang San shi yi-ge xuesheng.
    Z.S. be one-AN student
    (Z.S. is a student.)

Zhang San in (a) is Agentive (Fillmore), Affected (Halliday), and Agent (Chafe). Zhang San is doing something, engaged in an activity, and we shall adopt Chafe's term here, viz. Agent, for this role. Halliday assigns Affected to this role for reasons which are not clear to me. This is quite striking when we compare (a) with (b), in which Zhang San is described as Dative, Affected, and Patient. Here Zhang San is not engaged in any activity, he is only perceived as possessing a certain quality. Halliday equates this Patient with Agent in (a). It seems that there is nothing in common between them as far as notional role is concerned. Furthermore, if we are willing to postulate "volition" in the role "Agent," the contrast between them is quite apparent. Agent plays an "active" role, while Patient plays a "passive" role. We shall refer to Zhang San in (b) as Patient, following Chafe. It would be quite undesirable if we had to interpret Halliday's Affected role as merely capturing the traditional notion "subject of an intransitive verb (including adjectives)."

Zhang San in (c) functions as Dative, Affected, and Patient. Here he is not doing something nor perceived as possessing a quality. Something happened to him. Passivity is also apparent in this case, and Zhang San is conceived of as playing the identical role to that in (b). This role will be referred to in this thesis as Patient.

Zhang San in (d) plays the role Agentive, Causer, and Agent. Causer is defined in Halliday (1968) as Actor of a directed action and Initiator of non-directed action. In this instance, it is an Initiator, causing 'a person' to undergo the process of 'dying.' Thus this sentence is a causative sentence. Chafe's postulation of the derivational history of 'kill' as "process 'die' + causative" is in agreement with Halliday's analysis. The initiating actor of a causative construction is engaged in an activity and will thus be described as Agent, without differentiating it from the Agent as seen in (a). The difference of meaning is derivative from different semantic structures in question.

'A person' in (d) plays the role Dative, Affected, and Patient. As is apparent from the discussion in the last paragraph, the role of 'a person' here is identical to that of Zhang San in (c). Notionally, killing someone equals causing someone to die. This role will be referred to as Patient.

Zhang San in (e) plays the same role as in (d) but 'the car' here is Objective, Affected, and Patient. Fillmore postulates Objective here primarily for the reason that 'sell' takes only inanimate nouns (see next sub-section). This postulation predicts animateness of the object nouns but does not imply any difference involved in the "meaning" of these two verbs (or what Halliday refers to as verbal process, 1968:20). Halliday and Chafe, on the other hand, differentiate (e) from (d). Although Zhang San in both (d) and (e) is Causer, it is Actor of a directed action rather than Initiator. This means that Halliday does not conceive of the feature "causative" as present in (e). Similarly, Chafe specifies 'sell' as an intrinsic Process-action verb, without the feature "causative" as in 'kill.' In his framework, he allows for two types of Process-action verb, one inherent and the other derived. We shall follow Halliday and Chafe in differentiating the "verbal processes" involved in (d) and (e).

Zhang San in (f) is Agentive, Affected, and Agent. It is Affected in Halliday's framework because it is the subject of a non-directed action, similar to (a). This approach has the advantage of analyzing the property of the verb 'sing' as similar to that of 'cry' rather than 'kill' and 'sell'; 'sing' and 'cry' are both non-directed action verbs. However, if we look at the role of 'a song' in (f), viz. Factive, Range, and Complement, we observe that the role Range already indicates that the "verbal process" here must be distinct from that in (d) and (e). No Range occurs in a directed action. Redundancy can be avoided by recognizing the role of Zhang San here as Agent and by establishing a distinct role of object, as all these three scholars do. Note that the surface object in (d) is caused to undergo a process, but that in (f) cannot be similarly conceived of. It only specifies the scope of the activity in question. In this particular instance, it is in fact quite "empty" semantically. We shall look into this in greater detail below. Here we follow Halliday and refer to this type of object as Range.

The sentence in (g) poses many interesting questions. Zhang San is described as Dative, Affected, and Experiencer, and Li Si as Objective, Range, and Patient. They all agree in assigning a passive instead of active role to Zhang San, but the description of Li Si is varied. Fillmore's description, viz. Objective, does not quite reflect any semantic meaning, since objective is "semantically most neutral" (1968:25). This Objective, which is in the object position, cannot correspond to the Objective in (e) because Zhang San in (e) is Agent, who can dispose of an object, while Zhang San in (g) is Dative, which is an affected (i.e. passive) role itself. Therefore the relationship between Dative and Objective is not quite clear. Chafe, on the other hand, identifies the role of Li Si in (g) with that of Zhang San in (b). He recognizes that 'like' is a state verb, similar to 'tall,' and the patient which is directly associated with this state is Li Si, similar to Zhang San in (b). Therefore this means that Zhang San in (g) plays an even more "passive" role than Li Si in the sentence. This inference from his treatment may not be entirely groundless because of the fact that Patient in the object position generally specifies the "victim" of happenings, an interpretation inappropriate for a state verb. In his framework, a state verb cannot be associated with more than one Patient simultaneously. We may ask, who between the two is being in the state of 'like?' The answer is Zhang San. The feasibility of this answer is more conspicuous if we substitute 'like' with other state verbs such as 'love.' If A loves B, it doesn't follow that B is in love with A, but A must be in love with B. Li Si in (g) merely specifies the reaching point of Zhang San's affection. We shall describe objects of such state verbs as Goal and subjects as Patient. The role Goal will be discussed in detail in Chapter 7.

The sentence in (h) represents sentences with nominal predicates. Zhang San is postulated as Dative, Affected, and Patient. 'A student' is postulated as a nominal state verb by Chafe, corresponding exactly to the sentence in (b). Fillmore specifically creates a distinct category Essive for such a relation and does not relate it to any of the other sentence types. The meaning of this sentence seems to correspond to 'This thing is worth five dollars,' specifying the state of a noun. In Halliday's framework, Zhang San is Attribuant and 'a student' Attribute. We may analyze 'be' as a relational state verb, Zhang San as a Patient who is in the state of being identified in terms of Range, 'a student.'

As a conclusion of this comparative study, the semantic roles of the nouns occurring in sentences in (2) are defined as below,

(3) a. Agent
  b. Patient
  c. Patient
  d. Agent – Patient
  e. Agent – Patient
  f. Agent – Range
  g. Patient – Goal
  h. Patient – Range

Identical descriptions are observed for the pairs (b) and (c), (d) and (e). It does not follow from this that "meanings" involved are identical in each pair. Differences are indicated by other features in the semantic structures. For example, Patient in (b) has to do with State but Patient in (c) has to do with Process. Generally speaking the combinations of nominal roles and verbal features are sufficient to account for meaning differences in most cases.

2. The Role of Animateness in Fillmore's Case Categories

The feature "animate" defines all Fillmore's cases as below,

(4) a. Agentive: animate
     b. Dative: animate
     c. Objective: neutral
     d. Factitive: inanimate
     e. Instrumental: inanimate
     f. Benefactive: animate
     g. Locative: inanimate (typically)
     h. Comitative: animate
     i. Essive: neutral

This specification is less satisfactory for Transitivity relations than for Circumstantial relations, in that exceptions to (e), (f), and (h) are rare and also that the Circumstantial relations do not affect the specifications of individual verbs nor do they change categories depending on animateness. For instance, we observe that most Comitative nouns are animate, and if inanimate nouns are found to occur in identical syntactic environments, it is quite unlikely that they are to be reanalyzed as other relations such as Instrumental. In other words, no two Circumstantial relations are found to form an opposition in terms of animateness. The same cannot be said of Transitivity relations.

In the pair of sentences,

(5) a. Zhang Xiaojie hen bai.
         Zhang Miss very white
         (Miss Zhang is very fair.)
     b. Zhe-zhong zhi hen bai.
         this-kind paper very white
         (This kind of paper is very white.)

Miss Zhang plays the role Dative but 'paper' plays the role Objective. The only factor in this contrast which leads to this discrepant description is the feature "animate." In this sense, Dative and Objective form an opposition in terms of animateness. A legitimate question here is, how significant is this difference? Fillmore's description ignores the fact that the state (i.e. 'white') referred to in both cases is the same and that the semantic roles of these two nouns are identical, that is, both are ascribed with a certain characteristic. If 'white' in (a) is given the frame [__ O] and that in (b) [__ O], how do we relate them? It is more appropriate to assume both Dative and Objective in this instance under a general category, say Patient, leaving the feature "animate" as a further specification in different contexts.

It may be argued that it is precisely because 'white' can take both animate and inanimate Patients that the case frame in question should only be [__O], leaving animateness unspecified. However, note that in the sentences,

(6) a. Zhang Xiaojie hen pang.
         Zhang Miss very fat
         (Miss Zhang is very fat.)
     b. *Zhe-zhi zhu hen pang.

this-AN pig very fat
(This pig is very fat.)

c.   *Zhe-zhi kuaizi hen pang.
this-AN chopstick very fat
(This chopstick is very fat.)

d.   *Zhang Xiaojie hen fei.
Zhang Miss very fat
(Miss Zhang is very fat.)

e.   Zhe-zhi zhu hen fei.
this-AN pig very fat
(This pig is very fat.)

f.   *Zhe-zhi kuaizi hen fei.
this-AN chopstick very fat
(This chopstick is very fat.)

'Pang' — 'fat' requires human Patient and 'fei' — 'fat' animate non-human Patient. How important is the difference at the most abstract semantic level? A semantic theory must first capture their relatedness and have available in the theory a device to specify the difference. It is accidental, i.e. idiosyncratic, that 'white,' 'pang' — 'fat,' and 'fei' — 'fat' require different kinds of surface subjects. We shall regard the assignment of Dative and Objective in (5) as over-differentiation. The same situation is observed across Agentive and Objective, e.g.

(7) a.   Diren tui-le.
enemy withdraw-asp
(The enemy retreated.)

   b.   Chao-shui tui-le.
tide withdraw-asp
(The tide ebbed.)

'Enemy' is Agentive but 'tide' is Objective. It is felt that whereas only the phenomenon is reported in (b), some willful action has been performed in (a). Volition may come only from an Agent. However, this is not necessarily the case. (7.a) is in fact ambiguous; it may be either volitional or non-volitional. In the former interpretation, we may think of the intentional withdrawal of the enemy, and in the latter, only the enemy's motion and change of location are reported. When the sentence is reported in the latter interpretation, its status is no different from that of (7.b). Roughly speaking, the disappearance of something from the original location is all that is in question in both. The issue of "intentionality" will be further examined later (Chapter 4, Section 3). It is important to bring out the relatedness between these two sentences (both as Patient), and it is at the same time no less important to bring out the difference between them (one as Agent and the other Patient). We shall present a way in Chapter 4, Section 4 whereby this can be achieved.

The objects of action verbs are also differentiated into Dative and Objective according to animate and inanimate respectively, e.g.

(8) a.   Ta ba zei sha-le.
he p.t. thief kill-asp
(He killed the thief.)

   b.   Ta ba xin si-le.
he p.t. letter tear-asp
(He tore up the letter.)

'Thief,' being animate, is Dative, but 'letter' being inanimate, is Objective, but we understand that something has been done to them both, in a very similar way. There is a change of state involved in both cases. Thus both are described as Affected in Halliday (1968) and Patient in Chafe (1970). To differentiate them by means of Dative and Objective in this case would force the function of case-assignment into becoming a mechanism of sub-classifying action verbs to predict the animateness.

The last area in this connection has to do with Agentive and Instrumental. In the following sentences,

(9) a. Ta ba lazhu chui-mie le.
   he p.t. candle blow-extinguish asp
   (He blew out the candle.)

   b. Feng ba lazhu chui-mei le.
   wind p.t. candle blow-extinguish asp
   (The wind blew out the candle.)

'He' is Agentive and 'the wind' Instrumental in Fillmore's framework. This analysis cannot account for the fact that when real Instrumental occurs as the subject of a sentence, it implies a separate initiator of the action, as is the case below,

(10) a. Zhe-ba yaoshi kai che-men.
   this-AN key open car-door
   (This key opens the car-door.)

   b. Chezi ba huo yun-zou le.
   car p.t. goods transport-away asp
   (The car hauled away the goods.)

In these two sentences, an animate Agent is implied. Notice that no such an initiator is available for (9.b). The role Force is suggested in Huddleston (1970) for nouns such as 'the wind.' Agentive and Force will be the animate and inanimate realizations of a more general category, Causer. (For more detailed discussion, see Chapter 4, Section 2.)

What we have seen in this section is the over-differentiation of nominal roles in the case grammar. The factor behind this is the undue attention paid to the feature "animate." We follow Halliday and Chafe, and regard the selection of the feature "animate" as a secondary specification.

3. Summary of Transitivity Relations

The entire set of Transitivity relations postulated in this thesis is outlined in this section. Readers should refer to relevant sections in the following chapters for the definition and characteristics of these relations.

The outline below is oriented toward verb classifications. We follow Chafe (1970) and sub-categorize verbs into Action, State, and Process. Action verbs define activities, both physical and mental, State verbs define quality and condition, and Process verbs define change-of-state.

Different configurations of relations define different categories of verbs. For instance, verbs which take 'Agt + Pat' and those which take 'Agt + Goal' are defined as two sub-categories of Action verbs.

(a) *Action*:
   (i) Agt + ∅:   Ta zai ku.
                  he p.v. cry
                  (He is crying.)

    (ii) Agt + Pat: Ta zai sha ji.
                             he p.v. kill chicken
                             (He is killing chickens.)
    (iii) Agt + Range: Ta zai chang ge.
                             he p.v. sing song
                             (He is singing.)
    (iv) Agt + Goal: Ta zai zhao shu.
                             he p.v. look-for book
                             (He is looking for books.)

(b) *State*:
    (i) Pat + ∅:   Ta hen gao.
                             he very tall
                             (He is very tall.)
    (ii) Pat + Range: Zhe-liang che zhi san-bai-kuai qian.
                             this-AN car worth three-hundred-AN money
                             (This car is worth $300.)
    (iii) Pat + Goal: Ta hen xihuan pao-che.
                             he very like sportscar
                             (He likes sportscars.)

(c) *Process*:
    (i) Pat + ∅:   Ta si le.
                             he die asp
                             (He died.)
    (ii) Pat + Range: Men po-le yi-ge dong.
                             door break-asp one-AN hole
                             (The door got a hole in it.)
    (iii) Pat + Goal: Kedou hui bian qingwa.
                             tadpole will become frog
                             (Tadpoles will become frogs.)

(d) *Causer*:
    (i) Causer + Agt: Nei-jian huai xiaoxi shi ta da ku qilai.
                             that-AN bad news cause he great cry i.p.
                             (That bad news made him cry.)
    (ii) Causer + Pat   Zhang San shi ta hen shengqi.
              (state):   Zhang San cause he very angry
                             (Zhang San made him angry.)
    (iii) Causer + Pat   Kaihui shi ta wang-le chi fan.
              (process): meeting cause he forget-asp eat rice
                             (Meetings made him forget to eat.)

CHAPTER 4

Agent

The role Agent defines the subjects in the following sentences,

(1) a. Ta zai xiao.
he p.v. laugh
(He is laughing.)

b. Ta zai kan shu.
he p.v. read book
(He is reading.)

c. Ta pei wo liang-kuai qian.
he restore two-AN money
(He reimbursed me two dollars.)

d. Ta ba yifu tuo-le.
he p.t. clothes take-off-asp
(He took off his clothes.)

Action verbs, whether transitive or intransitive, must be specified with an Agent, as formulated in Diagram H.

(2) V $\longrightarrow$ V   agt
action   action   N

Diagram H

1. Agent, Patient, and Three Classes of Verbs

In our framework, the differences between Agent and Patient are characterizable as those between Action verbs and non-Action verbs.

Two features, viz. Active and Stative, are proposed in Lakoff (1966) which sub-categorize predicates (both verbs and adjectives) into two major classes. His criteria for the differentiation are primarily syntactic and consequently do not correspond exactly to our distinction between Action and non-Action. Some of his observations are given below, ("verb" is used below to include both traditional verbs and adjectives)

(1) a. Only Active verbs occur in the imperative construction.

b. Only Active verbs occur in the progressive.

c. Only Active verbs occur with manner adverbs such as 'enthusiastically' and 'carefully.' (Not applicable to adjectives.)

d. Only Active verbs occur embedded under verbs such as 'persuade' and 'remind.'

The sub-categorization of verbs shown in Diagram I is obtained accordingly.

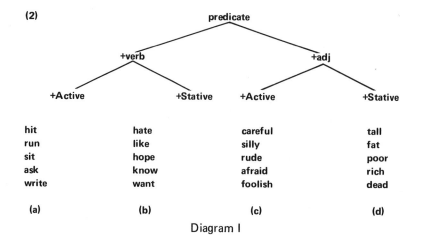

Diagram I

Semantically, only verbs in (a) define activity. The rest define mental or physical characteristics, i.e. states. The fact that verbs in (c) occur in identical syntactic environments (in English) to those in (a) does not entail any semantic relatedness between them. It seems that these syntactic tests involve other semantic properties. For instance, verbs in (d) are all "generic," and those in (c), when occurring in constructions listed in (1), are "non-generic." Observe that while stating 'John is careful,' we can assert 'careful' as John's disposition, we cannot do so when stating 'John is being careful.' Only "generic" states may occur attributively (e.g. John is a careful person). Moreover, verbs such as 'careful' and 'silly' can be either "generic" or "non-generic," others such as 'afraid' are necessarily "non-generic" (*John is an afraid boy).[1]

In our framework, Agent is associated with verbs in (a) and Patient with the others. Moreover, Action verbs specify what Agent can (though in some cases not necessarily) perform willfully and voluntarily. The criteria to distinguish Agent and Patient presented below are more or less directed towards this fundamental property of Agent.

(3) a.   Only Action verbs may occur in the progressive (not necessarily correspond-
          ing to English '-ing').
          (i) Ta zai ku.
               he p.v. cry
               (He is crying.)
          (ii) *Ta zai xiaozin.
               he p.v. careful
               (He is being careful.)
     b.   Only Action verbs may be embedded under such verbs as 'forget' and
          'remember.'
          (i) Ta wang-le wen Zhang San.
               he forget-asp ask Zhang San
               (He forgot to ask Zhang San.)

---

[1] Verbs given in (2.c) are 'behavioral' states, thus necessarily non-generic. 'Behavioral' in the sense that the Patient of these verbs can willfully (e.g. purposely) act as such; thus in 'John is being silly,' John has an absolute control over the state he is in.

I am grateful to Professor Chafe for directing my attention to this.

(ii) *Ta wang-le xihuan Zhang Xiaojie.
     he forget-asp like Zhang Miss
     (*He forgot to like Miss Zhang.)

(iii) Jide xie feng xin gei ta.
      remember write AN letter give he
      (Remember to write a letter to him.)

(iv) *Jide bu haipa.
     remember Neg afraid
     (*Remember not to be afraid.)

c. Only Action verbs may occur with Instrumental adverbs.

(i) Wo yong maobi xie.
    I use brush write
    (I'll write with a brush.)

(ii) *Wo yong qian you-qian.
     I use money have-money
     (I am rich with money.)

It is significant that a well-defined sub-category of verbs is entirely left out of discussion in Lakoff (1966). To this class belong such verbs as 'die,' 'break,' 'sink,' 'melt,' and 'fall,' in the intransitive usage. Lakoff's definition of Active and Stative cannot characterize these verbs, since they resemble both Active verbs (occurring in the progressive, in English) and Stative (not occurring in the other contexts).

These verbs are members of what is referred to as Process in Chafe (1970). They characterize neither activity nor state, but change-of-state. We shall refer to them as Process, and the nouns associated with them as Patient. Observe their characteristics in relation to our definition given in (3),

(4) a. *Ta zai si.
       he p.v. die
       (He is dying.)

   b. *Ta wang-le diao-xia-qu.
      he forget-asp fall-down-go
      (*He forgot to fall down.)

   c. *Bing yong reqi hua le.
      ice use heat melt asp
      (Ice melted with heat.)

This does not mean that these verbs can also be categorized as State verbs. There are systematic differences between them, as summarized below,

(5) a. Only State verbs may be modified by 'hen' — 'very.'

   (i) Ta hen shou.
       he very thin
       (He is very thin.)

   (ii) *Ta hen shang.
        he very injured
        (*He is injured a lot.)

   b. Only State verbs may be intensified through duplication.

   (i) Ta gao-gao de.
       he tall-tall m.p.
       (He is very tall.)

       (ii) *Chuan chen-chen de.
           boat sink-sink m.p.
           (*The boat sank very much.)

   c. Only Process verbs may be negated by 'meiyou' – (lit. have not, specifying "non-occurrence").

       (i)   *Ta meiyou keqi.
           he Neg-have polite
           (*He did not polite.)

       (ii) Men meiyou huai.
           door Neg-have break
           (The door didn't break.)

   d. Only Process verbs may be subject to number of occurrences.

       (i)   *Ta gaoxing-le liang-ci.
           he happy-asp two-time
           (He was happy twice.)

       (ii) Ta xing-le liang-ci.
           he wake-asp two-time
           (He woke up twice.)

Since change-of-state makes reference to states, a shift from State to Process is possible for many State verbs. Compare the following pairs of sentences,

  (6) a. Xiezi tai xiao.
        shoe too small
        (The shoes are too small.)

     b. Xiezi xiao le.
        shoe small asp
        (The shoes are too small now.)

     c. Tade toufa hen bai.
        his hair very white
        (His hair is grey.)

     d. Tade toufa bai le.
        his hair white asp
        (His hair became grey.)

A contrast of state is implied in (b) and (d) only (e.g. only (a) is appropriate when trying on shoes at a shop, since, (b) implies that the shoes used to fit). Thus although both State and Process specify Patient, the characteristics defined by them are different, the former specifying what state a Patient is in, and the latter what state a Patient enters.

In this section, we have defined Action, State, and Process as three sub-categories of verbs. Furthermore, Action verbs specify Agent and both State and Process specify Patient. This is shown in Diagram J.

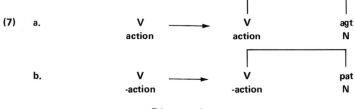

Diagram J

2. Inanimate Agent vs. Instrument

Agent is defined as animate in Fillmore (1968). It follows from this that if inanimate nouns occur in identical environments, they have to be assigned to other roles. As stated above, the subjects of Action verbs must be Agent, and since Agent is necessarily animate, inanimate subjects of Action verbs have to be defined otherwise. This role is usually defined as Instrument (cf. Fillmore 1968). We shall examine if this is feasible.

Inanimate subjects of Action verbs are generally of two categories; in one, the nouns may resume the role of Instrument in a prepositional phrase (its standard position), and in the other, no such syntactic connection is available. The first type is seen in (1) and the second in (2),

(1) a. Zhe-zhong jiandao bu nèng jian bu.
        this-kind scissors neg can cut cloth
        (This kind of scissors cannot cut cloth.)
    b. Kache ba dongxi yun-hui-lai le.
        truck p.t. thing transport-back-come asp
        (The truck hauled back the things.)
(2) a. Feng ba shu chui-dao le.
        wind p.t. tree blow-down asp
        (The wind blew down the tree.)
    b. Da-shui ba cunzi yan le.
        flood p.t. village drown asp
        (The flood drowned the village.)

A characteristic revealed by all these sentences is that there is a complete overlapping of activities between the subject nouns and the verb properties. For instance, 'jian' means 'to cut with scissors' and its subject can only be scissors, in the absence of an Agent. The range of activities of 'the wind' is again limited, all that is related to 'blowing.' An animate Agent is not subject to such restrictions.

Sentences in (1) can be related to sentences with animate Agent, e.g.

(3) a. Ta xihuan yong zhe-zhong jian-dao jian bu.
        he like use this-kind scissors cut cloth
        (He likes to cut cloth with this kind of scissors.)
    b. Ta yong kache ba dongxi yun-hui-lai le.
        he use truck p.t. thing transport-back-come asp
        (He hauled back the things with the truck.)

Note here that the execution and accomplishment of the Agent's activity depends on other elements, the Instrument (e.g. He cannot 'knife' except with a knife). On the other hand, the Instrument in (1) is not capable of fulfilling the intended function without an external initiator, the Agent. Therefore, subjects in (1) will be postulated as Instrument.

Sentences in (2) do not have Instrumental counterparts, but in some cases Agentive counterparts are found, e.g.

(4) a. Feng ba qi-qiu chui-guo-lai le.
        wind p.t. air-ball blow-over-come asp
        (The wind blew the balloon over.)
    b. Zhang San ba qi-qiu chui-guo-lai le.
        Z.S. p.t. air-ball blow-over-come asp
        (Z.S. blew the balloon over.)

Although an Agent occurs in (4.b), we understand that the Agent employs some other agency to accomplish the act, viz. 'wind' in this case. Therefore it appears that the status of the subjects in (2) parallels that of those in (1). However, some significant differences are observed. Firstly nouns such as 'the wind' and 'flood' cannot act as Instruments, e.g.

(5) a. *Ta yong feng ba qi-qiu chui-guo-lai le.
he use wind p.t. air-ball blow-over-come asp
(*He blew the balloon over with wind.)

b. *Ta yong da-shui ba cunzi yan le.
he use flood p.t. village drown asp
(*He drowned the village with flood.)

and secondly, subjects in (2) possess potency for certain phenomena without external initiators. For example, the wind blows and heat melts ice.

Thirdly, while animate Agent and the subjects in (2) may occur in the passive construction, true Instrument may not, e.g.

(6) a. Qi-qiu bei feng chui-guo-lai le.
air-ball p.p. wind blow-over-come asp
(The balloon was blown over here by the wind.)

b. *Bu bei jian-dao jian-po le.
cloth p.p. scissors cut-break asp
(*The cloth was slashed by the scissors.)

It would be difficult to specify the occurrence of verb-noun relations in the passive construction, if nouns such as 'the wind' and 'scissors' are treated alike. Sentences in (6) clearly indicate that animate Agent and such nouns as 'the wind' and 'water' in these particular contexts are sub-categories of a more general relation.

For these reasons, subjects in (2) are assigned the same status as animate Agent, at least in the areas of their inherent activities.

To capture this important aspect, we follow Chafe (1970) and specify Agent not with the feature "animate" but with "Potent." Nouns found in (2) are Potent nouns but those in (1) are non-Potent. Only Potent nouns may function as Agent. This role corresponds to Force in Huddleston (1970).

3.   Agent and Volition

"Volition" is sometimes used as a criterion to distinguish Agent from other roles (cf. G. Lee 1969 and Hall [Partee] 1965). A classic example is the pair of sentences below,

(1) a. Ta kan-le Zhang San yi-yan.
he look-asp Z.S. one-eye.
(He looked at Z.S.)

b. Ta kan-jian Zhang San.
he look-see Z.S.
(He saw Z.S.)

'Looking' is what one can do volitionally but not 'perceiving.' Two conclusions are usually drawn from this; that 'he' is Agent in (a) but Patient (or Experiencer in Chafe 1970) in (b), and that 'kan' — 'look' is an Action verb but 'kan-jian' — 'see' a State verb. A criterion of this approach will be returned to below.

In many cases, when a sentence is subject to both volitional and non-volitional readings, the different relations assigned are Agent and Instrument, so that in the sentences

(2) a. Ta xia-le Zhang San yi-tiao.
he frighten-asp Z.S. one-jump
(He frightened Z.S.)
b. Ta peng-le Zhang San yi-xia.
he bump-asp Z.S. one-moment
(He bumped Z.S.)

'Zhang San' is only conceived of as a physical object in the non-volitional reading, hence Instrument. This approach attempts to locate the source of "volition" in the different configurations of relations in the underlying structure. However, it meets with the following difficulty. Consider that the sentences,

(3) a. Ta shuai-po liang-ge wan.
he smash-break two-AN bowl
(He smashed two bowls.)
b. Ta tun-le yi-gen biezhen.
he swallow-asp one-AN safety-pin
(He swallowed a safety-pin.)
c. Ta tu-le yi-kou xue.
he spit-asp one-mouth blood
(He spat out a mouthful of blood.)

are subject to two readings, but the subject can in no way be described as Instrument in the non-volitional reading. It is obvious that 'he' above is engaged in activities such as 'smashing,' 'swallowing,' and 'spitting,' though not willfully.

Sentences in (3) differ from those in (2) in another respect. In the former, when they are interpreted volitionally we may ask the question "What did he do?," but we may at the same time ask the question "What happened to him?" when they are interpreted as non-volitional. On the other hand, in the case of (2), "What happened to him?" is inappropriate for 'he' but is appropriate for Zhang San in both readings. This means that subjects in (3) are actually not Agent but Patient in the non-volitional reading. However, this postulation entails that an Action verb is accompanied by an Agent in the volitional reading but a Patient in the non-volitional reading. Can it be that an Action verb is changed to a Process verb (hence accompanied by a Patient) if it is specified as non-volitional? There are many disadvantages in this approach.

Firstly, the difference between Action verbs and Process verbs in many cases would not be to capture the verb properties but the nominal roles. This approach destroys the syntactic patterns characterized by Action, Process, and State verbs in other cases. Secondly, this class of verbs would constitute an exception to our hypothesis that the nominal roles are uniquely determinable from the verb features. Thirdly, if we adopt this postulation, we have to be consistent and attempt to explain that the difference between volition and non-volition in every case is due to the difference between Action and Process. We fail this condition, because the subjects in (2) cannot be interpreted as Patient. Moreover, if the subjects in (3) are Patient, what role shall we assign to the objects? More Patients?

What we have seen so far are cases of the same verbs exhibiting ambiguity in terms of volition. There is another class of sentences which exhibit this contrast by verb derivations. This is seen in the following pairs of sentences,

(4) a.   Ta qie-le cai le.
          he cut-asp vegetable asp
          (He cut the vegetables.)
     b.   Ta cie-dao zijide shou.
          he cut-reach own hand
          (He (accidentally) cut his own hand.)
     c.   Ta ti xiao meimei.
          he kick little sister
          (He kicked the little sister.)
     d.   Ta ti-dao xiao meimei.
          he kick-reach little sister
          (He (accidentally) kicked the little sister.)

(a) and (c) refer to intentional acts but (b) and (d) to accidental events. The latter are always indicated by the verb 'dao' – 'reach.' This is an extremely productive process (e.g. this verb may occur with 'mo' – 'touch,' 'mai' – 'buy,' 'cai' – 'tread,' 'chuang' – 'bump,' 'lau' – 'scoop,' 'zhua' – 'catch,' 'zu' – 'rent,' etc.). In the non-volitional sentences here, the role Patient cannot be assigned to the subjects, since the question "What happened to him?" is not appropriate for (d). In fact (d) answers the question "What did he do?"

It was mentioned above (1) that the pair of verbs 'kan' – 'look' and 'kan-jian' – 'see' is usually analyzed as related but separate verbs; 'kan' as Action taking Agentive and 'kan-jian' as State taking Dative (cf. Y.C. Li 1970). The relationship between 'kan' and 'kan-jian' is in fact identical to that between the Action verbs and those plus the suffix 'dao' – 'reach' in (4). The speech of many Mandarin speakers does waver between the suffixes 'dao' and 'jian' in the context of 'kan' and 'ting' – 'listen' and to a less extent 'wen' – 'smell.' 'Wen' in fact almost always governs 'dao.' Viewing the morphological connection between 'kan,' 'ting,' and 'wen' on the one hand and 'kan-jian,' 'ting-jian,' and 'wen-dao' on the other in the greater context of Action verbs taking the suffix 'dao' in a well-defined environment (i.e. non-volitional) it is not difficult to judge that it misses an important fact to postulate 'kan' and 'kan-jian' as separate lexical verbs. The feeling that the subject of 'kan' and 'ting' is actively involved, while that of 'kan-jian' and 'ting-jian' is only passively involved is not unique to these verbs. It applies to all Action verbs which take 'dao' such as those in (4). We may refer to sentences containing Action verbs alone as activity sentences, and those containing Action verbs modified by suffixes such as 'dao' and 'jian' as resultative sentences. The difference between these two types of sentences is not so much connected with the nominal roles as with the different aspects of an event, which are expressed by different verbal processes. We shall postulate "non-volitional" as a verb inflectional feature and not change verb selectional features. The shift of the nominal features (i.e. from Agent to Patient-like) in (3) will be postulated as derivative of this derivational feature. This is formalized below,

(5) a.   V   V
          action   →   action
          root   *root + non-volitional*
          non-volitional

     b.   V   V
          action   →   action
          root + non-volitional   *root + dao*   /V = [–perception]

c.

V		V	
action	$\rightarrow$	action	
root + non-volitional		*root + jian*	/V = [perception]

Speakers who have 'kan-dao' and 'ting-dao' instead of 'kan-jian' and 'ting-jian' simplify their grammar by deleting the context in (5.c). The feature "non-volitional" is not realized morphologically in the case of verbs such as 'tun' — 'swallow,' 'tu' — 'spit,' and 'xia' — 'frighten,' and the realization is optional in the case of 'peng' — 'bump.'

"Volition" should be clearly distinguished from other features such as "wish" and "desire." For instance, "desire" is appropriate even for Patient, e.g.

(6) a. Ta xiang pang.
he think fat
(He would like to be fat.)
b. Ta xian si.
he think die
(He wants to die.)

"Volition" refers to intention or motivation to materialize something within the range of one's control. In (6), "desire" merely indicates the wish for the realization of something which is entirely beyond one's control. Furthermore "Volition" is an option for animate Agents only. Inanimate Agents are always understood non-volitionally.

Action verbs which are exclusively volitional are exemplified below

(7) a. Ta wang xia yi-tiao.
he towards underneath one-jump
(He jumped down.)
b. Ta ba men kai-kai.
he p.t. door open-apart
(He opened the door.)

In fact, most Action verbs are exclusively volitional.

The semantic relatedness between Patient and non-volitional (or accidental in particular) Agent is clearly suggested by similar syntactic environments in which they occur. The syntactic properties of non-volitional Agent is given below (cf. Section 1 of this chapter).

(8) a. Non-volitional Agent may not occur in the progressive.
(i) Ta zai qie dangao.
he p.v. cut cake
(He is cutting a cake.)
(ii) *Ta zai qie-dao dangao.
he p.v. cut-reach cake
(*He is cutting (by accident) a cake.)
b. Non-volitional Agent may not occur embedded under such verbs as 'forget' and 'remember.'
(i) Ta wang-le qie dangao.
he forget-asp cut cake
(He forgot to cut the cake.)
(ii) *Ta wang-li qie-dao dangao.
he forget-asp cut-reach cake
(*He forgot to cut (by accident) the cake.)

    c.   Non-volitional Agent may not occur in positive imperative.
        (i)   Da tade tou.
             hit his head
             (Hit his head!)
        (ii)   *Da-dao tade tou.
             hit-reach his head
             (*Hit his head by mistake.)
        (iii) Bie da-dao tade tou.
             Neg hit-reach his head
             (Don't hit his head by mistake.)

The relatedness here is in reference to Patient of Process verbs. Process verbs define 'happening,' and so do accidental events, whereas volitional activities define 'doing.'

4. Agent With Double Roles

Compare the following pair of sentences,

(1)   a.   Diren tui-le.
           enemy withdraw-asp
           (The enemy retreated.)
      b.   Chao-shui tui-le.
           tide-water withdraw-asp
           (The tide ebbed.)

A problem posed by these sentences is this: 'the enemy' is understood, in the volitional reading, as Agent and the verb 'withdraw' as Action, while 'the tide' is Patient and 'withdraw, ebb' here as a Process verb. How do we account for the relatedness of these two verbs in these two cases, especially as (a) is subject also to the non-volitional reading with 'the enemy' as Patient? In our framework, no Action verbs may be accompanied sometimes by Agent and sometimes by Patient freely.

Verbs such as 'kai' – 'open' and 'guan' – 'close' are similar to 'withdraw' in that they are accompanied by inanimate Patient in the most basic pattern (2.a), e.g.

(2)   a.   Men kai-le.
           door open-asp
           (The door opened.)
      b.   Ta kai-le men le.
           he open-asp door asp
           (He opened the door.)
      c.   Ta ba men kai-le.
           he p.t. door open-asp
           (He opened the door.)

but when an animate Agent is present, it is in the "ergative" relation with the Patient, as seen in (2.b) and (c). The verb 'withdraw' may also occur in the "ergative" construction, i.e.

(3)   a.   Ta tui-le piao le.
           he withdraw-asp ticket asp
           (He returned the ticket.)
      b.   Ta ba piao tui-le.

he p.t. ticket withdraw-asp
(He returned the ticket.)

Thus 'withdraw' in (3) can be analyzed as Process Action verb with the feature "causative" incorporated, similar to 'kai' in (2.b) and (c). In other words, 'withdraw' is basically a Process verb.

A solution to the volitional reading of (1.a) is suggested in Halliday (1968:188) and Huddleston (1970). According to their approach, we may say that while tides 'ebb' as a natural phenomenon, 'enemy' may 'withdraw,' i.e. willfully making themselves 'ebb.' Therefore 'withdraw' in (1.b) is a simple Process verb, but in (a) it is a Process Action verb, with identical Agent and Patient. The description of (1) is given below,

(1) a.   Volitional   = Agent/Patient (Process Action)
         Non-volitional = Patient (Process)
    b.   Patient (Process)

The two readings of (1.a) have the underlying structures[2] as given in figures 8 and 9.

Fig. 8

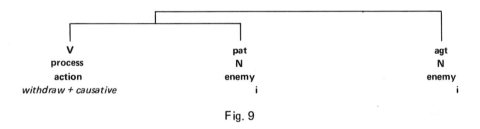

Fig. 9

The following pairs of sentences are similarly analyzed,

(4) a.   Zhang San ting-xia-lai le.
         Z.S. stop-down-come asp
         (Z.S. stopped.)
    b.   Huo-che ting-xia-lai le.
         train stop-down-come asp
         (The train stopped.)
    c.   Ta dong-le yi-xia.
         he move-asp one-moment
         (He moved.)

---

[2] Professor Chafe pointed out to me that an alternative would be to posit two verbs 'withdraw,' one Action and the other Process, the former being derived from the latter through the activization process, i.e.

    V   V
  process   →   action
  root   *root + activizer*

      d.   Cao dong-le yi-xia.
           grass move-asp one-moment
           (The grass moved.)

So far we have seen cases of the feature "causative" incorporated into Process verbs but retaining the same phonetic forms. Below is a case of lexical suppletion,

    (5) a.   Ta tiao-xia-qu le.
           he jump-down-go asp
           (He jumped down.)
        b.   Ta diao-xia-qu le.
           he fall-down-go asp
           (He fell down.)
        c.   Ta duo-qi-lai le.
           he hide-up asp
           (He hid.)
        d.   Ta ba xiezi cang-qi-lai le.
           he p.t. shoe hide-up asp
           (He hid the shoes.)

Essentially both (a) and (b) express the same verbal process, viz. downward movement, but while 'he' in (b) is Patient alone, 'he' in (a) is Agent and Patient simultaneously. (5.a) corresponds to the volitional reading of (1.a) and (5.b) to the non-volitional reading of (1.a).

    Double role is not restricted to Agent-Patient identity, nor the identity of roles within the Transitivity relations. Given below are cases of identity between the Transitivity and Circumstantial relations,

    (6) a.   Zhang San shou-dao yi-ben shu.
           Z.S. receive-reach one-AN book
           (Z.S. received a book.)
        b.   Zhang San ji-chu yi-ben shu.
           Z.S. mail-out one-AN book
           (Z.S. sent out a book.)

In (a), although no Benefactive phrase is present, we understand that Zhang San himself is the beneficiary, and we may assign to it both the Agent and Benefactive roles. (This type of Benefactive will be postulated as Goal in this thesis; see Chapter 7). On the other hand, Zhang San in (b) marks not only the Agent who did something but also the Source from which 'a book' has departed. Sentences in (6) are described as below,

    (6) a.   Agent = Benefactive (Goal)
        b.   Agent = Source

For an informative phenomenon of double roles involving Patient, Locative, and Instrument (Material), refer to Chapter 5, Section 4.

5. Agent and Causer

    The role Agent may occur in various contexts and is subject to different interpretations. In transitive sentences, a significant contrast is shown in (1.a) and (b)

    (1) a.   Ta ba men kai-le.
           he p.t. door open-asp
           (He opened the door.)

b.   Ta ba yifu tuo-le.
     he p.t. clothes take-off-asp
     (He took off his clothes.)

Although 'he' in both sentences is the Agent of a Process Action verb, the verbal processes involved are different. Whereas 'open' may occur without an Agent, 'take off' may not, e.g.

(2) a.   Men jintian bu hui kai.
         door today neg will open
         (The door won't open today.)
    b.   *Yifu jintian bu hui tuo.
         clothes today neg will take off
         (*Clothes won't take off today.)

This means that 'open' is inherently a Process verb, which requires the specification of a Patient only, not an Agent as well, so that the occurrence of 'he' in (1.a) is to fulfill the function of initiating the process which 'door' undergoes. In this sense, (1.a) but not (b) is a causative sentence, and the Agent plays the role of a "causer."

The difference is made explicit in Halliday's framework. Although 'he' is "causer" in both (1.a) and (b), it is Initiator of a non-directed action in (a) but Actor of a directed action in (b). The difference is further indicated by the roles the objects play. 'Door' is Actor of a non-directed action but 'clothes' is Goal. We shall follow Chafe (1970) and indicate the difference by different verb features; 'open' is a derived Process Action verb while 'take off' is an inherent one, as shown below,

(3) a.   V   V
         process   process
         Kai   →   action
         open   *kai + causative*

    b.   V
         process
         action
         tuo
         take off

The different features in Halliday's framework can be derived from the different semantic features involved here. 'He' in both (1.a) and (b) will be assigned the role Agent, and the 'causer' interpretation of 'he' in (a) is again derivative from the underlying structure as seen in (3.a).

However, by Causer in this section I am referring to the subjects of the following sentences,

(4) a.   Ta shi Zhang San hen bu gaoxing.
         he cause Z.S. very neg happy
         (He made Z.S. very unhappy.)
    b.   Ta shi Zhang San shu-le shi-kuai qian.
         he cause Z.S. lose-asp ten-AN money.
         (He made Z.S. lose ten dollars.)
    c.   Di-shangde xue shi ta pao-bu-kuai.
         ground-top-g.p. snow cause he run-neg-fast
         (Snow on the ground made him unable to run fast.)

According to Fillmore (1968), the verb 'shi' — 'cause' has the case frame $[-S + A]$. The specification S, i.e. Sentence, does not impose any constraints on the case relations occurring within this S, so that we find State verb in (a), Process verb in (b), and Action verb in (c). What is in question is the specification of Agentive for the subject of 'shi.' As pointed out above, the role Agent in many cases is subject to volitional and non-volitional interpretations. Neither of the animate subjects in (4) can be interpreted volitionally, and Agent in the strictest sense (i.e. Actor) cannot even occur with an Action verb in the lower sentence, e.g. (compare the English translations),

(5) a.   *Ta shi Zhang San xia-lai.
          he cause Z.S. down-come
          (He made Z.S. come down.)
    b.   *Ta shi Zhang San mai yi-ben shu.
          he cause Z.S. buy one-AN book
          (*He caused Z.S. to buy a book.)

One semantic property shared by all the subjects in (4) is that they indicate "cause" for the fact reported in the lower sentence. Causer in this sense can also be a whole sentence, e.g.

(6) a.   Jia-li mei ren shi ta hen bu fangxin.
          house-inside neg-have person cause he very neg at-ease
          (It makes him worried not to have anyone at home.)
    b.   Wai-tou you ren shuo-hua shi ta shui-bu-zhao.
          outside exist person talk cause he sleep-Neg-s.p.
          (It makes him unable to go to sleep to have someone talking outside.)

In Fillmore's framework, S can only be generated through the category Objective, to accommodate sentences in (4), but to accommodate those in (6), he would have to allow for the generation of S through Agentive. Consequently the category Agentive would be devoid of any significance.

Causer in this sense can even occur in the object position, e.g.

(7) a.   Ta hen danxin nide bing.
          he very worry your illness
          (He is very worried about your illness.)
    b.   Nide bing shi ta hen danxin.
          your illness cause he very worry
          (Your illness makes him very worried.)

These sentences are mentioned here (cf. Chapter 7, Section 4) to show that the roles Agent and Causer should be differentiated, in order to capture the relatedness of the pairs of sentences in (7). It should also be mentioned that not all objects of such State verbs as given above take Causer as objects, e.g.

(8) a.   Ta hen ke-lian Li Xiaojie.
          he very pity Li Miss
          (He pities Miss Li.)
    b.   *Li Xiaojie shi ta hen ke-lian.
          Li Miss cause he very pity
          (*Miss Li makes him pity.)

This will be dealt with at greater length in connection with Source and Goal (see Chapter 7, Section 4).

Causer contrasts with Agent in a causative construction, e.g.

(9) a. Zhang San shide ta hen zibei.
Zhang San cause-extent he very inferior
(Zhang San caused him to feel inferior.)

b. Zhang San nongde ta hen zibei.
Zhang San make-extent he very inferior.
(Zhang San made him feel inferior.)

'He' in (a) feels inferior because of Zhang San's merits over himself, but we understand in (b) that Zhang San must have acted or treated 'he' in such a way as to form an inferiority complex in 'he.' In Halliday's framework (1968), Zhang San in (9.a) may be described as Phenomenon/Causer and Zhang San in (b) as Causer.

There are two major syntactic differences between Agent and Causer. Agent may occur in the disposal construction, but Causer may not, i.e.

(10) a. *Zhang San ba ta shide hen zibei.
Zhang San p.t. he cause-extent very inferior

b. Zhang San ba ta nongde hen zibei.
Zhang San p.t. he make-extent very inferior
(Zhang San made him feel inferior.)

Secondly, Agent but not Causer may occur in the passive construction,

(11) a. *Ta bei Zhang San shide hen zibei.
he p.p. Zhang San cause-extent very inferior

b. Ta bei Zhang San nongde hen zibei.
he p.p. Zhang San make-extent very inferior
(He was made to feel inferior by Zhang San.)

What is established in this section is a new category Causer, which is distinct from Agent. Causer may be a noun, animate or inanimate, and it may also be a whole sentence. As will be seen in the following chapters, an S may also be generated through the categories Patient and Goal.

CHAPTER 5

Patient

The role Patient defines the subjects of the following sentences,

(1) *State verbs*:
   a. Nei-ke shu hen gao.
      that-AN tree very tall
      (That tree is very tall.)
   b. Xiao Ming hen ai tade gege.
      Xiao Ming very love his brother
      (Xiao Ming loves his brother very much.)
   c. Ren shi dongwu.
      man be animal
      (Man is an animal.)
   d. Niao you yumao.
      bird have feather
      (Birds have feathers.)

(2) *Process verbs*:
   a. Gou si-le.
      dog die-asp
      (The dog died.)
   b. Men po-le yi-ge dong.
      door break-asp one-AN hole
      (The door got a hole in it.)
   c. Kedou biancheng qingwa le.
      tadpole become frog asp
      (The tadpole became a frog.)

and the objects of the following,

(3) *Process-Action verb*:
   a. Mama sha-le yi-zhi ji.
      mother kill-asp one-AN chicken
      (Mother killed a chicken.)
   b. Ta ba yizi mai-le.
      he p.t. chair sell-asp
      (He sold the chair.)
   c. Ta ba shu fang-zai zhuozi-shang.
      he p.t. book put-l.v. desk-top
      (He put the book on the desk.)

Patient is the subject of State verbs in (1), the subject of Process verbs in (2), and the object of Process-Action verbs in (3). As a rough rule of thumb, the following questions can be asked about the Patient of a State verb, a Process, and a Process-Action verb, in that order,

(4) a. Ta zemme yang?
he how kind
(What is he like?)
b. Ta zemme le?
he how asp
(What happened to him?)
c. Zhang San ba ta zemme le?
Zhang San p.t. he how asp
(What did Zhang San do to him?)

Although Agent is predominantly animate, no such tendency is observed for Patient. However, the possibility is not excluded that certain State, Process, and Process-Action verbs may require animate, inanimate, or even human Patients. (Refer to Chapter 2, Section 2.) As pointed out in the last chapter, Agent in many instances is subject to Volitional and non-Volitional readings, but Patient, on the other hand, is always non-Volitional.

What qualifies a noun as the Patient of Process-Action is best defined in comparison with other relations which occur in the same surface position, viz. Range and Goal. For this reason, this point will be postponed until later (Chapter 6, Section 1 and Chapter 7, Section 3).

1. Patient vs. Experiencer

The verbs in the following sentences

(1) a. Ta xihuan pao-che.
he like sportscar
(He likes sportscars.)
b. Wo mingbai nide yisi.
I understand your meaning
(I understand what you mean.)
c. Li Si pa gui.
Li Si afraid ghost
(Li Si is afraid of ghosts.)

are what Dragunov refers to as non-action verbs (1958:101), which are distinct from his category of adjectives. Although he recognizes that non-action verbs and adjectives are related not only semantically but also syntactically, he does not set out to justify his postulation of separating them by means of the major dichotomy of predicators, viz. verbs vs. adjectives. One factor behind this analysis of his may be that non-action verbs are "transitive" in the traditional sense when adjectives are by his own definition intransitive.

In our framework, in which verbs (i.e. predicators) are classified into State, Process, and Action, this group of verbs is State. Briefly, State verbs are distinguished from Action and Process verbs by not taking aspectual inflections, e.g. (for detail, refer to Chapter 4, Section 1).

(2) a. *Zhang San xihuan-le pao-che.

Zhang San like-asp sportscar
(Zhang San liked sportscar.)
b.   *Zhang San xihuan-zhe pao-che.
Zhang San like-p.s. sportscar
(*Zhang San is liking sportscar.)

In Chafe (1970)[1] these are referred to as Experiential State verbs, which occur in the following semantic structure (that of 1.a).

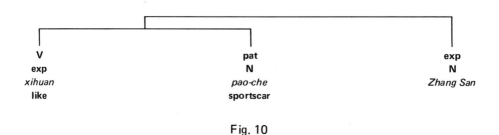

V	pat	exp
exp	N	N
xihuan	*pao-che*	*Zhang San*
like	sportscar	

Fig. 10

That is, the subjects of these verbs are assigned the role Experiencer instead of Patient, which is usually assigned to the subjects of State verbs.

We would like to ask, in what significant ways is Experiencer different from Patient of non-experiential State verbs? Note that in the following pairs of sentences,

(3) a.   Zhang San hen huanxi.
Zhang San very happy
(Zhang San is very happy.)
b.   Zhang San hen xihuan Li Xiaojie.
Zhang San very like Li Miss
(Zhang San is very fond of Miss Li.)
c.   Zhang San hen haipa.
Zhang San very afraid
(Zhang San is very scared.)
d.   Zhang San hen pa Li Xiaojie.
Zhang San very afraid Li Miss
(Zhang San is afraid of Miss Li.)

if Zhang San is described as Patient in (a) and (c) but Experiencer in (b) and (d) and Miss Li as Patient, then Zhang San in (a) and (c) is made to correspond to Miss Li. This treatment leaves the fact unexplained that Zhang San throughout all the sentences in (3) is the one whose mental disposition is affected, not Miss Li. To put it informally, if A is in the state of fearing B, it does not follow that B is also in a similar state, that B is in any way affected. There is only one Patient in (3), viz. Zhang San. This approach is explicit in Halliday's analysis. Zhang San is Affected in all the sentences in (3), and Miss Li is

---

[1] The same position is taken by Fillmore, in his lectures (Eng. 270) given at the University of California, Berkeley.

Phenomenon functioning as Range (i.e. Goal in our analysis in this case). The underlying structure of (1.a) in our re-analysis is given below,

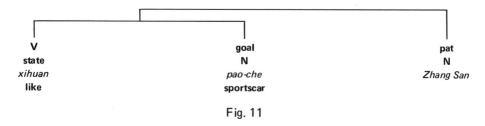

V	goal	pat
state	N	N
xihuan	*pao-che*	*Zhang San*
like	sportscar	

Fig. 11

In this way, we need not differentiate two types of 'like' (both 'huanxi'), one taking Patient and the other Experiencer.

These State verbs are different from others in that they take Goal. In most cases, e.g. 'love,' 'understand,' 'believe,' and 'hate,' Goal is obligatory. 'xihuan' — 'like' and 'pa' — 'afraid' seem to be the only cases with optional Goal. In (3.a) and (c), no Goal is implied or understood.

Another instance of Experiencer given in Chafe (1970) is seen below,

    (4) a.   Zhang San kan-jian yi-zhi niao.
             Zhang San look-perceive one-AN bird
             (Zhang San saw a bird.)
        b.   Zhang San ting-jian niao jiao.
             Zhang San listen-perceive bird call
             (Zhang San heard birds singing.)

The verbs are analyzed as Experiential Process, Zhang San as Experiencer, and the objects as Patient. It has already been argued (see Chapter 4, Section 3) that these verbs cannot be postulated as lexical verbs (i.e. they are compound verbs), and that the "passive" role of Zhang San here is shared by many other instances of Agent; that is, the Patient-like interpretation of Zhang San is not by any means due to the verbs being Process.

2. Sentential Patient

2.1. Easy and Difficult

It is a characteristic of many State verbs that they take a whole sentence as Patient. Straightforward examples are given below,

    (1) a.   Yi-nian nei xue-hao Yingwen hen nan.
             one-year within learn-good English very difficult
             (It is difficult to learn English well in one year.)
        b.   Ni jiao ta qu hao.
             you call he go good
             (It is better if you ask him to go.)

Typically, in the surface structure, the sentential Patient precedes the State verbs. The reverse order is rare, e.g.

    (2) a.   Hen nan jiao ta bu shuo-hua.
             very difficult call he Neg speak-word
             (It is difficult to ask him not to talk.)

    b.   Hao-xiang ta hen bu gaoxing.
         look-like he very Neg happy
         (It seems that he is very unhappy.)

Sentential Patient in this case corresponds to the Subject Complementation in Rosenbaum (1967). Head noun to the complementation may occur as an apposition, e.g.

    (3) a.   Yi-nian nei xue-hao Yingwen zhe-jian shi hen nan.
            one-year within learn-good English this-AN thing very difficult
            (The task of learning English well in one year is difficult.)
        b.   Ni bu ting-hua zhe-jian shi shi bu dui de.
            you Neg listen-word this-AN thing be Neg correct particle
            (The fact that you didn't listen was not right.)

Verbs such as 'difficult' and 'easy' are more versatile than others in that they may occur after the subject,

    (4) a.   Xue Zhongguo hua hen nan.
            learn China language very difficult
            (It is difficult to learn Chinese.)
        b.   Zhongguo hua hen nan xue.
            China language very difficult learn
            (Chinese is difficult to learn.)
        c.   Xue Zhongguo hua hen rongyi.
            learn China language very easy
             (It is easy to learn Chinese.)
        d.   Zhongguo hua hen rongyi xue.
            China language very easy learn.
            (Chinese is easy to learn.)
        e.   Xue Zhongguo hua hen kuai.
            learn China language very quick
            (It doesn't take long to learn Chinese.)
        f.   *Zhongguo hua hen kuai xue.
            China language very quick learn
            (Chinese doesn't take long to learn.)

(a) and (c) are apparent cases of Sentential Patient, but are (b) and (d) transformationally related to (a) and (c) respectively? Or instead of being (transformed) Subject Complementation, can they be cases of VP Complementation (Rosenbaum 1967), similar to sentences in (5)?

    (5) a.   Ta hen yuanyi qu.
            he very willing go
            (He is willing to go.)
        b.   Ta bu gaoxing qu.
            he Neg happy go
            (He doesn't feel like going.)

which have the phrase structure as given in figure 12.

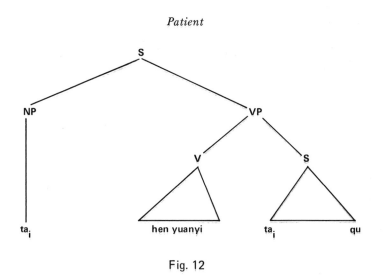

Fig. 12

This alternative analysis is attractive for the reason that it explains the ungrammaticality of (4.f) in a natural way, since while (6.a) and (b) occur and account for the source of (4.b) and (5.a), the non-occurrence of (6.c) accounts for that of (4.f)

(6) a. Zhongguo hua hen nan.
China language very difficult
(Chinese is difficult.)
  b. Ta hen yuanyi.
he very willing
(He is willing.)
  c. *Zhongguo hua hen kuai.
China language very fast
(*Chinese is fast.)

However, this alternative confronts difficulties in accounting for such cases as in (7)

(7) a. Ta xue-hao Zhongguo hua hen nan.
he learn-good China language very difficult
(For him to learn Chinese well is difficult.)
  b. Ta hen nan xue-hao Zhongguo hua.
he very difficult learn-good China language
(*He is difficult to learn Chinese well.)
  c. *Ta hen nan.
he very difficult
(He is difficult.)

It is clear here that (b) cannot be a case of VP Complementation, since (c), postulated as the matrix sentence of (b), is not acceptable. On the other hand, if (b) is derived from (a), we are able to specify for such verbs as 'difficult' and 'easy' that they do not accept animate Patient (they do in English, but with different meaning), because 'difficult' in (a) takes a whole sentence as Patient.

The phrase structure of (4.a) as postulated in this thesis is given in figure 13.

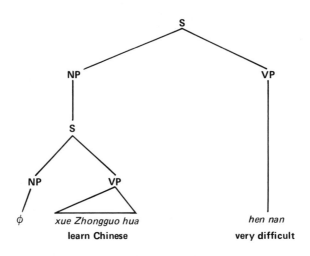

Fig. 13

A major transformation necessary to account for (4.b) and (7.b) is "predicate-lowering," which positions the predicate directly after the subject, after subject is formed (Agent as subject in 7.b, and Goal as subject in 4.b). Now compare the differences among the sentences below

(8)   a.   Hen nan xue-hao Zhongguo hua.
             very difficult learn-good China language
             (It is difficult to learn Chinese well.)

       b.   *Hen nan ta xue-hao Zhongguo hua.
             very difficult he learn-good China language
             (It is difficult for him to learn Chinese well.)

       c.   Zhongguo hua ta hen nan xue-hao.
             China language he very difficult learn-good
             (*Chinese, he is difficult to learn.)

       d.   *Zhongguo hua hen nan ta xue-hao.
             China language very difficult he learn-good
             (Chinese is difficult for him to learn well.)

(b) is unacceptable precisely because the higher predicate is lowered across the subject. In (c), the Goal, 'Chinese,' is topicalized, but the higher predicate 'difficult' is positioned after the subject, the Agent. (d) is ungrammatical, because it violates the condition that lowered predicates follow the subject. The violation can be stated as this: predicate-lowering is ordered to follow subject-formation, and topicalization to follow predicate-lowering. What is seen in (d) is that predicate-lowering applies after topicalization.

     Predicate-lowering is not applicable to all verbs which accept Sentential Patient. For instance, the position of 'fast' and 'slow' is limited, (cf. 4.e and f)

(9)   a.   Xue Zhongguo hua hen man.
             learn China language very slow
             (Learning Chinese takes a long time.)

b. *Zhongguo hua hen man xue.
   China language very slow learn
   (Chinese takes a long time to learn.)
c. *Hen man xue Zhongguo hua.
   very slow learn China language
   (It takes a long time to learn Chinese.)

In other words, they are restricted to the sentence-final position.

So far we have presented cases of 'difficult' and 'easy' where lowering is optional. In sentences below, lowering is obligatory,

(10) a. Ta hen rongyi ku.
        he very easy cry
        (He cries easily.)
     b. *Ta ku hen rongyi.
        he cry hen easy
        (For him to cry is easy.)
     c. Hua-ping hen rongyi po.
        flower-pot very easy break
        (Vases break easily.)
     d. *Hua-ping po hen rongyi.
        flower-pot break very easy
        (?For vases to break is easy. Cf. It is easy for vases to break.)

In the next section, we shall discuss more cases of obligatory lowering of predicates. This is not an ad hoc treatment of 'difficult' and 'easy' but is shared by other verbs.

2.2. Begin

In the sentences,

(1) a. Wanhui kaishi le.
       party begin asp
       (The party began.)
    b. Xianzai women kaishi jintiande wanhui.
       now we begin today's party
       (Now we begin tonight's party.)
    c. Tamen kaishi ba-cao le.
       they begin extract-grass asp
       (They began weeding.)
    d. *Tamen ba-cao kaishi le.
       they extract-grass begin asp
       (Their weeding began.)

we observe that 'begin' takes a simple Patient (a) but not a sentential Patient (d), and that the relationship between (a) and (b) is identical to that between the intransitive use and the transitive use of 'open' (i.e. as Process and Process-Action). The parallelism is shown below,

(2) a. Men shi ta kai de.
       door be he open particle
       (The door was opened by him.)

    b.   Jintiande zhenglun shi ta kaishi de.
         today's quarrel be he begin particle
         (Today's quarrel was started by him.)

    c.   *Ba-cao shi ta kaishi de.
         extract-grass be he begin particle
         (Weeding was started by him.)

Thus, postulating 'begin' as an inherent Process verb can account for both (1.a) and (1.b). In the latter it incorporates the feature "causative." Our task is to explain 'begin' in (c). To relate it to that in (a) and (b), we need to postulate that 'begin' in (c) is in fact a Process verb taking a sentential Patient. Its source, namely (1.d), is however ungrammatical and has to undergo obligatory predicate-lowering, analogous to the case of 'easy,' as seen in the last section.

    The description of begin-class verbs in Rosenbaum (1967) postulates cases such as (1.c) as Intransitive Verb Phrase Complementation but ignores related cases such as (1.a) and (b). Perlmutter (1968) establishes two types of 'begin' — one intransitive as in (1.a) and the other transitive as in (c). The underlying structures in his analysis are given below,

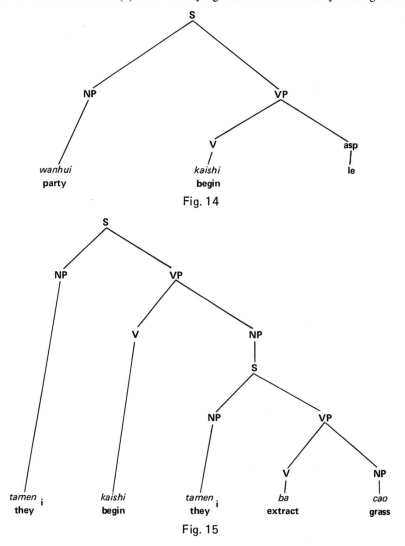

Fig. 14

Fig. 15

According to Perlmutter, 'begin' is subject to the "equi-subject deep structure constraint," since the sentences found in (3) are ungrammatical,

(3) a. *Wo kaishi ta ba cao.
I begin he extract grass
(*I began for him to weed.)

b. *Ta kaishi Zhang San xihuan ta.
he begin Zhang San like he
(*He began for Zhang San to like him.)

However, the following facts indicate that even Perlmutter's transitive 'begin' has to be analyzed as intransitive, that is, 'begin' in (1.c) is still a Process verb, taking a sentential Patient. The facts have to do with the active-passive pairings of sentences with transitive 'begin.' The following are the active instances of 'begin,'

(4) a. Dang-yuan zai 1965-nian kaishi piping zhe-xie ren.
party-member l.v. 1965-year begin criticise this-lot person
(Party members started to criticize these people in 1965.)

b. Ren-jia kaishi qifu tade haizi.
people start bully his child
(Other people started to bully his child.)

which have the passive counterparts as below,

(5) a. Zhe-xie ren zai 1965-nian kaishi bei dang-yuan piping.
this-lot person l.v. 1965-year begin p.p. party members criticize
(These people started to be criticized by party members in 1965.)

b. Tade haizi kaishi bei ren-jia qifu le.
his child begin p.p. people bully asp
(His child began to be bullied by other people.)

If we assume that passive sentences are derived from active sources, sentences in (5) have to be derived from (4). Should the underlying structure of (4) be similar to that given in figure 15, 'begin' would be the main verb, and we would expect (6) to be the passive sentences of (4),

(6) a. *Zhe-xie ren zai 1965-nian bei dang-yuan kaishi piping.
this-lot person l.v. 1965-year p.p. party-member begin criticize

b. *Tade haizi bei ren-jia kaishi qifu le.
his child p.p. people begin bully asp

which are ungrammatical. On the other hand, if sentences in (4) start out with sentential Patients, the passive transformation is inapplicable to the higher S because it contains the Process verb 'begin' and (6) would not result. The transformation is, on the other hand, applicable to the lower S, and the desired result is guaranteed after the higher predicate, viz. 'begin' is lowered to follow the subject. The derivation of (4.b) is demonstrated in (7).

(7) a. [Ren-jia qifu tade haizi] kaishi le.
people bully his child   begin asp

b. [Tade haizi bei ren-jia qifu] kaishi le. (passive)
his child p.p. people bully   begin asp

c. Tade haizi kaishi bei ren-jia qifu le. (predicate lowering)
his child begin p.p. people bully asp

Predicate lowering is obligatory. Ordering is crucial here: passive has to precede predicate-lowering.

There is another argument against the transitive treatment of 'begin.' The following sentences are instances of Rosenbaum's Object Noun Phrase Complementation,

(8) a. Zhang San xihuan chang-ge.
         Zhang San like sing-song
         (Zhang San likes to sing.)
    b. Zhang San bu xiangxin wo hui chou-yan.
        Zhang San Neg believe I can smoke-cigarette
        (Zhang San doesn't believe that I can smoke.)

If both (1.c) and (8.a) are analyzed as complementation structures, to differentiate them by different labels and by different ad hoc underlying structures is merely noting their different syntactic characteristics. It does not explain the difference. Compare that in (9),

(9) a. Zhang San lian chang-ge dou xihuan.
         Zhang San include sing-song all like
         (Zhang San even likes singing.)
    b. *Tamen lian ba-cao dou kaishi le.
        they include extract-grass all begin asp
        (They even began weeding.)

'sing (song)' in (a) functions as an object but 'weed' in (b) does not. This means that 'sing (song)' is derived from a nominal node (Goal in our analysis) and that 'to weed' is not traceable to similar node. Thus the structure given in figure 15 is inappropriate for (1.c). It should be postulated for sentences such as in (8).

What has been established about 'begin' is that in all the syntactic environments in which it occurs, it is an inherent Process verb, taking either a simple noun or a sentence as Patient. When a sentential Patient occurs, Predicate-lowering is obligatory. This transformation is briefly diagrammed in figure 16.

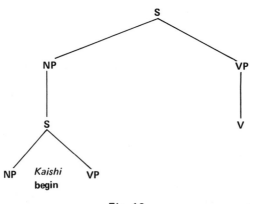

Fig. 16

2.3. An Analysis of Modals

It is well-known that many modals are subject to quite distinct interpretations. It will be postulated here that ambiguities of modals are accounted for by different semantic structures. Two such structures are recognized: in one modals take simple Patient and in the other sentential Patient.

First consider that in the following sentences

(1) a. Wo xiang ta hui shuo Fawen.
   I think he can/will speak French.
   b. Ta neng chi-fan.
   he can eat-rice
   (He can/may eat.)

The modals are subject to two interpretations (as indicated by the English translations), but in (b), when they are modified by 'very,' there is only one interpretation, namely, that of ability and not prediction,

(2) a. Ta hen hui shuo hua.
   he very can speak speech
   (He talks well.)
   b. Ta hen neng chi fan.
   he very can eat rice
   (He can (really) eat (a lot).)
   c. *Ta hen hui ji xin lai.
   he very can mail letter come
   (*He will write (home) very well.)

We shall say that sentences in (1) are ambiguous between "internal" modality and "external" modality. "Internal" refers to Patient's inner ability and capacity, while "external" refers to probability and permissibility of events.

The syntactic environments of "internal" 'hui' are identical to State verbs such as 'like' and 'afraid' and, moreover, this 'hui' and 'like' are mutually exclusive, e.g.

(3) a. Ta hui xihuan zhu-zai zher.
   he will like live-l.v. here
   (He will enjoy living here.)
   b. *Ta hen hui xihuan shuo Fawen.
   he very can like speak French
   (*He can like speak French a lot.)

Furthermore, the same transformation applies to both this 'hui' and 'xihuan,' e.g.

(4) a. Ta lian youyong dou bu hui.
   he include swim all Neg can
   (He can't even swim.)
   b. Ta lian youyong dou bu xihuan.
   he include swim all Neg like
   (He doesn't even like swimming.)
   c. *Ta lian zhidao dou bu hui.
   he include know all Neg will
   (He won't even know.)

State verbs are in many cases generic[2] and incompatible with time references, e.g.

---

[2] Non-generic State verbs include 'afraid,' 'disappointed,' 'angry,' 'satisfied,' and 'pleased.' These may occur with time reference,
   (i) Ta changchang hen shengqi.
   he often very angry
   (He is often angry.)
   (ii) Ta zuotian hen gaoxing.
   he yesterday very happy
   (He was very happy yesterday.)

(5) a.   *Ta mingtian hen hui youyong.
           he tomorrow very can swim
           (He can swim very well tomorrow.)
     b.   *Ta mingtian hen xihuan youyong.
           he tomorrow very like swim
           (*Tomorrow he likes swimming.)
     c.   Ta mingtian hui zhidao.
           he tomorrow will know
           (He will know tomorrow.)

These syntactic characteristics clearly establish that 'hui' meaning "ability" is a State verb which resembles 'like' in every respect, whereas 'hui' meaning "prediction" is a totally different type of State verb. The former takes a simple Patient and a Goal. Goal, as has been briefly mentioned above in connection with 'like,' may be a noun or a sentence. This 'hui' takes a simple noun phrase as Goal only in limited contexts, e.g.

(6) a.   Zhang San hui Ewen.
           Zhang San can Russian
           (Zhang San knows Russian.)
cf. b.   Ta shemme dou hui.
           he what all can
           (He can do everything.)

The latter 'hui' takes a sentential Patient, and obligatorily. This is evidenced by the following pairs of sentences,

(7) a.   Ta hui ba dan nong-po.
           he will p.t. egg make-break
           (He will break the eggs.)
     b.   Dan hui bei ta nong-po.
           egg will p.p. he make-break
           (The eggs will be broken by him.)

This kind of pairing is not possible with State verbs taking Goal, e.g.

(8) a.   Ta hen hui mai dongxi.
           he very can sell thing
           (He is good at selling things.)
     b.   *Dongxi hen hui bei ta mai.
           thing very can p.p. he sell
           (*Things are very good at being sold by him.)
     c.   Ta hen xihuan mai dongxi.
           he very like sell thing
           (He likes selling things.)
     d.   *Dongxi hen xihuan bei ta mai.
           thing very like p.p. he sell
           (*Things like to be sold by him.)

The active-passive pairings, as seen in (7), have already been shown in connection with 'begin,' to indicate sentential Patient (refer to the last section).

The underlying structures of these two kinds of 'hui' are given below. Figure 17 represents (4.a), an instance of Goal 'hui,' and figure 18 represents an instance of sentential Patient 'hui.' (Negation in both sentences is ignored.)

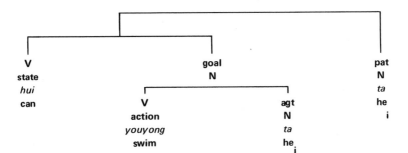

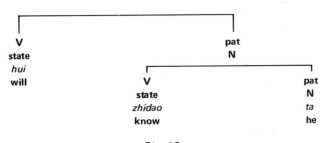

Fig. 17

Fig. 18

Examples to show that the modals 'neng' and 'keyi' (both "permission") also take sentential Patient are given below,

(9) a.   Ta keyi ba chezi kai-zou.
          he may p.t. car drive-away
          (He may drive the car away.)
     b.   Chezi keyi rang ta kai-zou.
          car may let he drive-away
          (The car may be driven away by him.)
     c.   Ni bu neng ba che kai-zou.
          you Neg can p.t. car drive-away
          (You mustn't drive the car away.)
     d.   Chezi bu neng rang ni kai-zou.
          car Neg can let you drive-away
          (The car mustn't be driven away by you.)

'Keyi' is different from 'neng' and 'hui' in that it can take a sentential subject in the surface structure, e.g.

(10) a.   Ni zhe-yang zuo bu keyi.
          you this-kind do Neg may
          (Your doing it like this is not allowed.)
     b.   *Ni zhe-yang zuo bu neng.
          you this-kind do Neg can
          (Your doing it like this is not allowed.)
     c.   *Ta zhe-yang zuo bu hui.
          he this-kind do Neg will
          (That he does it like this won't happen.)

Furthermore, compare the following,

(11) a.   Ni zhe-yang zuo bu xing.
           you this-kind do Neg permissible
           (For you to do it like this is not allowed.)
     b.   *Ni bu xing zhe-yang zuo.
           you Neg permissible this-kind do
           (You are not permitted to do it like this.)
     c.   Ni bu neng zhe-yang zuo.
           you Neg can this-kind do
           (You mustn't do it like this.)

'xing' and 'neng' are semantically similar, both referring to "permission" in the affirmative and "prohibition" in the negative, and they are in complementary distribution. It may be possible that they form a suppletive pair, 'neng' is realized when predicate-lowering has applied and 'xing' is realized otherwise.

Just as 'hui' and 'neng' exhibit ambiguity between "ability" and "prediction" and between "capacity" and "permission" respectively, 'keyi' is ambiguous between "capacity" and "permission," as shown below,

(12) a.   Che keyi kai-de gen huoche yiyang kuai.
           car may drive-extent with train same fast
           (Cars may/can drive as fast as trains.)
     b.   Wo keyi yi-tian kan liang-ben shu.
           I may one-day read two-AN book
           (I may/can read two books a day.)

"Ability" and "capacity" refer to the state of a Patient, while "prediction" and "permission" refer to "speech act" (Cf. Boyd and Thorne 1969). Let us refer to the former property as "internal modality" and the latter "external modality." "Internal modality" has a noun phrase as Patient and "external modality" a whole sentence.

3.   Sentential Predicate vs. Possessive Patient

Under discussion in this section are the following two sets of sentences,

(1) *State verbs*:
     a.   Ta duzi e.
           he stomach hungry
           (He is hungry.)
     b.   Ta tou tong.
           he head ache
           (He has a headache.)
(2) *Process verbs*:
     a.   Ta diu-le yi-ben shu.
           he lose-asp one-AN book
           (He lost a book.)
     b.   Ta si-le fuqin.
           he die-asp father
           (He lost his father.)

These verbs, whether State or Process, are specified in our grammar to be accompanied by single nouns but are found to be associated with two above. This observation may not seem so apparent in (1) as in (2), since the two nouns in each sentence occur consecutively and can be postulated as holding a "possessive" relationship between them, with the genitive particle 'de' deleted. In fact, in this analysis, sentences in (2) can be similarly treated, i.e. the possessor and the possessed noun are "discontinuous" in the surface structure. This approach then needs to establish Possessive Patient in the underlying structure. The source sentences for (1) and (2) might be

(3) a. Tade duzi e.
   his stomach hungry
   (He is hungry.)
   b. Tade tou tong.
   his head ache
   (He has a headache.)
(4) a. Tade yi-ben shu diu le.
   his one-AN book lose asp
   (He lost a book.)
   b. Tade fuqin si le.
   his father die asp
   (His father died.)

However, arguments will be given below for abandoning such a postulation. Process verbs will be discussed first.

Note that the Patient in (2) is 'he' so that all the sentences in (2) can be answers to "What happened to him?" whereas the Patient in (4) is what follows the genitive particle. Sentences here cannot be answers to the question given above. Thus "theme" or "focus of interest" is different in these two cases. However, in a grammar which allows for meaning contribution by transformation, this shift of focus can be accounted for (cf. Chomsky 1969). In other words, when the possessor is promoted to become the surface subject, it must necessarily bear the feature "focus."

Secondly, the occurrence of adverbs reveals a drastic difference between the two structures. The sentences below mean quite different things,

(5) a. Ta you diu-le yi-ben shu.
   he again lose-asp one-AN book
   (He lost a book again.)
   b. Tade shu you diu le.
   his book again lose asp
   (One of his books got lost again.)

(a) implies that a different book is lost, whereas (b) means that the same book is lost again. The occurrence of 'again' in some instances of Possessive Patient results in ungrammaticality,

(6) a. Ta you si-le yi-ge erzi.
   he again die-asp one-AN son
   (He lost another son.)
   b. *Tade yi-ge erzi you si le.
   his one-AN son again die asp
   (*One of his sons died again.)

'Losing' allows for recurrence but not 'dying.' There is nothing inconceivable about (a) and we understand that the sentence means something like 'The dying of a son happened again to him.' This interpretation is what is intended by "Sentential Predicate."

Thirdly, some instances of Possessive structure do not find counterparts in which the possessor and the possessed noun are discontinuous, e.g.

(7) a. Kong-zi de houyi si le.
        Confucius's descendant die asp
        (Confucius's descendant died.)

     b. *Kong-zi si-le houyi.
        Confucius die-asp descendant
        (*Confucius lost his descendant.)

Similarly, cases are found where the latter structure lacks a possessive counterpart, e.g.

(8) a. Zui can de jiu shi taitai si-le zhangfu.
        most sad m.p. just be wife die-asp husband
        (The saddest thing is when a wife loses her husband.)

     b. *Zui can de jiu shi taitaide zhangfu si le.
        most sad m.p. just be wife's husband die asp
        (*The saddest thing is when a wife's husband dies.)

     c. Nei-ke shu jintian diao-le shi-pian yezi.
        that-AN tree today fall-asp ten-AN leaf
        (Ten leaves fell from that tree today.)

     d. ?? Nei-ke shude shi-pian yezi jintian diao le.
        that-AN tree's ten-AN leaf today fall asp
        (?That tree's ten leaves fell today.)

(8.d) is strange for the reason that it implies that the tree had only ten leaves to begin with.

All these argue for the separation of (2) and (4) as far as their semantic structures are concerned. Furthermore, we cannot analyze sentences in (2) as having the structure "Patient-Verb" followed by a certain type of object, for in that case a constant assignment of the role Patient is made impossible in relating sentences in (2) with the following,

(9) a. Shu diu le.
        book lose asp
        (The book is lost.)

     b. Fuqin si le.
        father die asp
        (The father died.)

We want to be able to say that 'book' and 'father' in both (2) and (9) are Patient.[3]

---

[3] Our discussion here touches upon one of the most hotly debated topics in recent Chinese linguistics in Mainland China (refer to Yu Wen Hui Bian Vol. 9). Chinese linguists there can be divided into two groups, namely structuralists and semanticists, according to their analysis of the sentence
     Wang Mian qi-sui si-le fuqin.
     Wang Mian seven-age die-asp father
     (Wang Mian lost his father when he was seven.)
The former postulate (i) and the latter (ii)
(i) subject – verb – object
(ii) subject – verb – subject
An important difference is that the former recognize that 'die' may be used intransitively (in most cases) and transitively, while the latter do not recognize this shift of verb categories.

Therefore, it is proposed that sentences in (2) are instances of Sentential Predicate, accompanied by an Experiencer. The underlying structure of (2.b) is as given in figure 19.

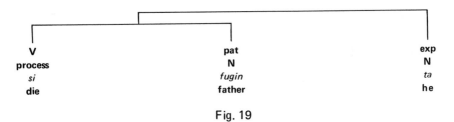

V	pat	exp
process	N	N
si	*fugin*	*ta*
die	father	he

Fig. 19

What we need to state here is that Experiencer, the higher Patient who is affected by the event expressed in the lower sentence, has priority over a lower Patient in the "subject hierarchy." The role Experiencer is taken from Chafe (1970), but with different application in this thesis. It can also be understood as Patient predicated by a sentence.

It is a general tendency in Chinese for indefinite nouns to occur after the verb, regardless of types of verbs, in the surface structure, e.g.

(10) a.   Zuotian si-le yi-ge ren.
           yesterday die-asp one-AN person
           (A man died yesterday.)
     b.   Jintian lai-le liang-ge ren.
           today come-asp two-AN person
           (Two people came today.)

Therefore it is merely a coincidence that sentences in (2) resemble those with the structure "subject-verb-object." On the other hand, there is a syntactic mechanism available to bring the indefinite noun in front of the verb, by introducing the "existential operator" (Allan 1971) e.g.

(11) a.   Zuotian you yi-ge ren si le.
           yesterday exist one-AN person die asp
           (Yesterday someone died.)
     b.   Jintian you liang-ge ren lai.
           today exist two-AN person come
           (Today two people came.)

Similarly, this transformation is applicable to (2), i.e. (2.b has to be excluded since its lower Patient is definite).

(12) a.   Ta you yi-ben shu diu le.
           he exist one-AN book lose asp
           (He lost a book.)
     b.   Ta you yi-ge erzi si le.
           he exist one-AN son die asp
           (He lost a son.)

It should be clear from this that if (2) is derived from (4), then the relatedness of (2) and (9) cannot be accounted for. A problem here, however, is that while the theme in (2) is 'he,' it changes to the indefinite noun in (12). Nonetheless, the relatedness of (2) and (12) is evidenced by the fact that while (6.a) cannot be changed to (6.b), it finds an existential counterpart, i.e. compare

(13) a.   Ta you you yi-ge erzi si le.
          he again exist one-AN son die asp
          (He lost another son.)

     b.   *Ta you yi-ge erzi you si le.
          he exist one-AN son again die asp
          (*One of his sons died again.)

     c.   Ta you you yi-ben shu diu le.
          he again exist one-AN book lose asp
          (He lost another book.)

Both (a) and (c) refer to a different 'son' and 'book,' in agreement with the interpretation in Sentential Predicate.

Next, we shall examine cases of Sentential Predicate in which State verbs occur, as exemplified in (1). It should be clear that if sentences in (1) contain Possessive Patients with deleted genitive particle, there should be two major constituents in each sentence, viz. the possessed noun with the possessor and the State verb. It will be demonstrated below that the constituent-breaking (IC cut) should be between the possessor and the possessed noun. In other words, 'he' in (1) should be the Experiencer and in the remainder of the sentences the Sentential Predicate. Sentences in (1) will be contrasted with ordinary possessive structures, such as given in (14),

(14) a.   Tade duzi hen zhang.
          his stomach very full
          (He feels very full.)

     b.   Tade shou hen tong.
          his hand very painful
          (His hand is very painful.)

In the first place, various adverbs can be inserted between the Experiencer and the Sentential Predicate, but not between the possessor and the possessed noun, e.g.

(15) a.   Ta you tou tong le.
          he again head ache asp
          (He has a headache again.)

     b.   Ta tou you tong le.
          he head again ache asp
          (He has a headache again.)

     c.   Ni hai tou tong ma?
          you still head ache particle
          (Do you still have a headache?)

     d.   Ni tou hai tong ma?
          you head still ache particle
          (Do you still have a headache?)

(16) a.   *Ta you shou tong le.
          he again hand ache asp
          (His hand is aching again.)

     b.   Ta shou you tong le.
          he hand again ache asp
          (His hand is aching again.)

   c.   *Ni hai shou tong ma?
       you still hand ache particle
       (Is your hand still aching?)

It is a general rule in Chinese that adverbs occur directly in front of verbs, even in cases where the domain of adverbs governs nouns,[4] yet in the case of Sentential Predicate, they occur in two positions, either in front of a verb or in front of a noun followed by a verb. The only way to capture the situation is to state that adverbs occur in front of a predicate. There are two predicates in (15), one predicating the higher Patient 'he' and the other predicating the lower Patient 'head.' The ungrammaticality of (16.a) and (c) is then systematically accounted for; they contain only one predicate, and adverbs must occur in front of it.

Similarly, modals, which have been analyzed as a higher predicate taking Sentential Patient, can be lowered to precede a Sentential Predicate, e.g.

(17) a.   Fangxin! Wo bu hui tou tong.
         at ease, I Neg will head ache
         (Don't worry, I won't get a headache.)
      b.   *Fangxin! Wo bu hui shou tong.
         at ease, I Neg will hand ache
         (Don't worry, my hand won't ache.)

Secondly, the difference between Sentential Predicate and Possessive Patient is clearly indicated in complementation constructions. It is a well-known fact (see Rosenbaum 1967) that in the following sentence

(18) Wo juede hen gaoxing.
     I feel very happy

equi-NP deletion has applied to the subject of the embedded sentence. Now, consider that in the sentences

(19) a.   Wo juede duzi e.
         I feel stomach hungry
         (I feel hungry.)
      b.   Wo juede tou tong.
         I feel head ache
         (I have a headache.)
      c.   *Wo juede shengin di.
         I feel voice low
         (I feel that my voice is low.)
      d.   Wo juede wode shengin di.
         I feel my voice low
         (I feel that my voice is low.)

---

[4] Compare the following
(i) Zhang San gen Li Si dou yao lai.
     Zhang San and Li Si all want come
     (Both Zhang San and Li Si want to come.)
(ii) Shu gen bi wo dou yao mai.
     book and pen I all want buy
     (I want to buy both books and pens.)
The domain of 'all' applies to nouns only, yet it occurs before the verbs.

if the higher Patient is a simple noun and the lower Patient is a possessive NP, no deletion can take place (cf. c and d). However, equi-NP deletion has taken place in (a) and (b). This must mean that the subject of the embedded sentence is a simple noun and not a possessive NP. This supports our postulation that sentences in (1) contain a sentential Patient while those in (14) contain Possessive Patient.

It is not claimed here that sentences in (1) are distinct from those in (3). The latter are in fact derived from the former by undergoing a transformation which introduces what I have called "pseudo-genitive" (see Teng 1970, footnote 17). Essentially, the genitive particle 'de' is optionally inserted between two nouns, i.e.

(20) $NP_1 + NP_2 \Rightarrow NP_1$ de NP_2

This is a late rule and accounts for the occurrence of 'de' in the following sentences, in addition to those in (3),

(21) a.   Ni bie sheng tade qi.
          you don't form his anger
          (Don't be angry with him.)
     b.   Wo lai bang nide mang.
          I come help your busy
          (Let me help you.)

That 'de' in (3) is a "pseudo-genitive" while that in (14) is a genuine genitive is evidenced in conjoining deletion. Compare the following,

(22) a.   Zhang Sande duzi hen e, Li Si ye shi.
          Zhang San's stomach very hungry, Li Si also be.
          (Zhang San is very hungry, so is Li Si.)
     b.   *Zhang Sande duzi hen e, Li Side ye shi.
          Zhang San's stomach very hungry, Li Si's also be
     c.   Zhang Sande shou hen chang, Li Side ye shi.
          Zhang San's hand very long, Li Si's also be
          (Zhang San's hand is very long, so is Li Si's.)
     d.   *Zhang Sande shou hen chang, Li Si ye shi.
          Zhang San's hand very long, Li Si also be
          (*Zhang San's hand is very long, so is Li Si.)

At the stage of deleting the identical elements, 'de' in (a) must be absent, to account for its grammaticality and the ungrammaticality of (b). However 'de' is specified in the underlying structure, it must have been introduced by the stage of conjoining deletion and is not deletable. Moreover, notice that while (23.a) is ambiguous, (23.b) is not,

(23) a.   Wo juede Zhang Sande piqi hen huai, Li Si ye shi.
          I feel Zhang San's temper very bad, Li Si also be
          (I feel Zhang San is bad-tempered; Li Si too.)
     b.   Wo juede Zhang Sande shengin hen di, Li Si ye shi.
          I feel Zhang San's voice very low, Li Si also be
          (I feel Zhang San's voice is very low; Li Si too.)

Li Si in (a) can be the higher Patient, corresponding to 'I' or the lower Patient, corresponding to Zhang San, whereas Li Si in (b) can only be the higher Patient. To get the meaning that Li Si is the lower Patient in (b), 'de' has to be retained. This shows that both (22.a) and (23.a) contain Sentential Predicate, in which 'de' is inserted by a late transformation, whereas 'de' in (22.c) and (23.b) is a genuine genitive.

Therefore, the underlying structures of (1.b) and (14.b) are specified as in figures 20 and 21 (genitive simplified).

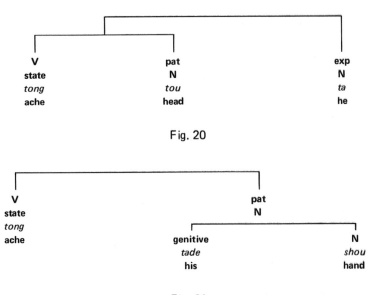

Fig. 20

Fig. 21

Sentences with Sentential Predicate correspond to the well-known "double-subject" constructions in Japanese (see Fillmore 1968:65 for a brief discussion of this) and are recognized as such by many Chinese scholars. It may be informative to look at L. Wang's position on this. He claims that Sentential Predicate

Is restricted to a very narrow range of reference, e.g. 'Ta duzi e-le' (He is hungry) and 'Ta danzi xiao' (He is timid). I cannot agree to extend the range, because the phrases 'duzi e' (hungry) and 'danzi xiao' (timid) are in fact equivalent to single lexical items. It is quite feasible to establish that these phrases refer to activities or qualities of the nouns identified as the subjects (1956:175, my translation).

What is claimed is that these phrases (or sentences) are already idiomaticized (cf. Chafe 1968). Idioms, though syntactically resembling phrases and sentences, correspond to lexical items in reference. Our task here is to determine what are and what are not idioms.

An idiom can be defined as "a constituent or series of constituents for which the semantic interpretation is not a compositional function of the formatives of which it is composed" (Fraser 1970). This can be best understood as the following diagram (from Weinreich 1966)

$$\frac{A+B}{a\ \ b} = \frac{A+B}{X} \neq \frac{A+B}{a+b}$$

(A,B = item, word: a,b,X = sense, meaning)

In most cases of idioms, a literal counterpart is available, as can be inferred from Weinreich's diagram. According to these two criteria, what qualifies as our Sentential Predicate, according to the syntactic tests discussed above, falls into two groups, e.g.

(24) a. Group A: danzi xiao-'timid,' erduo ruan-'indicisive,' xin du-'cruel,' duzi da-'pregnant,' yan hong-'jealous,' lianpi hou-'thick-skinned.'

      b.   Group B: duzi e-'hungry,' piqi huai-'bad-tempered,' tou tong-'headache,' jixing hao-'good memory,' xingzi ji-'impatient,' yao suan-'backache.'

Those in Group A, when not interpreted literally, will be defined as idioms, but those in Group B as Sentential Predicate. Idioms generally characterize personality and temperament by means of physical description in the literal sense. Sentential Predicate is characterized by the semantic property of referring to temperament and physical condition, and very rarely physical description, which is usually rendered by Possessive Patient. Like L. Wang, Chao (1968:94 ff) does not differentiate between idiom and Sentential Predicate.

    Idioms and Sentential Predicate start out with different semantic specifications (e.g. 'duzi da' — 'stomach big=pregnant' is specified identically as 'huaiyun' — 'pregnant'), but before reaching the transformational component, they share identical structures (refer to Chafe 1968 for a systematic account of this). This explains why they behave alike syntactically.

    Only State and Process verbs are observed to occur in Sentential Predicate. This has to be specified for the generation of well-formed semantic structures. Since Action verbs do not occur in this construction, we may generalize and say that this particular underlying configuration indicates an event or happening affecting a patient or a Patient experiencing a certain state.

4. Existential Agent and Existential Patient

    By existential sentences, I shall here arbitrarily restrict our discussion to those in which 'zai' — 'zhe' alternation is observed, e.g.

    (1) a.   Zhuxi zuo-zai tai-shang.
              chairman sit-l.v. platform-top
              (The chairman is sitting on the platform.)
        b.   Tai-shang zuo-zhe zhuxi.
              platform-top sit-p.s. chairman
              (On the platform is sitting the chairman.)
        c.   Dianxian-shang ting-zhe liang-zhi niao.
              cable-top stop-p.s. two-AN bird
              (On the cable are sitting two birds.)
        d.   You liang-zhi niao ting-zai dianxian-shang.
              exist two-AN bird stop-l.v. cable-top
              (There are two birds sitting on the cable.)

and not consider those in which 'zai' and 'you' alternate (refer to Y.C. Li (1972) for this topic), e.g.

    (2) a.   Shu zai zhuo-shang.
              book l.v. table-top
              (The book is on the table.)
        b.   Zhuo-shang you shu.
              table-top exist book
              (On the table there is a book.)

However, I am not unaware of nor denying the relatedness between these two constructions.

'Zhuxi' — 'chairman' and 'niao' — 'bird' in (d) will be referred to as "Existential Agent"; here we are not reporting any activity performed by the Agent, but rather we are describing a state which results from such an activity. As Lü comments, "Once an activity has been accomplished, a state results" (1942:57).

Corresponding to Existential Agent, Existential Patient is seen below,

(3) a. Qiang-shang gua-zhe hua.
   wall-top hang-p.s. painting
   (On the wall hangs a painting.)
 b. Zhuo-shang fang-zhe shu.
   table-top place-p.s. book
   (On the table lies a book.)

In these sentences, we understand that the Patient is now so located as a result of the activity of an unspecified Agent. They find 'zai' counterparts, i.e.

(4) a. Hua gua-zai qiang-shang.
   painting hang-l.v. wall-top
   (The painting is hung on the wall.)
 b. Shu fang-zai zhuo-shang.
   book place-l.v. table-top
   (The book is placed on the table.)

as well as Agentive counterparts, i.e.

(5) a. Ta ba hua gua-zai qiang-shang.
   he p.t. painting hang-l.v. wall-top
   (He hung the painting on the wall.)
 b. Ta ba shu fang-zai zhuo-shang.
   he p.t. book place-l.v. table-top
   (He placed the book on the table.)

An important issue involved here is whether the Existential Patients in (3) are Patients of State verbs or of Process-Action verbs. If the former analysis is adopted, we will have to establish two types of such verbs, one State and the other Process-Action. In fact, the traditional treatment is to establish two types, one intransitive and the other transitive (Lü 1946:110). We have noted that when a traditional transitive verb is related to an intransitive verb, the derivational relationship can be understood as that of "causation." In other words, the intransitive verb is "basic" and the transitive is "derived" (e.g. 'kai' — 'open,' 'guan' — 'close,' 'ting' — 'stop,' and 're' — 'hot, to heat'). A parallel postulation for such verbs as 'gua,' 'fang' and 'tie' in (3) seems highly inappropriate. In the first place, they do not behave like State verbs, since they occur with aspects, nor can they be understood as Process verbs, since they do not imply "happening" or "change-of-state." Secondly, although both (2.a) and (4.b) mean that the book is now placed on the desk because of external instigation, the former is "state-oriented" (i.e. a pure State verb) while the latter is "action-oriented." This is indicated by the fact that adverbs may occur with the latter but not with the former,

(6) a. *Shu pingpingde zai zhuo-shang.
   book flatly l.v. table-top
   (*The book is flatly on the table.)

    b.   Shu pingpingde fang-zai zhuo-shang.
        book flatly place-l.v. table-top
        (The book is placed flat on the table.)

    c.   *Xiangpian waiwaide zai men-shang.
        picture crooked-ly l.v. door-top
        (*The picture is crookedly on the door.)

    d.   Xiangpian waiwaide tie-zai men-shang.
        picture crookedly paste-l.v. door-top
        (The picture is pasted crooked on the door.)

It is also important to note that such adverbs also occur in Agentive counterparts, viz.

(7) a.   Ta ba shu pingpingde fang-zai zhuo-shang.
        he p.t. book flatly place-l.v. table-top
        (He placed the book flat on the table.)

    b.   Ta ba xiangpian waiwaide tie-zai men-shang.
        he p.t. picture crooked-ly paste-l.v. door-top
        (He pasted the picture crooked on the door.)

This means that as long as we derive sentences in (6) from those in (7), no separate and ad hoc restriction on the occurrence of such adverbs needs to be stated. The "deactivated" sense (Chafe 1970) of these verbs in (3) and (4) follows from the Agent being unspecified. We shall consequently postulate that Existential Patient above is Patient of Process-Action verbs.

However, this postulation works well only for those cases in which 'zai'-'zhe' alternation is found and which find Agentive counterparts. Consider now in the following sentences,

(8) a.   Shengzi-shang gua-zhe yi-zhi bianfu.
        rope-top hang-p.s. one-AN bat
        (On the rope hangs/is hung a bat.)

    b.   Shan-shang gai-zhe yi-ceng xue.
        mountain-top cover-p.s. one-layer snow
        (The mountain is covered with a layer of snow.)

    c.   Wu-li ji-zhe hen duo ren.
        house-inside crowded-p.s. very many person
        (The house is crowded with people.)

the nouns in question are unlikely to be Existential Patient, since the "understood" Agent is not available (to get the same meaning), although (7.a), for example, are ambiguous. The bat (alive or dead) can be hung there by an Agent, or else it (necessarily alive) can hang on there of its own accord. In the former interpretation, we can postulate the role Existential Patient, and in the latter, we have to treat it as Existential Agent. The other sentences do not have Agentive counterparts, i.e.

(9) a.   *Ba xue gai-zai shan-shang.
        p.t. snow cover-l.v. mountain-top
        (*Cover the mountain with some snow.)

    b.   *Ba hen duo ren ji-zai wu-li.
        p.t. very many person crowd-l.v. house-inside.
        (*Get many people crowded into the house.)

Even if an Agent could be found, the meaning would be entirely different.

Our problem here is the treatment of these nouns as Existential Agents. Lü suggests that

Verbs in these sentences can be used either transitively or intransitively ... but not every case is easily differentiated ... and these sentences (i.e. indeterminable cases) can be analysed as $V^{a/b}S$ (V^bS = our Existential Patient, V^aS = our Existential Agent) .. then the problem appears simple (1946:110, my translation).

The problem is not that simple. His postulation entails the establishment of two sets of such verbs (transitive and intransitive), and the connection between them is not clearly defined.

A solution is made possible when we utilize the notion "double role" (see Chapter 4, Section 4). All the verbs in (8) are intrinsic Process-Action verbs. Compare the following sentences with those in (8),

(10) a.   Ta ba tanzi gai-zai shen-shang.
          he p.t. blanket cover-l.v. body-top
          (He spread the blanket on himself.)
     b.   Ta ba shenti ji-guo-qu.
          he. p.t. body crowd-over-go
          (He squeezed in.)

Thus, in the case of (8.a) for instance, we recognize the verb only in the capacity of Process-Action, and we understand the bat to be playing the role of both Agent and Patient (i.e. it is hung there as a result of hanging itself there).

All verbs in this type of Existential sentences specify "locational displacement," and this process requires Patients which undergo the displacement. This general property of these verbs cannot be stated if they are analyzed as merely "intransitive" when occurring in the context given in (8).

In this section, we have observed three types of Existential sentences, those specifying Agent only (1), those specifying Patient only (3) and (4), and those specifying both Agent and Patient (8). Their underlying structures are given in figure 22 (locative simplified).

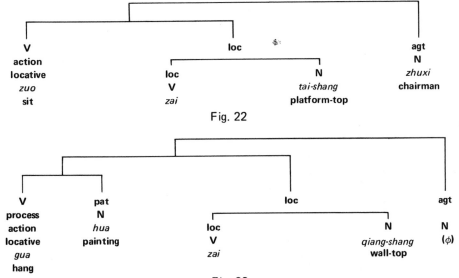

Fig. 22

Fig. 23

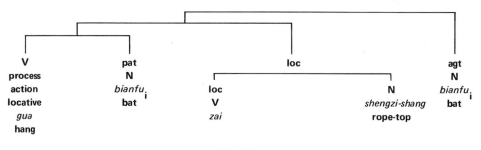

Fig. 24

In each underlying structure, there are two Noun-nodes, and either of them may be selected as the surface subject (or topic).

In place of 'zhe,' we find 'man' — 'full' in these Existential sentences, e.g.

(11) a. Jiangtai-shang zuo-man-le xuesheng. (agt)
           platform-top sit-ful-asp student
           (The whole platform is seated with students.)
      b. Shujia-shang fang-man-le shu. (pat)
           bookshelf-top place-full-asp book
           (The bookshelf is loaded with books.)
      c. Xiyuan-li ji-man-le ren. (agt/pat)
           theatre-inside crowded-asp person
           (The theatre is crowded with people.)

'Man' may be derived from full-fledged adverbs in the sentences below,

(12) a. Jiangtai-shang manmande zuo-zhe xuesheng.
           platform-top fully sit-p.s. student
           (The platform is fully seated with students.)
      b. Shujia-shang manmande fang-zhe shu.
           bookshelf-top fully place-p.s. book
           (The bookshelf is loaded with books.)

In the following sentences, however, it is difficult to determine whether the nouns are Locative or Patient,

(13) a. Luguan dou zhu-man-le.
           hotel all live-full-asp
           (The hotel is fully occupied.)
      b. Weizi dou zuo-man-le.
           seat all sit-full-asp
           (Seats are all occupied.)
      c. Pingzi dou zhuang-man-le.
           bottle all load (fill)-full-asp
           (Bottles are all filled.)

They look like Patient, because, firstly, locativizers are absent and, secondly, the surface structure here resembles some others with normal Patient, e.g.

(14) a. Shujia dou bai-wai le.
           bookshelf all place-crooked asp
           (Bookshelves are all placed crooked.)

    b.   Weizi dou zuo-huai le.
        seat all sit-bad asp
        (Seats are all broken (from people sitting on them).)

and, thirdly, these nouns can occur in 'ba' (disposal)-constructions, e.g.

  (15) a.   Tamen ba weizi zuo-man le.
          they p.t. seat sit-full asp
          (They took all the seats.)
      b.   Tamen ba pingzi zhuang-man le.
          they p.t. bottle fill-full asp
          (They filled the bottles.)

Since Patient occurs after 'ba' very frequently, these nouns are also felt to be Patient. However, the following observations favor the analysis that they are Locatives. In the first place, a separate Existential Agent or Patient may occur in such sentences, e.g.

  (16) a.   Luguan dou zhu-man-le ren.
          hotel all live-full-asp person
          (The hotels are all fully occupied with people.)
      b.   Weizi dou zuo-man-le ren.
          seat all sit-full-asp person
          (Seats are all full (with people).)
      c.   Pingzi dou zhuang-man-le shui.
          bottle all fill-full-asp water
          (The bottles are all filled with water.)
      d.   Shu-jia dou fang-man-le shu.
          book-shelf all place-full-asp book
          (The bookshelf is filled with books.)

Moreover, these sentences can be transformed into 'ba'-construction (the definiteness of the Agent nouns is adjusted below).

  (17) a.   Nei-xie ren ba luguan dou zhu-man le.
          that-lot person p.t. hotel all live-full asp
          (Those people occupied the whole hotel.)
      b.   Nide shu ba shujia dou fang-man le.
          your book p.t. bookshelf all place-full asp
          (Your books filled the whole bookshelf.)

If 'shu-jia' – 'bookshelf' in (b) is analyzed as Patient, then we are forced to interpret 'shu' – 'book' as Agent. This is obviously unsatisfactory. As we have observed earlier (Chapter 2, Section 5.2), 'ba' may take Locative. When Locatives are so accusativized, the locativizers have to be deleted.

    Sentences in (16) do not necessarily argue that their surface object (in c and d) has to be Patient. In fact, it finds Agentive counterparts, with the object functioning as a type of Instrument, e.g.

  (18) a.   Ta yong shu ba shujia dou fang-man le.
          he use book p.t. bookshelf all place-full asp
          (He filled the whole bookshelf with books.)
      b.   Ta yong tang ba pingzi dou zhuang-man le.
          he use sugar p.t. bottle all fill-full asp
          (He filled the bottle with sugar.)

Furthermore, note the position of this type of Instrument (or Material) when co-occurring with true Instrument,

    (19) a.   Ta yong shuang shou ba shujia dou fang-man-le shu.
                he use both hand p.t. bookshelf all place-full-asp book
                (He used both hands to fill the bookshelf with books.)
        b.   Ta yong shuang shou ba shu dou fang-zai shujia-shang.
                he use both hand p.t. book all place-l.v. bookshelf-top
                (He used both hands to put the books onto the bookshelf.)

In other words, this type of Instrument has to be accusativized (pre-verbally) or occur post-verbally in the presence of true Instrument. Although we understand that 'book' and 'sugar' in (18) are the material for such activities as 'placing' and 'loading or filling', they are simultaneously the objects which undergo "locational displacement," i.e. Existential Patient in our analysis. Again, the notion "double role" can be employed to account for this complex role of 'book' and 'sugar,' i.e. both are Material/Patient. The role Material is made more prominent in the structure seen in (18) and the role Patient is made more prominent in (16).

    At the same time, it may not be entirely farfetched to claim that 'bookshelf' and 'jar' in (18) also play a double role. 'Bookshelf' as Locative in (19.b) is clear, and in (18.a) and (b) we also understand that they undergo a change-of-state, from 'empty' to 'full.' They are Locative/Patient. So that sentences in (18) can answer such questions as the following (only when Instrument is absent).

    (20) a.   Shu/shujia zemme le?
                book/bookshelf how asp
                (What happened to the books/bookshelf?)
        b.   Ta ba shu/shujia zemme le?
                he p.t. book/bookshelf how asp
                (What did he do to the books/bookshelf?)

Recall (in the introductory section of this chapter) that such questions are always directed to Patient. Since these Locative and Material are also Patient, it accounts systematically for the syntactic fact that they may be accusativized in these constructions. Otherwise, we would have to leave it as an idiosyncratic fact and an exception to the general pattern that Locative and Material are not accusativized.

    Thus to conclude all the foregoing observations, we shall postulate the nouns in (13) as Locative and the post-verbal nouns in (16.c) and (d) as Existential Patient. In fact, all verbs in this type of Existential sentences can take either Locative or Patient as the direct object, e.g.

    (21) a.   Ni zhuang tang, wo zhuang mianfen.
                you load sugar, I load flour
                (You load the sugar, and I load the flour.)
        b.   Ni zhuang nei-liang che, wo zhuang zhei-liang che.
                you load that-AN car, I load this-AN car
                (You load that car, and I load this car.)
        c.   Ni tie hong zhi, wo tie bai zhi.
                you paste-on red paper, I paste-on white paper
                (You paste on the red paper, and I the white one.)

    d. Ni tie menkou, wo tie chuangzi.
        you paste-on door, I paste-on window
        (You paste (it) on the door, and I on the window.)

Other verbs lack this versatility, e.g.

(22) a. Ta ba shu diu-zai zhuozi-shang.
        he p.t. book throw-l.v. table-top
        (He threw the book on the table.)
     b. Ta diu shu.
        he throw book
        (He threw the book.)
     c. *Ta diu zhuozi. (as related to a)
        he throw table
        (*He threw the table.)

CHAPTER 6

Range

The role Range defines the post-verbal nominal elements in the following sentences,

(1) *State*:
    a.   Zhe-liang che zhi san-qian yuan.
        this-AN car worth three-thousand dollar
        (This car is worth 3000 dollars.)
    b.   Ta shen gao liu chi.
        he body tall six foot
        (He is six-feet tall.)
    c.   Nei-wei xiaojie xing Gao.
        that-AN lady surname Gao
        (That lady is named Gao.)
    d.   Wo qian ta *shi-kuai qian*.
        I owe he ten-AN money
        (I owe him ten dollars.)
    e.   Ta shi Zhang Xiaojie.
        she be Zhang Miss
        (She is Miss Zhang.)
    f.   Ta you yi-bu xin che.
        he has one-AN new car
        (He has a new car.)

(2) *Process*:
    a.   Men po-le yi-ge dong.
        door break-asp one-AN hole
        (The door got a hole in it.)
    b.   Ta shu-le shi-kuai qian.
        he lose-asp ten-AN money
        (He lost ten dollars.)
    c.   Wo ying-le ta *shi-kuai qian*.
        I win-asp he ten-AN money
        (I won ten dollars from him.)
    d.   Ta pang-le shi-bang.
        he fat-asp ten-pound
        (He gained ten pounds.)

(3) *Action*:
    a.   Zhang San chang-le yi-shou ge.
        Zhang San sing-asp one-AN song
        (Zhang San sang a song.)
    b.   Ta zuo-le yi-ge meng.
        he make-asp one-AN dream
        (He had a dream.)

c. Ta xihuan tan zhengzhi.
   he like talk politics
   (He likes to talk about politics.)
d. Women mingtian qu pa-shan.
   we tomorrow go climb-mountain
   (We are going to climb mountain tomorrow.)
e. Ta hui shuo Faguo hua.
   he can speak France language
   (He can speak French.)
∙f. Tamen zai wan pai.
   they p.v. play card
   (They are playing cards.)

The term "Range" is taken directly from Halliday (1967-8). It corresponds (only roughly) to the Factitive case in Fillmore (1968) and Complement in Chafe (1970). As defined by Halliday, Range "specifies the extent of its (i.e. that of verbal process) scope or reference" (1967a:58). Thus the sole function of it is to add "specifications" to what is implied by the verbs in question. In some cases, as will be discussed below, the overlapping of content between Range and verbs is so great that the informational content of Range appears to be weakened, and consequently there is a semantic shift, from specific to general (e.g. 'fan' — 'rice' to 'food'), in this particular construction. This role has been traditionally designated as "Cognate Object" (cf. Chao 1968:312, Jespersen 1924:137ff).

It follows from the property of Range that the scope of specifications in general is extremely limited, so that in the above examples, the only way to specify 'worth' is by mean of money or something valuable in terms of money, to specify a 'surname' by means of a name, and to specify 'damage' by means of an actual result of such a damage. In the area of Action verbs, the specifications are more varied but nonetheless fall into several well-defined categories.

1. Range and Patient Compared

One major difference between Range and Patient of Process verbs is that the former is "effected" while the latter is "affected" (cf. Fillmore 1968:4). In the following pair of sentences containing Process verbs,

(1) a. Men po-le yi-ge dong. (Range)
       door break-asp one-AN hole
       (The door got a hole in it.)
    b. Yizi huai-le yi-zhi jiao. (Patient)
       chair bad-asp one-AN leg
       (The chair has a broken leg.)

'hole' is resultative of the verbal process, something "created," while 'leg' is pre-existent, something to which an event can happen. Thus they behave differently syntactically, e.g.

(2) a. *Yi-ge dong po le.
       one-AN hole break asp
       (*A hole broke.)
    b. Yi-zhi jiao huai le.
       one-AN leg bad asp
       (A leg is broken.)

    c.   *Mende dong po le.
         door's hole break asp
         (*The door's hole broke.)
    d.   Yizide jiao huai le.
         chair's leg bad asp
         (The chair's leg is broken.)
    e.   *Ta ba dong da-po le.
         he p.t. hole hit-break asp
         (*He broke the hole.)
    f.   Ta ba jiao da-huai le.
         he p.t. leg hit-bad asp
         (He broke the leg.)

An "effected" noun cannot undergo a change-of-state (a), cannot be genitivized (c), and cannot be "executed" (e).

In the area of Action verbs, the difference between Range and Patient is well-defined. Patient must necessarily undergo a change-of-state, whereas Range does not. Change-of-state here is loosely defined to cover not only the change of an intrinsic state, such as from 'alive' to 'dead,' but also the change in location. In other words, Patient must be "disposed" of in a certain manner, i.e. someone must do something "to" or "with" it.

Let us first look at effected Patient of Action verbs. Effected Patient is always associated with "effective" or "creation" verbs such as 'gai' — 'build,' 'zau' — 'manufacture,' 'xie' — 'write,' and 'zuo' — 'make,' as seen below,

    (4) a.   Ta gai-le yi-dong fangzi.
              he build-asp one-AN house
              (He built a house.)
         b.   Ta xie-le yi-feng xin.
              he write-asp one-AN letter
              (He wrote a letter.)
         c.   Ta zuo-le yi-jian yifu.
              he make-asp one-AN dress
              (He made a dress.)

"Creation" is a type of change-of-state, from non-existence to existence. Compare these sentences with those containing "executed" Patient, e.g.

    (5) a.   Ta mai-le yi-dong fangzi.
              he sell-asp one-AN house
              (He sold a house.)
         b.   Ta shao-le yi-feng xin.
              he burn-asp one-AN letter
              (He burned a letter.)
         c.   Ta si-le yi-jian yifu.
              he tear-asp one-AN dress
              (He tore up a dress.)

That these Patients are "disposed of" is clear. What "effected" and "executed" Patients have in common is that they both can occur in 'ba'-construction, e.g.

    (6) a.   Ta ba nei-feng xin xie le.
              he p.t. that-AN letter write asp
              (He wrote that letter.)

b. Ta ba nei-feng xin shao le.
   he p.t. that-AN letter burn asp
   (He burned that letter.)

And in turn, (6.b) can answer the questions,

(7) a. Nei-feng xin zemme le?
      that-AN letter how asp
      (What happened to that letter?)
   b. Ta ba nei-feng xin zemme le?
      he p.t. that-AN letter how asp
      (What did he do to that letter?)

Such questions are not appropriate for (6.a) since questions in (7) presuppose the existence of the Patient, which is not available for "effected" Patient.

Now compare these Patient sentences with Range sentences as the following, (with so-called Cognate objects)

(8) a. Ta chang-le ge.
      he sing-asp song
      (He sang.)
   b. Ta bu shuo hua.
      he Neg speak speech
      (He won't talk.)

Range can be definite but cannot occur in 'ba'-construction,

(9) a. Ta chang-le Faguo ge.
      he sing-asp France song
      (He sang a French song.)
   b. *Ta ba Faguo ge chang le.
      he p.t. France song sing asp
      (He sang the French song.)
   c. Ta shuo-le Faguo hua.
      he speak-asp France language
      (He spoke French.)
   d. *Ta ba Faguo hua shuo le.
      he p.t. France language speak asp
      (He spoke French.)

This is the first area of difference between Patient and Range. Secondly, Range cannot occur in what can be referred to as the counterpart of English "pseudo-cleft" construction (cf. Peters and Bach 1968), e.g.

(10) a. Ta xie de shi xin.
       he write m.p. be letter
       (What he wrote was a letter.)
    b. Ta si de shi yifu.
       he tear m.p. dress
       (What he tore up was a dress.)
    c. *Ta shuo de shi hua.
       he speak m.p. be speech
       (*What he uttered was speech.)

    d.   *Ta chang de shi ge.
          he sing m.p. be song
          (What he sang was a song.)

What is being "clefted," the focus, is always "new" information or contrastive. Range (as Cognate objects) cannot be "clefted" since it can never be contrastive (let us limit our discussion to indefinite nouns), e.g.

(11) a.   Ta xie de bu shi xin, shi baogao.
          he write m.p. Neg be letter, be report
          (What he wrote was not a letter but a report.)
     b.   *Ta shuo de bu shi hua, shi ???
          he speak m.p. Neg be speech, be
          (Cf. *He didn't speak, he said . . .)

What is "uttered" must be an "utterance," and if "utterance" is negated then the act of "uttering" is also denied. Therefore, while Range is predictable to a significant degree, Patient is not. To put it informally, while we can predict that when one utters, one utters in terms of utterances, we cannot predict that a letter is written whenever one writes. The issue involved is best explicated by Halliday. He states that "Cognateness is best thought of as 'extension inherent in the process' leading to a mutual expectancy of collocation between the noun and the verb involved" (1967a:59). Much redundancy of information appears especially when Range is in the indefinite.

    On the other hand, (10.c) and (d) are ungrammatical for the reason that what is pre-supposed in the verb is first abstracted out of it (by means of clefting) and then specified again. These sentences are no different from '*What he dreamed was a dream' or even '*The sex of John's wife is female.'

    While (10.c) and (d) are ungrammatical, the following are grammatical,

(12) a.   Ta shuo de shi nei-ju hua.
          he speak m.p. be that-sentence speech
          (That was what he said.)
     b.   Ta chang de shi nei-shou ge.
          he sing m.p. be that-AN song
          (That was the song he sang.)

in which the Range is definite, also "actual" (see section on "actual" and "virtual" below). However, this fact does not refute our explanation above. Note that in (13), which underlie (12),

(13) a.   Ta shuo-le nei-ju hua.
          he speak-asp that-sentence speech
          (He said that.)
     b.   Ta chang-le nei-shou ge.
          he sing-asp that-AN song
          (He sang that song.)

(8) is pre-supposed, that is, 'hua' — 'utterance, speech' and 'ge' — 'song' are pre-supposed. The demonstrative in (13) merely specifies the identification of such an utterance or song. When (13) is negated, the pre-supposition is not denied, so that in

(14) a.   Ta mei shuo nei-ju hua.
          he Neg speak that-sentence speech
          (He didn't say that.)

b. Ta mei chang nei-shou ge.
    he Neg sing that-AN song
    (He didn't sing that song.)

the demonstrative is negated but not the Range. This is the case in one of the two readings. Sentences in (14) are ambiguous, depending on whether the negation governs the demonstrative only or the whole sentence, in the latter interpretation it is the denial of the sentences as previously asserted. Such an ambiguity is observed in all sentences with nominal modifications, e.g.

(15) a. Ta mei mai xin che.
         he Neg buy new car
         (He didn't buy a new car.)
     b. Ta mei shao zuotian xie de xin.
         he Neg burn yesterday write m.p. letter
         (He didn't burn the letter he wrote yesterday.)
     c. Ta mei mai xin che, zhi mai-le jiu che.
         he Neg buy new car, only buy-asp old car
         (He didn't buy a new car, only a used one.)

In (15.a), if negation governs the whole sentence, there is no pre-supposition, and (15.c) would be ungrammatical if its first clause were intended in this reading. (15.c) has only one reading in which all elements but 'new' are pre-supposed. In other words, the relevance of information (i.e. focus) does not concern 'buy' or 'car' but 'new' or 'old.'

Thus when the focus in (14) is on the demonstrative, (14.b), for example, means 'He sang a song, but not that one.' Similarly, in (12), the focus is on the demonstrative, not the Range. This is clearly seen in their negative counterparts, i.e.

(16) a. Ta shuo de bu shi nei-ju hua, shi lingwai yi-ju.
         he speak m.p. Neg be that-sentence speech, be another one-sentence
         (What he said was not that, but something else.)
     b. Ta chang de bu shi nei-shou ge, shi lingwai yi-shou.
         he sing m.p. Neg be that-AN song, be another one-AN
         (The song he sang is not that one, but another one.)

While the act of "uttering" is negated in (11.b), which results in ungrammaticality, it is not negated in (16.a), as is evidenced by yet another specification of utterance in the second clause.

In this section, the semantic and syntactic distinctions of Patient and Range are discussed. Patient is defined as a noun which undergoes a certain kind of change-of-state, instigated by Agent. Range, on the other hand, only functions to specify the scope of Agent's activities. Our aim here is only to demonstrate the differences without looking specifically at the properties of Range, which will be the scope of discussion in the next sections.

2. "Actual" and "Virtual"

In this section, I shall state how "actual" and "virtual" are used in this thesis (these two terms are taken directly from Frei 1956). First, it is necessary to review how the notions "definite" and "indefinite" are currently understood and used, whose interplay with "actual" and "virtual" is complex and often confused by many linguists (refer to Frei 1956 for this point). This does not mean that the notions "definite" and "indefinite" are postulated here as primitive semantic notions, in terms of which "actual" and "virtual" are definable. Quite the contrary, as will be demonstrated below, the latter will be seen to be primitive notions, in terms of which the former are defined.

2.1. Definite and Indefinite Defined

The common assumption is that "definite" has a specific referent, beings or things, for both the speaker and the hearer. In this sense the italicized nouns in the following sentences are definite,

(1) a. *Taiyang* chu-lai le.
      sun out-come asp
      (The sun came out.)
   b. *Ta* yao zou le.
      he want go asp
      (He is going now.)
   c. *Wo* yao zou le.
      I want go asp
      (I am going now.)
   d. *Ma* chu-lai le.
      horse out-come asp
      (The horse came out.)
   e. *Nei-ge ren* hao pang.
      that-AN person very fat
      (That man is very fat.)

There are diverse factors which contribute to the definiteness of nouns. In (a) there is only one thing in the real world as far as the speaker and the hearer are concerned which is referred to as 'the sun,' so that when 'the sun' is uttered, a direct and specific referent is available. Let us call this the "absolute" condition. 'The wind,' 'the rain,' 'the moon,' 'London,' 'the President,' etc. belong to this category. Of course, proper nouns are strictly not as "absolute" as the other items above, since the experiential components of the speaker and of the hearer may vary considerably, so that when the speaker assumes too much, the "absolute" condition may fail. In that case, a definite noun (e.g. Johannesburg) for the hearer may simply be vague. It does not result in an indefinite noun: the hearer is simply confused, whereas an indefinite noun, which is to be understood positively, conveys adequate information for the purpose of communication.

The absolute condition may also be satisfied linguistically, i.e. introduced in previous utterances. This very condition triggers the anaphoric process. The pronoun in (b) is intended as such a case. Another interpretation of this pronoun is to be equated with the 'I' in (c). The latter pronoun is definite by virtue of the fact that the speaker is referring to himself, who must necessarily be directly referrable (and also visible) to the hearer. Let us call this the "relative" condition; relative, since it is much more liable to break down than the "absolute" condition and also since it relies on the assistance of other factors such as gestures (in life context) and "relative clauses" or "demonstratives" (in linguistic contexts). It is a common experience of us all to start with 'He . . .' or 'That man . . .' and receive the response 'Who . . .?' when these nouns satisfy only the "relative" condition, i.e. pointing or referring to someone. The pronouns 'I' and 'you' (or their plural counterparts) never fail to specify the referent, since the confrontation (not necessarily physical) between the speaker and the hearer (more appropriately "addressee") constitutes one of the prerequisites of linguistic communication. The third person pronouns, as should be clear from the foregoing discussions, have double sources, one as pronominalized form (because of previous occurrence), and the other as deictic reference (often replaceable by 'that man,' 'this man,' etc.). 'I' and 'you' never function as pronominalized forms.

(1.d) is grammatical only if 'horse' is interpreted "definite," i.e. non-generic and directly visible to at least the speaker and/or anticipated by both.

Indefinite nouns, on the other hand, do not have specific referents, so that in the sentences below,

(2) a. Ta zai qi jiaotache.
        he p.v. ride bicycle
        (He is riding a bicycle.)
    b. Ta jiancha-wan jiaotache le.
        he inspect-finish bicycle asp
        (He finished inspecting bicycles.)
    c. Jiaotache hen gui.
        bicycle very expensive
        (Bicycles are very expensive.)

'bicycle' receives various interpretations: most likely singular in (a), plural in (b), and "generic" in (c). Other interpretations are possible (e.g. 'two' in (a), singular in (b), and definite in (c) and dependent on contexts.) When nouns are modified by numerals alone, they are usually designated as indefinite, e.g.

(3) a. Ta yao zhao yige yongren.
        he want look-for one-AN servant
        (He wants to look for a servant.)
    b. Ta chi-le yige pingguo.
        he eat-asp one-AN apple
        (He ate an apple.)
    c. Ta zai chao yige cai.
        he p.v. fry one-AN vegetable
        (He is cooking a dish.)

In (a), no specific 'servant' is being sought for. All that the speaker and the hearer are certain of is that anyone can qualify as a candidate. The reference is thus "random" (Chafe 1970). "Unspecified" rather than randomness is seen in (b) and (c), where the only information given is that an 'apple' is consumed and a 'dish' is being prepared.

What we have seen so far is summarized in (4),

(4) a. "Definite" characterizes "non-generic" and "specified."
    b. "Indefinite" characterizes "generic," "random," and "unspecified."

Let us now look at the surface realizations of these notions, to see whether the notions "definite" and "indefinite" articles can be established in Chinese.

Dragunov states that

As is well-known, in Chinese, just as in many other languages, demonstrative pronouns often function as definite articles, and moreover are in this sense in opposition with the indefinite article, 'yige-ge.' Naturally, when 'zhe(ge)-'this' and 'na(ge)-'that' are used in this supplementing function, they lose their own distinct tones (1958:205, my free translation).

There are many serious problems with this postulation. In the first place, and this is straightforward, the properties "definite" and "indefinite" are present without such articles (cf. 1.a, b, and 2). In fact, the occurrence of such articles would result in ungrammaticality, e.g.

(5) a.   *Zhege taiyang chu-lai le.
         this-AN sun out-come asp
         (*This sun came out.)
    b.   *Yibu jiaotache hen gui.
         one-AN bicycle very expensive
         (A bicycle is very expensive.)

Secondly, they (e.g. 'zhe' — 'this' and 'yi' — 'one,a') do not stand in opposition, i.e. they are not in complementary distribution (as English 'the' and 'a' are). Most obvious is the fact that 'zhege' — 'this-AN' is a variant of 'zheige' or 'zhe yige' — 'this one-AN', in the latter the so-called definite and indefinite articles occur consecutively. Furthermore, in the following sentences, these so-called articles occur with definite nouns,

(6) a.   Ta chang de shi yi-shou Faguo guo-ge.
         he sing m.p. be one-AN France national-anthem
         (What he sang was the French national anthem.)
    b.   Ta you yao chang nei-shou Faguo guo-ge.
         he again want sing that-AN France national-anthem
         (He wants to sing the French national anthem again.)

Dragunov is not unaware of these phenomena. He cites the following examples (p. 44),

    c.   Huran lai-le ge Wang Shu-li.
         suddenly come-asp AN Wang Shu-li
         (Suddenly Wang Shu-li appeared.)
    d.   Zhongguo chu-le ge Mao Ze-dong.
         China emerge-asp AN Mao Tse-tung
         (Mao Tse-tung emerged in China.)

and comments that

> It (i.e. indefinite article preceding proper nouns) points out that, although the person referred to is already known to the speaker, he appears in a new situation in this sentence; therefore an indefinite article is required before this proper noun (1958:44, my translation).

Lü also noticed this peculiar pattern, but, instead of probing into the matter as Dragunov does, discards this pattern as an "extended" usage of the indefinite article (1945). Examples (6.a) and (b) go beyond the semantic range of Dragunov's explanation (i.e. cannot be explained as "unexpected appearance"). We shall return to this point further below.

What I am questioning is the status of the definite and indefinite articles. I am not claiming that definite and indefinite as semantic notions, as defined in (4), are not valid in Chinese. When we dispense with the articles (which impose on us the concept that the indefinite article marks an indefinite noun and the definite article a definite noun, contradicting such facts as in (5) and (6), we are free to construct various configurations of several notions to account for various types of communication between the speaker and the addressee. In addition to the concepts "demonstrative" and "number," we need only "actual" and "virtual." These latter terms are taken from Frei (1956), but my usage may depart somewhat from his original scheme.

A noun will be referred to in this thesis as "actual" if reference to it is available to the speaker or the addressee or both. As far as the speaker is concerned, an "actual" noun must have a specific referent in mind. Knowledge of its existence must also be present in his mind. Existence here should not be taken as existence in the real world. It is existence in the speaker's world. Thus an "actual" noun may simply be conceived of or imagined by him. A "virtual" noun, on the other hand, lacks this particular referent. No image of it exists in the speaker's mind.

Thus, when one says 'I am looking for a house,' he may be either trying to locate or identify a particular house he is supposed to visit or simply looking around for a suitable one to purchase; in the former interpretation 'a house' is "actual" but in the latter it is "virtual." Such questions as 'What is the address?' and 'Who lives there?' are relevant only if 'a house' is meant as "actual," and on the other hand, such questions as 'How many rooms do you need?' and 'What area would you prefer?' are relevant only if it is intended as "virtual."

"Actual" should not be equated with "pre-supposition of existence," since in either interpretation the existence of 'a house' is pre-supposed by the speaker. One does not set out to seek something without at the same time assuming that it can be found. This is an instance where a noun may be either "actual" or "virtual" even though its existence in the real world is pre-supposed. Cases where nouns may be either "actual" or "virtual" but without existence in the real world can be exemplified by such contrastive sentences as 'We must build one of the houses this year' and 'We must build a house this year.' The reference to 'house' in the former sentence is "actual" (a particular one out of a group of houses already planned) and the reference to 'house' in the latter is "virtual" (no pre-conceived plan is available). Yet in both cases 'house' is non-existent in the real world. All that is required to make a non-existent thing "actual" is that pre-conception is present in the speaker's mind. Such a pre-conception does not even have to be shared by the hearer.

"Actual" and "virtual" correspond to "specific" and "non-specific" in Dean (1968) and Karttunen (1968), but the latter seems to define "specific" and "non-specific" slightly differently from the former. For example, the sentence 'I talked with a logician' is ambiguous for Karttunen; the object can be "specific" or "non-specific." In our framework it can only be "actual," since a direct confrontation with someone necessarily constitutes a positive knowledge (in a very loose sense) about this person. Later reference to him should always be available to the speaker. Again in the sentence 'There is a cockroach in my soup,' 'a cockroach' is "non-specific" for Karttunen. To us, it can only be "actual." To utter such a sentence, the speaker must have seen a cockroach there. He may not be able to identify or describe it, but in his mind, in his experience, this particular cockroach is singled out against others.

In the following discussion, generally only sentences with 'I' as the subject are given. This is intentional, since "actual" and "virtual" are strongly speaker-oriented and if third person subject is used, confusion may result as to whether something is "actual" in reference to the present speaker or to the subject who may have originally uttered the sentence to the present speaker, who now reports it. For example, in the following conversation,

A to B: What are you doing?
B to A: I am looking for a pen. (meant as "actual")
A to C: He is looking for a pen.

When A mentions 'a pen' to C, it is most likely to be "virtual" for both A and C, because B has not revealed enough information for A to think otherwise. On the other hand, in the next version of the same event, i.e.

> A to B: What are you doing?
> B to A: I am looking for my red pen. (actual)
> A to C: He is looking for a pen.

'pen' must be "actual" for B, but when A transmits it to C after withholding some information, it is most likely to be "virtual" for C. Thus by using 'I' as the subject, the reference should be transparent as regards the speaker, and the loss of fidelity can be avoided.

Nouns are "definite," as in (1), precisely because they are "actual" for both the speaker and the addressee, in that they both know exactly what is being referred to. This does not mean that certain nouns, e.g. 'the sun,' are inherently definite. 'The sun' is a part of everyone's life experience (or so assumed by the speaker), so that the speaker assumes that it must be "actual" for the addressee. The appropriateness of such an assumption is entirely at the speaker's disposal, so that when he addresses a child who is without any knowledge of 'the sun,' it has first to be defined and identified (i.e. a process of making it "actual"). This is why on occasion, we have to have proper nouns "actualized" first before conversation can assume its proper course (e.g. medical terms).

It takes little reflection to realize that "demonstratives" are always "actual." In a sense, the personal pronouns 'I', 'you,' and 'he' (in the deictic usage, not as anaphoric) are also demonstratives: 'I' as 'the one who is speaking,' and 'you' as 'the one being spoken to.' The gestures used in referring to 'that person,' 'this person,' and 'he' are often also used in referring to 'I' and 'you'; the extent of the use is dependent on different cultural backgrounds. This may be a factor behind the fact that pronouns are closely bound to demonstratives in Chinese, e.g. (a is to be understood in the context when a salesman quotes prices for three pens held by three people, including himself)

(7) a. Wo zhe-zhi san yuan; ni nei-zhi si yuan; ta nei-zhi . . .
　　　I this-AN three dollars; you that-AN four dollars; he that-AN . . .
　　　(This one is three dollars; that one is four; that one . . .)
　　b. Wo-zher you zhi; ni-ner you shu; ta-ner you . . .
　　　I-here exist paper; you-there exist book; he-there exist . . .
　　　(Here is some paper; there are some books; over there are . . .)

Very frequently, what is being talked about is neither definite nor indefinite for both the speaker and the addressee, but halfway. A common situation is when something is "actual" for the speaker but "virtual" for the addressee. In the surface structure, such nouns occur as indefinite, e.g.

(8) a. Wo zai zhao yige dongxi.
　　　I p.v. look-for one-AN thing
　　　(I am looking for something.)
　　b. Wo zheng zai gen yige ren shuo-hua.
　　　I just p.v. with one-AN person speak-speech
　　　(I am talking to someone.)

In (a), the speaker must know what he is looking for (if he is a well being) but he does not bother or intend to let the addressee know what it is. In (b), it is apparent that the speaker is talking to a certain person, but he probably assumes that the addressee would not know who it is even if he discloses the identity. In both situations then, what is "actual" for the speaker is "virtual" for the addressee. To characterize nouns only by means of definite and indefinite necessarily fails to account for this phenomenon. Even more importantly, such a postulation is not capable of explicating the ambiguity of such sentences as,

(9) a. Wo zai zhao yi-zhi qingwa
        I p.v. look-for one-AN frog
        (I am looking for a frog.)

    b. Wo yao qu kan yige dianying.
        I want go look one-AN movie
        (I want to see a movie.)

(a) may mean either the speaker is looking for a frog missing from his collection or he is hunting for one to add to his collection; in the former 'frog' is "actual" and in the latter "virtual." "Virtual" in this particular instance corresponds to Chafe's "random" (1970), meaning 'any.' In (b) 'movie' is "actual" if the speaker has already decided on a particular one, but "virtual" (i.e. random) if he has not. Although the distinction is meant by the speaker, his intention is not always explicit as far as the addressee is concerned. Misunderstanding consequently results (to (b), 'Which film?' is asked when "virtual" is intended.)

Cases where what is "actual" for the addressee but "virtual" for the speaker can be exemplified by the following dialogue,

(10) a. Wo you yige didi dao Taiwan qu le.
         I have one-AN brother to Taiwan go asp
         (I have a brother, who went to Taiwan.)

     b. Ni nei-wei didi dao Taiwan qu zuo shemma?
         you that-AN brother to Taiwan go do what?
         (What did your brother go to Taiwan for?)

'Brother', obviously "actual" for the speaker in (a), is presented as "virtual" to the addressee, since perhaps the speaker's brother and the addressee are not acquainted. Our concern is how this "virtual" brother is referred to by the previous addressee now the speaker in (b). Note that he uses the demonstrative 'that' to introduce a so-called definite noun, since such a definite noun (your brother) is "actual" only for the addressee in (b).[1] Very often, phrases such as 'my grandfather' and 'John's uncle' are made seemingly "actual" (or definite in the usual analysis) for the other party but are in fact "virtual." They seem to be "actual" only because of the actual reference to 'I' and 'John.'

The "virtual" reference of 'brother' in (b) is especially conspicuous when the addressee has more than one brother, but such is not the only possible interpretation (the addressee would have said 'Wode yige didi' — 'one of my brothers' in such a case). We shall see below that 'you' — 'have, there is' preceding a number does not always denote a sub-set. To show that the demonstrative 'that' does not necessarily govern a so-called definite noun only under the condition of "sub-set," compare (10) with (11) below,

(11) a. Wo you yige xuesheng jiao Pan Taitai.
         I have one-AN student call Pan Mrs.
         (I have a student, whose name is Mrs. Pan.)

---

[1] Prof. Chafe pointed out to me that 'brother' in (b) is "actual" for the speaker in (b) when he utters the sentence. In this interpretation, we have to differentiate two types of "actual," one real world "actual" and the other linguistic "actual" (i.e. what is being actualized in the linguistic contexts). 'Brother' in (a), then, is real world and that in (b) linguistic. A difference is that linguistic "actual" is less stable than real world "actual" and tends to be referred to as "virtual."

    b.   Nei-wei Pan Taitaide chengji zemma yang?
         that-AN Pan Mrs.-g.p. grades how kind
         (How are Mrs. Pan's grades?)

In (b), 'that' governs a unique noun (Chafe 1970). In (10.b) and (11.b), 'he,' 'she,' 'your brother,' or 'Mrs. Pan' can be used directly, but then the distinction is obscured.

    The last possibility in the various configurations of the values "actual" and "virtual" is that in which what is "virtual" for the speaker is also "virtual" for the addressee. This is an extremely common situation and will not be elaborated. "Relayed" message of "third person" report has more often than not this property, e.g.
(12 is intended as a report on the message obtained in 9)

    (12) a.   Ta zai zhao yi-zhi qingwa.
             he p.v. look-for one-AN frog
             (He is looking for a frog.)
         b.   Ta yao qu kan yige dianying.
             he want go look one-AN movie
             (He wants to see a movie.)

Even if the reference in (9) is meant to be "actual" by the speaker, it is received as "virtual" by the addressee in (9), now the speaker in (12). The "actual" reference can in no way be recovered in (12).

    What has been discussed so far is summarized below (Case C is uncertain, see footnote 1)

Sentence No.	1	8	10.b	12
Speaker	Actual	Actual	Virtual	Virtual
Addressee	Actual	Virtual	Actual	Virtual
	(A)	(B)	(C)	(D)

Case (A) defines the traditional notion "definite" and case (D) "indefinite" and case (C) "definite". "Generic" is a sub-type of case (D), when number is absent. "Random" is another sub-type of case (D), when number is present. In the surface structure, these four cases of reference do not have to be marked in any specific way, i.e. even nouns in the plain form are subject to various interpretations, e.g. in (13)

    (13) a.   Wo zhao-dao qingwa le.
             I look-for-s.p. frog asp
             (I found the frog.)
         b.   Wo zai zhao qingwa.
             I p.v. look-for frog
             (I am looking for a frog.)
         c.   Wo xihuan qingwa.
             I like frogs.

'frog' may be interpreted as case (A) in (a), case (B) or case (D) "random" in (b), and case (D) "generic" in (c). When a demonstrative is present,

    (14) a.   Wo zhao-dao nei-zhi qingwa le.
             I look-for-s.p. that-AN frog asp
             (I found that frog.)
         b.   Wo zai zhao nei-zhi qingwa.
             I p.v. look-for that-AN frog
             (I am looking for that frog.)

c. Wo xihuan nei-zhi qingwa.
    I like that-AN frog
    (I like that frog.)

'frog' has to be interpreted as case (A) in all these sentences. This is simply due to the semantic function of demonstratives, i.e. always "actual." When number is present,

(15) a. Wo zhao-dao yi-zhi qingwa le.
         I look-for-s.p. one-AN frog asp
         (I found a frog.)

    b.   Wo zai zhao yi-zhi qingwa.
         I p.v. look-for one-AN frog
         (I am looking for a frog.)

    c.   *Wo xihuan yi-zhi qingwa.
         I like one-AN frog
         (I like a frog.)

'frog' has to be case (D) "random" in (a) and case (B) or case (D) "random" in (b). (c) is ungrammatical for the fact that 'like' is a generic verb and is thus incompatible with the number 'one,' not because of the fact that Chinese "indefinite" article cannot mark "generic" as the English counterpart can. The latter position would undoubtedly be advocated by Dragunov, since he comments that "the scope of 'indefinite article' is not entirely the same in Chinese as in European languages" (1958:45, Footnote 1, my translation).

2.2. The Role of "Actual" and "Virtual" in the Accusative Construction

The accusative (or ergative in Frei 1956) construction in Chinese has been studied from many angles and in many frameworks. It can be studied from the viewpoint of noun-type, verb-type, verb-complex, etc. In this section we will study the constraints that hold on certain Transitivity roles in the accusative construction and how the distinction between "actual" and "virtual" pertains to the constraints.[2]

First, let us examine a set of sentences, given in (1) and (2).

(1) a. Ni qu sha nei-zhi ji.
        you go kill that-AN chicken
        (Go and kill that chicken.)

    b. Ni qu ba nei-zhi ji sha-le.
        you go p.t. that-AN chicken kill-asp
        (Go and kill that chicken.)

---

[2] In Karttunen (1968), the following claim is made,
"Certain sentence types seem to imply that indefinite noun phrases are non-specific. This is the case with (i) interrogative, (ii) imperative, and (iii) existential sentences." (p.9)
As pointed out before, his "non-specific" seems to correspond to our "virtual." If this correspondence can be established, what he claims is entirely counter-factual. Consider the following,
(i) Do you want to buy a car?
(ii) Please move a desk outside!
(iii) Here is a book.
In (i), the speaker may intend to sell his own car; in (ii) the speaker has a particular desk in mind; and in (iii) the speaker has apparently seen a book. In our framework, all these nouns are "actual." Reference to these nouns is made in the following continuation sentences,
(i') It's only one year old.
(ii') It's the one by the window.
(iii') It's written by Hardy.

    c.   Ni qu sha yi-zhi ji.
        you go kill one-AN chicken
        (Go and kill a chicken.)
    d.   *Ni qu ba yi-zhi ji sha-le.
        you go p.t. one-AN chicken kill-asp
        (Go and kill a chicken.)

(2) a.   Wo mài-le yi-ben shu.
        I sell-asp one-AN book
        (I sold a book.)
    b.   Wo ba yi-ben shu mài-le.
        I p.t. one-AN book sell-asp
        (I sold a book.)
    c.   Wo mǎi-le yi-ben shu.
        I buy-asp one-AN book
        (I bought a book.)
    d.   *Wo ba yi-ben shu mǎi-le.
        I p.t. one-AN book buy-asp
        (I bought a book.)

The sentences in (1) are all imperative sentences and all involve the verb 'kill,' but whereas (a) has the ergative counterpart, (c) does not. The ungrammaticality of (d) is explained by the constraint that only "actual" nouns may be accusativized. Such nouns may be "actual" for both the speaker and the hearer (a and b) or for the speaker alone (2.a). In (2), the pairs of sentences differ only as regards verbs, thus the ungrammaticality of (d) has to be explained by the verb property. To capture the situation, H. Wang (1959) proposes the following,

> The object in ba sentences must fulfill one of the following two conditions:
> (A) it must refer to specific person(s) or items(s).
> (B) It must refer to person(s) or item(s) which "existed" before the action, whether the latter are specific or not! (Translation from POLA 1:4, p.75)

Condition (A) accounts for (1.d), and Condition (B) is intended to account for (2.d). According to him, 'a book' in (2.d) "can only exist through the action of 'buy'. Therefore 'a book' is originally non-existent with respect to 'I' " (ibid, Footnote 19). He further reasons that if an item does not exist, it cannot be disposed of, hence accusativization cannot apply. In fact, his "existence" condition is applicable to certain "effected" or "created" objects and not to the object of 'buy.' When one sets out to buy something, "actual" or "virtual," he must pre-suppose the existence of it in the real world. The following sentences specify "effected" objects,

(3) a.   Wo gai-le yi-dong fangzi.
        I build-asp one-AN house
        (I built a house.)
    b.   *Wo ba yi-dong fangzi gai-le.
        I p.t. one-AN house build-asp
        (I built a house.)
    c.   Wo xie-le nide jieshao xin.
        I write-asp your introduce letter
        (I wrote your reference letter.)
    d.   Wo ba nide jieshao xin xie-le.
        I p.t. your introduce letter write-asp

(I wrote your reference letter.)

but contrary to his claim, (d) is grammatical. Here we notice that the "effected" object in (a) is "virtual" but is "actual" in (c), (already in the speaker's mind before he executed it). Thus what is at issue in (3) is not "existence" but "actual" or "virtual." Furthermore, the following sentences

(4) a.   Wo kan-le nide shu.
         I look-asp your book
         (I read your book.)
    b.   Wo ba nide shu kan-le.
         I p.t. your book look-asp
         (I read your book.)
    c.   Wo kan-le nei-ge nu-ren.
         I look-asp that-AN woman
         (I looked at that woman.)
    d.   *Wo ba nei-ge nu-ren kan-le.
         I p.t. that-AN woman look-asp
         (I looked at that woman.)

all specify "existent" as well as "actual" objects, but (d) is ungrammatical. Therefore, H. Wang's conditions fail completely.

I propose the following conditions:

(5) a.   An accusativized object must be "actual," for both the speaker and the hearer, or for the speaker alone.
    b.   An accusativized object must be a Patient.
    c.   In volitional and completed events, an accusativized object must be "actual" at the time of action and not at the time of utterance. (This has to do with the two dimensions of "actual.")

Condition (a) is clear. It explains why (1.b) but not (d) is grammatical. When one says

(6) a.   Wo ba yi-jian shi wang-le.
         I p.t. one-AN thing forget-asp
         (I forgot something.)
    b.   Wo ba yi-jian shi gao-wang le.
         I p.t. one-AN thing cause-forget asp
         (I forgot something.)

at that moment he must have realized what he forgot (otherwise he would not remember that he forgot something). Thus the object is "actual" for the speaker and "virtual" for the hearer. Moreover, when one says to another

    c.   Ni bie ba yi-jian shi wang-le.
         you Neg p.t. one-AN thing forget-asp
         (Don't forget something.)

he is actually reminding the other not to forget what they have been discussing together, hence "actual" for both of them. Condition (a) also explains the ungrammaticality of (d) below,

(7) a.   Ni zuotian mai-le nide che meiyou?
         you yesterday sell-asp your car Neg
         (Did you sell your car yesterday?)

> b. Ni zuotian ba nide che mai-le meiyou?
>   you yesterday p.t. your car sell-asp Neg
>   (Did you sell your car yesterday?)
> c. Ni zuotian mai-le ji-bu che?
>   you yesterday sell-asp how-many-AN car
>   (How many cars did you sell yesterday?)
> d. *Ni zuotian ba ji-bu che mai-le?
>   you yesterday p.t. how-many-AN car sell-asp
>   (How many cars did you sell yesterday?)

In (a), 'car' is "actual" and thus can be accusativized, whereas in (c) no specific reference is made to any car, and the ergative construction is not appropriate.

Condition (b) is seen to function in (2) to (4). In (4), the same surface verb actually has two quite different properties (compare the English translations). In (a), the Agent goes through the book and tries to assimilate the message expressed in it. In this way, the book is perceived (not literally) to have undergone a change-of-state, from strange to familiar (actually it is the Agent that has undergone this change). Thus the book plays the role of Patient. The situation in (d) is quite different. The woman only specifies the termination point of the Agent's gaze, and is not affected in any way by the Agent's action. It plays the role of Goal. Goal is not to be accusativized. The difference between 'buy' and 'sell' as given in (2) can be analogously understood. When one sells something, he has it at his disposal, (hence Patient), but when one buys something, it is the seller and not the buyer who disposes of it. The object of 'buy' is Goal, as will be further discussed in the section on Goal.

To see the relevance of condition (c), observe that although (2.b) is grammatical, (8.b) is not, which is in no obvious way different,

> (8) a. Wo mai-le san-ben shu.
>   I sell-asp three-AN book
>   (I sold three books.)
>   b. *Wo ba san-ben shu mai-le.
>   I p.t. three-AN book sell-asp
>   (I sold three books.)

Moreover, the following sentences are grammatical,

> (9) a. Wo jintian san-ben shu dou mai-le.
>   I today three-AN book all sell-asp
>   (I sold all three books today.)
>   b. Wo jintian ba san-ben shu dou mai-le.
>   I today p.t. three-AN book all sell-asp
>   (I sold all three books today.)

There are significant differences between (8.a) and (9.a). In the former, the speaker merely reports the range of his achievement, whereas the speaker in the latter reports the accomplishment of his task. In other words, at the time of selling, the speaker in (8) did not have any specific books he had to sell (hence "virtual" at that time), whereas the speaker in (9) had in mind three specific books he wanted to sell (hence "actual"), although at the time of utterance, the Patient is "actual" for both the speakers. (Incidentally, (8) specifies that only three books are sold, whereas no such specification is necessary in (9). In the latter, more than three may have been sold, but the three intended ones must be included.)

It should be noted that condition (c) is not superfluous to (a). Sentences in (6) specify non-volitional completed events, yet the accusativized object is "actual" only at the time of utterance. It is accusativized due to condition (a) and not (c). In fact, the ambiguity of many action sentences between the volitional and non-volitional readings corresponds precisely to the "actual" and "virtual" distinction at the time of action and not of utterance. For example, the following sentences are ambiguous,

(10) a. Wo ba hua-ping nong-po le.
         I p.t. vase make-break asp
         (I broke a vase.)
     b. Wo ba lian-pen ti-fan le.
         I p.t. basin kick-turn-over asp
         (I kicked the basin over.)

When volitional events are involved, the Agent must know which vase or basin (hence "actual") he intended to break or kick, but if non-volitional or accidental events are involved, the Agent did not have such knowledge (hence "virtual"). However, at the time of utterance both objects are "actual" We may postulate, then, that objects in both volitional and non-volitional events are accusativized due to the feature "actual," but in different dimensions, the latter at the time of utterance only. Furthermore, it may be possible to reduce the features "volitional" and "non-volitional" to the more primitive features "actual" and "virtual," at the time of action, not utterance.

2.3. "Actual," "Virtual," and "Anticipation"

In this section, I would like to look at the question of how to characterize pre-verbal and post-verbal subjects in the so-called existential and appearance sentences. The most systematic accounts on this subject are given in Chao (1968:76ff) and Mullie (1932:160ff). Chao accounts for the different positions in terms of "definite" and "indefinite." Stating the differences of such sentences as (Chao's translation)

(1) a. Ke lai le.
         guest come Li
         (The guests (I invited) have come.)
    b. Lai ke le.
         come guest Li
         (We have some guests.)

Chao specifies that "There is a very strong tendency for the subject to have a definite reference and the object to have an indefinite reference" (1968:76). In this section, we have attempted to redefine "definite" and "indefinite." To characterize the sentences in (1), we can specify 'guest' in (a) as "actual" for both the speaker and the hearer and that in (b) as "actual" for the speaker and "virtual" for the hearer. However, this is unsatisfactory for other cases such as

(2) a. Taiyang chu-lai le.
         sun out-come asp
         (The sun has come out.)
    b. Chu taiyang le.
         out (appear) sun asp
         (The sun has come out.)

    c.   Yu kaishi xia le.
        rain begin fall asp
        (The rain started to fall.)
    d.   Kaishi xia yu le.
        begin fall rain asp
        (It started to rain.)

Here, both the 'sun' and 'the rain' are "actual" for both the speaker and the hearer, yet they may occur either pre-verbally or post-verbally.

Dragunov (1958) also raises objections to the analysis of (1) as originally given in Mullie (1932). Dragunov states that

> The fundamental difference between these two sentences does not lie in the fact that the subject is "definite" (or determinate as defined in Mullie) in the former but is "indefinite" (or indeterminate) in the latter, but in the fact that the former is a bi-constituent sentence, answering "Who came?" and the latter is a uni-constituent sentence, answering "What is it?" (1958:110, Footnote 1, my translation).

It is not clear what he means by "bi-constituent" and "uni-constituent" but it seems from the quotation that he would analyze 'guest' in (1.a) as the only "new" element, while both 'guest' and 'come' in (b) are "new." While this is a plausible approach to (1), it does not quite capture the difference in (2). In the first place, (b) and (d) can occur without any pre-supposition (e.g. announced by newspaper or weatherman). They are both all "new" sentences. On the other hand, (a) and (c) are usually uttered in the context when 'the sun' and 'the rain' are anticipated. Compare the naturalness of the following sentences,

   (3) a.   Women deng-le ban-tian taiyang cai chu-lai.
          we wait-asp half-day sun only-then out-come
          (We waited a long time before the sun came out.)
      b.   *Women deng-le ban-tian cai chu taiyang.
          we wait-asp half-day only-then out sun
          (We waited a long time before the sun came out.)

"Anticipation" is also present in (1.a), but not (b).

There is another way to understand Dragunov's comment, namely, that many nouns can have either "concrete" or "abstract" reference. In the "concrete" reference, nouns can further be specified as "actual" or "virtual," but nouns in the "abstract" reference can only be "virtual," since the question of "referent" is beside the point in this respect. In English, this point is illustrated by the pair 'priest' and 'priesthood.' Thus 'ke' may refer to 'a guest' or to the general notion of entertaining guests (cf. 'qing ke'-lit. 'invite guest' — 'feasting'). The situation is best illustrated by 'fan,' which may mean either 'rice' (concrete) or 'food' (abstract). In the following sentences

   (4) a.   Kai fan le.
          begin rice asp
          (The meal started.)
      b.   *Fan kai le.
          rice begin asp
          (The meal started.)
      c.   Women kai fan le.
          we begin rice asp
          (We started the meal.)

d. *Women ba fan kai-le.
    we p.t. rice begin-asp
    (We started the meal.)

'fan' refers to the abstract sense and thus cannot occur pre-verbally (b) nor accusativized (d). It is "virtual." Now in the sentences below

(5) a. Lai yi-diar fan!
        come little rice
        (Give us some rice.)
    b. Fan lai le.
        rice come asp
        (The rice is coming.)
    c. Wo chao-le fan le.
        I fry-asp rice asp
        (I fried some rice.)
    d. Wo ba fan chao-le.
        I p.t. rice fry-asp
        (I fried the rice.)

'fan' means 'rice' and can occur pre- or post-verbally as well as accusativized. The construction 'chi-fan' -lit. 'eat rice' is ambiguous, meaning either 'eat some rice' or 'eat (food), i.e. act of eating.' In our analysis, when such nouns occur in the concrete sense, they may play the role of Patient or Goal, but they function as Cognate Range (i.e. cognate object) when in the abstract sense. Therefore, 'chang-ge' — 'lit. sing song,' 'xie-zi' — 'write word,' 'nian-shu' — 'read book,' 'shuo-hua' — 'talk word,' etc. may function in either sense.

Cf. (6) a. Wo xiao shihou nian-le shu.
            I little when read-asp book
            (I studied when I was little.)
        b. *Wo xiao shihou ba shu nian-le.
            I little when p.t. book read-asp
            (I studied when I was little.)
        c. Wo zuotian nian-le shu. (ambiguous)
            I yesterday read-asp book
            (Yesterday I read the book. / I studied.)
        d. Wo zuotian ba shu nian-le. (unambiguous)
            I yesterday p.t. book read-asp
            (I read the book yesterday.)

(5.b) illustrates the notion "anticipation" adequately. When some rice ("virtual") is asked for in (5.a), the nouns occur post-verbally, but when it is served, it occurs pre-verbally (b), because it is anticipated, not because it is "definite" (Chao). It cannot be the rice which the speaker specified or had knowledge of.

Thus just in the case where "event" (or reality) matches "anticipation" do subjects occur pre-verbally in these sentences. Now let us see what "anticipation" involves. One may anticipate something "actual" (e.g. the sun to appear) or something "virtual" (any blue bird to appear), and when the event is realized as anticipated, the anticipated noun is in a sense no longer "new" to the concerned party. Thus, it qualifies as a "topic." However, the distinction between "actual" and "virtual" is valid only during the period of anticipation. Once the event has happened, even anticipated "virtual" nouns become "actual." This notion has been frequently touched upon earlier. Therefore in the sentences below

(7) a.   Lai le yi-ge ren.
      come asp one-AN person
      (There comes a man.)
   b.   You yi-ge ren lai le.
      exist one-AN person come asp
      (Someone is coming.)
   c.   *Lai le Zhang San.
      come asp Zhang San
      (There comes Zhang San.)
   d.   Zhang San lai le.
      Zhang San come asp
      (Zhang San is coming.)

(b) involves "virtual" anticipation and (d) "actual" anticipation, but at the time of utterance (i.e. after the events have happened) both nouns are necessarily "actual."

When proper nouns occur post-verbally, there is a contrast in the surface structure, e.g.

(8) a.   Zhongguo chu le Mao Ze-dong.
      China appear asp Mao Ze-dong
      (Mao Tse-tung came forth in China.)
   b.   Zhongguo chu le yi-ge Mao Ze-dong.
      China appear asp one-AN Mao Ze-dong
      (A person called Mao Tse-tung came forth in China.)
   c.   Gangcai zhi lai le Zhang Xiansheng.
      just-now only come asp Zhang Mr.
      (Only Mr. Zhang came just now.)
   d.   Gangcai zhi lai le yi-wei Zhang Ziansheng.
      just-now only come asp one-AN Zhang Mr.
      (Only someone called Mr. Zhang came just now.)

that is, proper nouns may or may not be modified by one. Meanings are, however, clearly distinct. For example (supposing (a) and (b) are uttered when listing one well-known figure from each country), if the speaker chooses (a), he is assuming that the hearer also knows of Mao. In this case, Mao is "actual" for both of them, and cannot be modified by "one." If he chooses (b) he is assuming that the hearer does not have knowledge of this person. Thus Mao in (b) is "actual" for the speaker yet "virtual" for the hearer. The situation is clearer if the terms "actual" and "virtual" are replaced by "known" and "unknown" respectively. A similar distinction is also observed between (c) and (d); in the former Mr. Zhang is "known" to both the speaker and the hearer. The latter sentence is ambiguous. In one reading, Mr. Zhang is "known" only to the hearer, and in the other, Mr. Zhang is "unknown" to both the speaker and the hearer, when he first appeared, but by the time the speaker utters the sentence in the second interpretation, he already learned of this person's identity. Thus Mr. Zhang was "unknown" to the speaker when the event happened but "known" when the speaker utters this sentence to the hearer.

We may account for the second reading of (d) (which is the more likely one) in the following manner. The sentence is contracted from two (co-ordinated) sentences, viz. (a) and (b) below

(9) a. Gangcai zhi lai le yi-ge ren.
        just-now only come asp one-AN person
        (Only one person came just now.)
    b. Nei-ge ren xing Zhang.
        that-AN person surname Zhang
        (That man is called Zhang.)
    c. Gangcai zhi lai le yi-ge ren, xing Zhang.
        just-now only come asp one-AN person, surname Zhang
        (Only one person came just now, whose name is Zhang.)

If reduction instead of contraction takes place, (c) results.

When "anticipation" is absent, the normal pattern is that "virtual" nouns occur post-verbally and "actual" nouns pre-verbally. This is particularly clear in "disappearance" and "existential" sentences, e.g.

(10) a. Pao le yi-zhi tuzi.
         run asp one-AN rabbit
         (One rabbit escaped.)
     b. You yi-zhi tuzi pao le.
         exist one-AN rabbit run asp
         (One rabbit escaped.)
     c. *Pao le nei-zhi tuzi.
         run asp that-AN rabbit
         (That rabbit escaped.)
     d. Nei-zhi tuzi pao le.
         that-AN rabbit run asp
         (That rabbit escaped.)

(11) a. Zhuo-shang you yi-ben zidian.
         desk-top exist one-AN dictionary
         (There is a dictionary on the desk.)
     b. You yi-ben zidian zai zhuo-shang.
         exist one-AN dictionary l.v. desk-top
         (A dictionary is on the desk.)
     c. *Zhuo-shang you nei-ben zidian.
         desk-top exist that-AN dictionary
         (*There is that dictionary on the desk.)
     d. Nei-ben zidian zai zhuo-shang.
         that-AN dictionary l.v. desk-top
         (That dictionary is on the desk.)

(b) and (d) sentences above are all "actual," though the former are "actual" only for the speaker. The ungrammaticality of (c) sentences indicates the non-occurrence of "actual" nouns in the post-verbal position. "Disappearance" sentences contradict our postulation that nouns in completed events are always "actual," that is, at the time of utterance. Clearly, 'rabbit' in (10.a) is "virtual" (the speaker only noticed one missing). (b) on the other hand contains an "actual" noun but does not express "anticipation." Moreover, 'rabbit' in both (a) and (b) must refer to a particular set. (If there were only one, it would have been "actual" for the speaker.) Note that this is not a necessary condition for "appearance" sentences (cf. 7.a and b).

The difference between (11.a) and (b) is not to be accounted for by "actual" and "virtual" in the sense defined above. This is because nouns in "existential" sentences are necessarily "actual," if they are modified by numbers, i.e. when they are not "generic." Assertion of the existence of an object pre-supposes foreknowledge, and foreknowledge constitutes "actual." Thus in the following sentences,

> (12) a. Tushuguan-li yinggai you yi-ben Zhongwen zidian.
>   library-inside ought exist one-AN Chinese dictionary
>   (There ought to be a Chinese dictionary in the library.)
>   b. Zhuo-shang yaoshi you yi-ben zidian, yiding shi wode.
>   desk-top if exist one-AN dictionary, certain be my
>   (If there is a dictionary on the desk, it must be mine.)

nouns are not "actual," since no assertion of existence is made.[3]

(a) and (b) differ in at least two areas. Firstly, 'book' in (a) cannot refer to "one of a set," while that in (b) must. Compare

> (13) a. Hezi-li you yi-kuai qian.
>   box-inside exist one-AN money
>   (There is a dollar in the box.)
>   b. *You yi-kuai qian zai hezi-li.
>   exist one-AN money l.v. box-inside
>   (*A dollar is in the box.)

It does not make sense to talk of 'one particular dollar' (not a dollar bill). Secondly, and this is more fundamental and important, (11.a) asserts "existence" and (b) "location." Although assertion in general of "existence" is made in reference to location (cf. Lyons 1967), assertion of location pre-supposes existence (in the broadest sense, i.e. including both physical and "conceived"). Therefore the existence of 'dictionary' is asserted in (a) (i.e. non-existent as far as the speaker is concerned before the utterance) but is pre-supposed in (b), (i.e. already existing in the speaker's mind before the utterance). Only in this broadest sense can the distinction of "virtual" and "actual" be postulated between (a) and (b).

This understanding enables us to see more clearly why (c) is ungrammatical. One of the well-formedness conditions of the short NP 'that dictionary' is its very existence (in this particular context, created by previous discourse, not deictic reference). Therefore, contradiction arises. Existential and locative sentences are usually postulated as

---

[3] Actually (a) is ambiguous. 'Dictionary' can be "actual" or "virtual." The distinction corresponds to the two meanings of 'ought to,' one meaning "obligation" and the other "logical necessity," as roughly translated below

(i) The library ought to have a Chinese dictionary (virtual).

(ii) A (certain) Chinese dictionary ought to be in the library (since I put it there just this morning) (actual).

In (i), the modal negates the existence in reality (it ought to have one, since/and it doesn't), hence the noun is "virtual." Note also that when the modal is interpreted as "obligation," 'library' can be "generic," but not as "necessity," e.g.

(iii) A library ought to have a Chinese dictionary.

(iv) *?A (certain) Chinese dictionary ought to be in a library.

transformationally related (i.e. due to different subject selections; cf. Lyons 1967, Huang 1966, and Y.C. Li 1972). This approach reflects some misunderstanding of the fundamental issues behind existential and locative sentences. They express different meanings and cannot be derived from the same underlying structures, when we operate within the theory that different underlying structures reflect different meanings.

3. Cognate Object as "Actual" and "Virtual"

The striking "emptiness" or "redundancy" of Range as Cognate object is illustrated in the sentences below,

(1) a. Ta zai xie zi.
he p.v. write word
(He is writing.)

b. Ta zai chi fan.
he p.v. eat rice
(He is eating.)

c. Ta bu nian shu le.
He Neg read book asp
(He stopped schooling.)

d. Other compounds: chang ge-'sing song,' zou lu-'walk road,' jiao shu-'teach book,' shui jiao-'sleep nap,' shu hua-'talk word,' kan shu-'read book.'

Note incidentally that the English translations here contain only simple Action verbs. (b) and (c) are ambiguous sentences. This involves, as I remarked earlier, a semantic shift from specific to general reference. In the specific interpretation, (b) and (c) mean 'He is eating rice' and 'He stopped reading a book' respectively, and they mean 'He is eating' and 'He quit school' in the general (i.e. abstract) interpretation. I shall postulate that the nouns in question are Patient in the specific reading but Range in the general reading. In the following sentences, 'fan' can only mean 'food,'

(2) a. Wo gen ta chi-guo fan.
I with he eat-exp rice
(I have dined with him before.)

b. Ni chi fan chi-le shemme dongxi?
you eat rice eat-asp what thing
(What did you eat when you ate?)

c. Ni xihuan chi shemme fan?
you like eat what rice
(What kind of food do you like to eat?)

On the other hand, 'fan' can only mean 'rice' below,

(3) a. Fan ta dou chi le.
rice he all eat asp
(He ate all the rice.)

b. Ta ba fan dou chi le.
he p.t. rice all eat asp
(He at up all the rice.)

c. Fan dou bei ta chi le.
rice all p.p. he eat asp
(All the rice was eaten up by him.)

> d. Ta chi de shi fan.
>   he eat m.p. be rice
>   (What he ate was rice.)

This means that 'fan' as Range cannot be "topicalized" (a), nor "accusativized" (b), nor "passivized" (c), nor "clefted" (d), while Patient occurs freely in these constructions.

The difference between Patient and Range is more clearly shown by the following pairs of sentences,

> (4) a. Ta chi-wan fan le.
>   he eat-finish rice asp
>   (He finished the rice/He finished eating.)
>   b. Ta chi-bao fan le.
>   he eat-full rice asp
>   (He ate enough.)
>   c. Ta he-wan jiu le.
>   he drink-finish wine asp
>   (He finished the wine/He finished drinking.)
>   d. Ta he-zui jiu le.
>   he drink-intoxicated wine asp
>   (He was drunk.)

(a) and (c) are ambiguous between Patient and Range, and (b) and (d) can only be interpreted as containing Range object. In the former two, each interpretation corresponds exactly to one of the two meanings of 'wan' — 'finish,' either 'to complete' (when Range) or 'to exhaust' (when Patient). When sentences in (4) refer to the completion of particular activities, the objects are necessarily abstract (hence "virtual"), which is the only possible interpretation of (b) and (d). Compare the "accusativized" versions of (4),

> (5) a. Ta ba fan chi-wan le.
>   he p.t. rice eat-finish asp
>   (He finished the rice.)
>   b. *Ta ba fan chi-bao le.
>   he p.t. rice eat-full asp
>   (He ate enough.)
>   c. Ta ba jiu he-wan le.
>   he p.t. wine drink-finish asp
>   (He finished the wine.)
>   d. *Ta ba jiu he-zui le.
>   he p.t. wine drink-intoxicated asp
>   (He was drunk.)

Although (4.a) and (c) are ambiguous, (5.a) and (c) unambiguously specify Patient. This is in agreement with our postulation above that Range may not be accusativized.

Frei remarks that "In expressions of the type 'chi-fan' — 'to eat' (lit. eat-rice), 'shuo-hua' — 'speak' (say-word). . . the object is virtual . . . when it is convertible into an ergative construction, however, the complement of 'ba' can only be actual, i.e. an indication" (1956:84). Can we, then, establish that Range is always "virtual" and because of that, cannot occur in the constructions shown in (5.b) and (d)? A logical conclusion to be drawn from such a postulation is that the role Range could be dispensed with and be replaced by, say, "virtual Patient." Unfortunately, this is not workable. Compare the following sentences,

(6) a.   Ta ba nei-ge mimi shuo le.
         he p.t. that-AN secret speak asp
         (He disclosed that secret.)
    b.   *Ta ba Faguo hua shuo le.
         he p.t. France language speak asp
         (He spoke French.)

If we say that such verbs as 'shuo' — 'speak, talk' always take Patient, (a) and (b) should receive identical descriptions, since they both contain definite nouns as objects. How in this theory do we account for the grammaticality of (a) and the ungrammaticality of (b)? Obviously, both objects are "actual." Again, in the sentences

(7) a.   Ta xie de shi yi-feng xin.
         he write m.p. be one-AN letter
         (What he wrote was a letter.)
    b.   *Ta xie de shi yi-ge zi.
         he write m.p. be one-AN word
         (What he wrote was a word.)

both objects in (a) and (b) are "virtual" (and "indefinite" on the surface), but they behave differently. In our postulation, on the other hand, this is all predicted, because the nouns in (6.b) and (7.b) are Range, which does not occur in such constructions.

Our observation, then, is that Range may be "actual" or "virtual." In this way, Range contrasts with Patient. More importantly, this contrast is observed with the same verbs. In other words, these verbs function in two capacities, as Action verbs and Process-Action verbs, as indicated below,

(8) ' shuo' — 'speak,' 'xie' — 'write,' 'chi' — 'eat,' 'nian' — 'read.'
    a.   *Taking Cognate-objects* (i.e. Range):

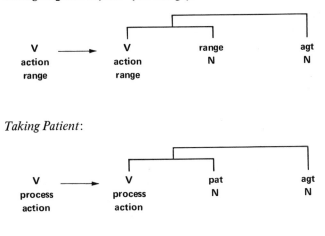

    b.   *Taking Patient*:

Diagram K

These verbs (in 8) are unique, in that generally when the same verbs are observed to function in different capacities, most notably transitive and intransitive, the relation is accountable for in terms of "causative," as illustrated between each pair of sentences below,

(9) a. Fan hen re. (State)
        rice very hot
        (Rice is hot.)
    b. Ta zai re fan.
        he p.v. hot rice
        (He is heating the rice.)
    c. Che ting-xia-lai le. (Process)
        car stop-down-come asp
        (The car stopped.)
    d. Ta ba che ting-xia-lai.
        he p.t. car stop-down-come
        (He stopped the car.)
    e. Ma zai pao. (Action)
        horse p.v. run
        (The horse is running.)
    f. Tamen zai pao ma.
        they p.v. run horse
        (They are racing horses.)

This relation, apparently, is inappropriate between (8.a) and (b); there is no "causative" meaning involved. Furthermore, for those verbs which are not involved in "class" derivations, unique "transitivity relations" are specifiable. For example, 'sha' — 'kill' and 'mai' — 'sell' always take Patient, 'tan' — 'talk' and 'jiao' — 'teach' always take Range, and 'mo' — 'touch' and 'ti' — 'kick' always take Goal (to be discussed later). 'Shuo' — 'speak' etc. are the only cases which can take either Range or Patient. The determination of Range or Patient is not entirely dependent on the nature of the nouns in question (cf. 4). But when these verbs are specified as Range, there is only a limited range of nouns which may accompany them.

Range, when occurring with Action verbs, is not restricted to Cognate objects. Strictly speaking, Range in the following sentences contrasts with that in (1)

(10) a. Ta xie-le Riben zi.
         he write-asp Japan word
         (He wrote some Japanese words.)
     b. Ta chi-le Riben fan.
         he eat-asp Japan rice
         (He ate Japanese food.)

If we follow Halliday's definition of cognateness as "extension inherent in the process" (1967a:59), Range in (1) is Cognate while that in (10) is non-cognate. However, if we analyze, as we should, such expressions as 'Japanese food' as forming the structure "modifier + head," the "head" nouns in (10) are precisely the Cognate objects in (1). Since this is the case, it is feasible to establish the Range in (10) also as Cognate, but with modifier. The modifier "actualizes" Range, so that Range can be "topicalized" and "clefted" but not "accusativized" or "passivized" (cf. 3), e.g.

(11) a. Riben hua ta hui shuo.
         Japan language he can speak
         (He can speak Japanese.)

    b.   Ta hui shuo de shi Riben hua.
          he can speak m.p. be Japan language
          (What he can speak is Japanese.)
    c.   *Ta ba Riben hua shuo le.
          he p.t. Japan language speak asp
          (He spoke Japanese.)
    d.   *Riben hua bei ta shuo le.
          Japan language p.p. he speak asp
          (Japanese was spoken by him.)

We have seen in this section that the distinction between "actual" and "virtual" accounts for the non-occurrence of such nouns as 'fan' meaning 'food' (i.e. generalized) in topicalization and clefting, but its non-occurrence in accusativization and passivization has to be accounted for by the distinction between Range and Patient.

4. Verbalized and Nominalized Range (and the Notion of Cognate Instrument)

I remarked in the last section that Cognate Range such as 'rice,' 'word,' and 'song' are generalized, because their reference in that particular context is "virtual," and also because their meaning is to a large extent specified by the verbs concerned. We may refer to such a type of Range as nominalized Range. In this section, we shall look at cases of Range where just the opposite is true, i.e., the verbs are general in reference while the Range alone specifies the informational content. We shall refer to this type as verbalized Range.

Consider the following sentences,

(1) a.   Ta zai zuo meng.
          he p.v. make dream
          (He is dreaming.)
    b.   Ta zai zuo mai-mai.
          he p.v. make buy-sell
          (He is doing business.)
    c.   Ta zai zuo shi.
          he p.v. make thing
          (He is working.)

'Zuo' in these sentences is extremely vague and empty in reference. It may be considered as a verbalized extension of the Range involved.

This type of Range is much more "frozen" syntactically than Cognate Range, e.g.

(2) a.   *Meng ta zuo le.
          dream he make asp
          (He had a dream.)
    b.   *Ta zuo de shi meng.
          he make m.p. be dream
          (*What he had was a dream.)
    c.   *Ta ba meng zuo le.
          he p.t. dream make asp
          (He had a dream.)
    d.   *Meng bei ta zuo le.
          dream p.p. he make asp
          (*Dream was had by him.)

However, "frozenness" (from Fraser 1970) varies according to individual items.

(3)   Ta zuo de shi mai-mai.
         he make m.p. be buy-sell
         (What he is doing is business.)

Modification to this type of Range is nonetheless permitted,

(4) a.   Ta zuo-le e-meng.
         he make-asp bad-dream
         (He had a nightmare.)
    b.   Ta zuo da mai-mai.
         he make big buy-sell
         (He is doing big business.)

Once modification is added, it can be clefted (cf. Section 1).

(5) a.   Ta zuo de shi e-meng.
         he make m.p. be bad-dream
         (What he had was a nightmare.)
    b.   Ta zuo de shi yi-ge e-meng.
         he make m.p. be one-AN bad-dream
         (What he had was a nightmare.)

Next, in the following sentences,

(6) a.   Ta kan-le yi-yan.
         he look-asp one-eye
         (He took a look.)
    b.   Ta ti-le yi-jiao.
         he kick-asp one-leg
         (He gave a kick.)
    c.   Ta da-le yi-quan.
         he hit-asp one-fist
         (He gave a punch.)
    d.   Ta yao-le yi-kou.
         he bite-asp one-mouth
         (He took a bite.)
    e.   Ni gen ta shuo yi-sheng.
         you with he speak one-voice
         (Speak a word to him.)

we observe that the objects specify means (i.e. Instrument) by which the action concerned is carried out. These are designated as Cognate objects in Chao (1968:313). Syntactically, these behave like the type of Cognate objects discussed in the last section, e.g.

(7) a.   *Yi-yan ta kan le.
         one-eye he look asp
    b.   *Ta kan de shi yi-yan.
         he look m.p. be one-eye
    c.   *Ta ba yi-yan kan le.
         he p.t. one-eye look asp

    d.   *Yi-yan bei ta kan le.
        one-eye p.p. he look asp

These objects can never be "actual," so that they never, as the other type does, occur in the topicalization or cleft constructions. However, there are significant differences between these two types of Cognate objects. I shall refer to the type of objects as seen in Section 3 as Cognate objects and that in (7) above as Cognate Instrument. Contrast between these two is available with the verb 'shuo' — 'speak,' as shown below,

(8) a.   Ni qu gen ta shuo yi-sheng.
        you go with he speak one-voice
        (Go and tell him.)
    b.   Ni qu gen ta shuo yi-ju hua.
        you go with he speak one-sentence speech
        (Go and talk to him.)

The message conveyed in (a) is rather incomplete (the action involved is no different from 'to utter'); the speaker seems to have something in mind which he does not specify probably for the reason that both the speaker and the addressee share this knowledge. On the other hand, what is to be uttered in (b), though unspecified also, is left entirely to the addressee's decision. This is why (9.a) is grammatical while (b) is not,

(9) a.   Ni qu gen ta shuo yi-sheng zai-jian.
        you go with he speak one-voice good-bye
        (Go and say good-bye to him.)
    b.   *Ni qu gen ta shuo yi-ju hua zai-jian.
        you go with he speak one-sentence speech good-bye
        (*Go and talk to him good-bye.)

Upon comparing (9.a) and (8.b) more closely, it will be revealed that the status of 'Goodbye' in the former corresponds to "speech" in the latter. In other words, 'Goodbye' in (9.a) is in fact the Range, not "voice" as suggested by Chao. 'Sheng' — 'sound, voice' in (8.a) is not even an object (or occurring in an NP-code) in the surface structure. Compare the following ('lian' preposes objects)

(10) a.   *Ta lian yi-sheng dou bu shuo.
         he even one-voice all Neg speak
         (*He doesn't even speak a voice.)
    b.   Ta lian yi-ju (hua) dou bu shuo.
         he even one-sentence (speech) all Neg speak
         (He doesn't even speak a word.)

Whereas Cognate objects are in a sense closer to Patient, Cognate Instrument is closely associated with (manner) adverbs, especially Instrument,

(11) a.   Ta yi-jiao ti-guo-qu.
         he one-leg kick-over-go
         (He gave a kick.)
    b.   Ta yi-quan da-guo-qu.
         he one-fist hit-over-go
         (He gave a punch.)

    c.   Ta da-sheng yi-jiao.
        he big-voice one-shout
        (He gave a loud cry.)

Moreover, Cognate Instrument may occur as Instrument proper,

  (12) a.   Ta yong jiao yi-ti.
           he use leg one-kick
           (He gave a kick.)
      b.   Ta yong quantou yi-da.
           he use fist one-hit
           (He gave a punch with his fist.)
      c.   Ta yong zui yi-yao.
           he use mouth one-bite
           (He took a bite.)

However, the difference between (12) and (6) should not be ignored; the former stresses the "action" aspect (how the action is conducted) whereas the latter stresses the "result" aspect (what has been done). Nonetheless, the Instrumental interpretation of both sets of sentences is clear.

    A final difference to be noticed is that while Cognate objects freely admit classifiers (AN), Cognate Instruments do not, e.g.

  (13) a.   Ta xie-le yi-ge zi.
           he write-asp one-AN word
           (He wrote a word.)
      b.   *Ta ti-le yi-zhi jiao.
           he kick-asp one-AN leg
           (He gave a kick.)
      c.   *Ta kan-le yi-zhi yan.
           he look-asp one-AN eye
           (He took a look.)

This restriction indicates that 'leg' and 'eye,' when occurring in (6), are not nominal elements. Cognate Instrument, then, may be analyzed as "objectivized adverb." These nouns are "Cognate" because they specify the basic Instrument (i.e. in "unarmed" contexts). In this sense, they are also "inherent in the process." (One cannot look except with eyes, etc.)

    The fact that Chao analyzes Cognate Instrument as Cognate object indicates that Chao's scope of this category differs from that of Fillmore, Halliday, Chafe, and even Jespersen. Chao's defining scope of Cognate object is this:

A cognate object may consist of an expression for
(a) the number of times of an action,
(b) its duration,
(c) its extent,
(d) the course of locomotion, or, less often, its destination (1968:312).

It can thus be seen that "cognate object" is defined by Chao adverbially whereas the others specify it as a verb-noun relation, which is also the approach in this thesis. Even here, Chao is not consistent, for he includes 'shui-jiao' — 'sleep nap' (Chao's gloss p.313) in the list together with 'ti yi-jiao' — 'give a kick.' 'Shui-jiao' is a true cognate object construction. Its various syntactic characteristics are given below,

(14) a.   Ta shui-le wujiao.
          he sleep-asp nap
          (He had a nap.)

     b.   Ta shui-le yi-ge jiao.
          he sleep-asp one-AN nap
          (He had a sleep.)

     c.   Ta lian jiao ye bu shui.
          he even nap also Neg sleep
          (He doesn't even want to sleep.)

     d.   Ta shui de shi wujiao.
          he sleep m.p. be nap
          (??What he had was a nap.)

The Range object above can be modified (a and b), preposed (c) and clefted (d). Cognate Instrument, as has been shown in this section, cannot occur in these constructions.

As regards derivation, I shall postulate that Cognate Instrument as seen in (6) is objectivized from Instrument constructions as seen in (12). For sentences such as (6.a), objectivization is obligatory. Objectivization of Circumstantial relations is always an idiosyncratic fact and has to be treated as such. The following sentences show some such cases,

(15) a.   Jintian wo shui shafa. (Locative)
          today I sleep sofa
          (I'll sleep on sofa today.)

     b.   Women chi guanzi qu. (Locative)
          we eat restaurant go
          (Let's go and eat in a restaurant.)

     c.   Wo chi da wan. (Instrument)
          I eat big bowl
          (I'll eat with a big bowl.)

     d.   Wo bang nide mang. (Goal)
          I help your busy
          (I'll help you.)

This process is neither productive nor predictable.

CHAPTER 7

Source and Goal

The notions "Source" and "Goal" are systematically presented in Gruber (1965) and extensively discussed in lectures (Eng. 270) given by Fillmore at University of California, Berkeley (Spring 1970). The role "Goal" also occurs in Halliday's grammar (see Halliday 1967a), but does not correspond to Gruber's definition. In Halliday's framework, Goal defines the object of a directed action (e.g. Mary washed the clothes).

In this thesis, our definition of Goal does not uniquely correspond to either Gruber's or Halliday's. As will be seen below, two types of Goal are postulated here, viz. Transitivity Goal and Circumstantial Goal, and the latter is more in line with Gruber's definition, while the former is presented as a new proposal. Transitivity Goal stands in opposition to Patient and Range and is thus within the scope of Transitivity, while Circumstantial Goal stands in opposition to Source.

1. General Properties of State, Source, and Goal

At the most fundamental and apparent level, we may conceive of an object as either being stationary or undergoing a change of location (i.e. locational displacement). When it undergoes a locational displacement we can talk of the initial location and the terminal location. Let us name the former "Source" and the latter "Goal." When an object undergoes this change, it is Patient, the definition of which is in agreement with that of the Patient of a Process-Action verb. Thus in the following sentences,

(1) a. Qiu cong zhuo-shang gun-dao di-xia.
        ball from table-top roll-reach floor-bottom
        (The ball rolled to the floor from the table.)
    b. Ta ba qiu cong zhuo-shang tui-dao di-xia.
        he p.t. ball from table-top push-reach floor-bottom
        (He pushed the ball down to the floor from the table.)

'the ball' is Patient, 'the desk' is Source, and 'the floor' is Goal.

When an object is stationary, where it is located will be referred to as State. Thus in the following sentences,

(2) a. Qiu zai zhuo-shang.
        ball l.v. table-top
        (The ball is on the table.)
    b. Qiu zai di-shang.
        ball l.v. floor-top
        (The ball is on the floor.)

'the ball' is Patient, and both 'on the desk' and 'on the floor' are States.

With these notions extended slightly, we may postulate that State verbs and Process verbs define State and Goal respectively. For instance, in

(3) a. Li Xiaojie hen gao.
   Li Miss very tall
   (Miss Li is very tall.)
   b. Li Xiaojie hen gaoxing.
   Li Miss very happy
   (Miss Li is very happy.)

'Miss Li' is presented as being (in a sense stationary) in the states of 'tall' and 'happy.' Whether states are generic (a) or non-generic (b) is immaterial for our description here. In this way, sentences in (3) are to be understood in the same way as those in (2). On the other hand, Process verbs as in

(4) a. Li Xiaojie gao le.
   Li Miss tall asp
   (Miss Li grew taller.)
   b. Li Xiaojie bing le.
   Li Miss ill asp
   (Miss Li became ill.)

indicate a change from one state to another. Moreover, they refer only to the terminal states, and the initial states are merely implied. Therefore, Process verbs define Goal. In this sense, Miss Li in (4) is to be understood in the same way as 'the ball' in (1). Again, whether the Goal states are "relative" (a) or "absolute" (b) (for an extensive discussion of these notions, refer to Chafe 1970) is immaterial to our discussion here.

In a simple-verb construction, the verb indicates either the State a Patient is in or the State a Patient enters (i.e., Goal). No verb is observed to indicate the State a Patient departs from (i.e. Source). In other words, we may hypothesize that in the construction "Noun + Verb" the only impossible interpretation is that the Noun lacks the property as identified by the verb. This is similar to the constraint in nominal compounds (e.g. 'toffee candy' and 'mushroom soup'); which excludes the reading that the head noun lacks the property as identified by the modifying noun.

Not only Patient but also Agent is describable in reference to State, Source, and Goal. However, this does not mean that when an Agent occurs, reference to these notions must also be present, although it is true that if a Patient occurs, State, Source, or Goal also occurs. In sentences below

(5) a. Zhang San Xiao le.
   Zhang San laugh asp
   (Zhang San laughed.)
   b. Li Si chang-le yi-shou ge.
   Li Si sing-asp one-AN song
   (Li Si sang a song.)

Source and Goal are absent, but when Source and Goal occur with an Agent in the absence of a separate Patient, the Agent must necessarily also function as a Patient, i.e. playing a double role, e.g.

(6) a. Ta zou-dao jiangtai-shang.
   he walk-reach platform-top
   (He walked to the platform.)

  b. Ta cong jiangtai-shang zou-xia-lai.
      he from platform-top walk-down-come
      (He walked down from the platform.)

in which 'the platform' is Goal in (a) and Source in (b). At the same time, we understand that in both cases, the Agent himself undergoes a locational displacement. Thus the Agent is also playing the role of Patient. The only, but significant, difference between 'he' in (6) and 'the ball' in (1) is that while the latter undergoes a locational displacement due to an external force (hence Patient), the former identifies himself with the force (hence Agent). When Patient itself is also the Agent, "volition" is a necessary condition.

  Agent is also describable in terms of State, when an action is in the so-called "progressive" aspect. (Refer to Joos 1964 for an insightful presentation of the "progressive," his "temporary," aspect.) There are two primary patterns in Mandarin to indicate "progressive," as shown,

  (7) a. Ta chi-zhe fan (ne).
          he eat-p.s. rice particle
          (He is eating.)
      b. Ta zai chi fan.
          he p.v. eat rice
          (He is eating.)

Details aside, I would only like to state that the suffix 'zhe' in fact marks an action as a type of State (de-activated, see Chafe 1970), and the Agent involved therein is understood as a Patient, whereas the prefix 'zai' specifies the "continuing" nature of an event, in which the Agent can be understood as engaged in an activity. The distinction is often obscured, as in (7). Let us look at some decisive cases. First, note the contrast in the following pair,

  (8) a. Ta chuan-zhe duanku.
          he wear-p.s. shorts
          (He is wearing shorts.)
      b. Ta zai chuan duanku.
          he p.v. wear shorts
          (He is putting on shorts.)

No activity is reported in (a), since only the result of the Agent's earlier activity is now the concern. In (b), no result is yet available since the action is still making headway. To put it plainly, the shorts are on him already in (a) but not in (b), at least not completely and properly. These two sentences are negated differently, i.e.,

  (9) a. Ta mei chuan-zhe duanku.
          he Neg wear-p.s. shorts
          (He is not wearing shorts.)
      b. Ta bu zai chuan duanku.
          he Neg p.v. wear shorts
          (He is not putting on shorts.)

Secondly, compare the grammaticality of the following sentences,

  (10) a. Ta zuo-zhe.
           he sit-p.s.
           (He is sitting.)

   b.   *Ta zai zuo.
       he p.v. sit
       (He is sitting.)

   c.   *Ta si-zhe baozhi.
       he tear-p.s. papers
       (He is tearing papers.)

   d.   Ta zai si baozhi.
       he p.v. tear papers
       (He is tearing papers.)

'Sit' is a static verb (no action involved) and 'tear' a dynamic verb (physical action required). Here we note that the suffix 'zhe' does not occur with a verb which requires action and which can be repeated over and over again, whereas the prefix 'zai' is incompatible with a non-action verb. This point is further supported by the occurrence of this suffix with (some) obviously State verbs, but not the prefix, e.g.

(11) a.   Li Xiaojie bing-zhe.
       Li Miss ill-p.s.
       (Miss Li is ill.)

      b.   *Li Xiaojie zai bing.
       Li Miss p.v. ill
       (Miss Li is ill.)

Thus, suffix 'zhe' de-activates an action into a state, and consequently the original Agent is depicted as a Patient.

To conclude this section, the parallelism between Agent and Patient, in terms of State, Source, and Goal, is shown in the following pairs of sentences,

(12) a.   Zhang San *tang-zhe* (state)
       Zhang San lie-p.s.
       (Zhang San is lying.)

      b.   Zhang San *hen gao*.
       Zhang San very tall
       (Zhang San is very tall.)

      c.   Zhang San tang-dao *chuang-shang* le (goal)
       Zhang San lie-reach bed-top asp
       (Zhang San lay on the bed.)

      d.   Zhang San *gao* le.
       Zhang San tall asp
       (Zhang San grew taller.)

      e.   Wo ba *ta* tui-dao *qian-tou* (patient-goal)
       I p.t. he push-reach front-side
       (I pushed him to the front.)

      f.   Wo ba *tang* nong-*re* le.
       I p.t. soup make-hot asp
       (I heated the soup.)

2. Transitivity Goal

The role Transitivity Goal defines the object of the following sentences,

(1) *State verbs*:
      a.   Ta hen xihuan Li Si.
       he very like Li Si

(He likes Li Si a lot.)

b. Ta zhidao wode mingzi.
    He know my name
    (He knows my name.)

c. Zhang San hen xiang Li Si.
    Zhang San very resemble Li Si.
    (Zhang San looks very much like Li Si.)

d. Li Si hui *kai che*.
    Li Si can drive car
    (Li Si knows how to drive a car.)

(2) *Process*:

a. Kedou bian-cheng qingwa le.
    tadpole change-become frog asp
    (The tadpole changed into a frog.)

b. Bing hua-cheng shui le.
    ice melt-become water asp
    (Ice melted into water.)

c. Ta cheng-wei chumingde yinyue-jia.
    he become-as famous musician.
    (He became a famous musician.)

d. Tade lian bian-hong le.
    his face change-red asp
    (His face reddened.)

(3) *Action*:

a. Ni bie da ta!
    you don't hit he
    (Don't hit him.)

b. Wo mai-le yi-ben shu.
    I buy-asp one-AN book
    (I bought a book.)

c. Ta zai zhao shu.
    he p.v. look-for book
    (He is looking for a book.)

Goal in the above sentences specifies the terminal point of the property expressed by the verb. The State verbs above are "directed" in Halliday's sense (1967a), as opposed to "non-directed" State verbs, such as 'tall' and 'big.' Thus, for instance, when a Patient is in the State of being 'fond' (1.a) or 'in love,' the range of the 'fondness' or 'love' has to extend over to a recipient (i.e. Goal). These Goal State verbs require, as their semantic well-formedness, the specification of Goal, as indicated in Diagram L.

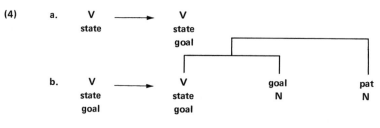

Diagram L

The specification of Goal in this case is uni-directional, in that if A likes or loves B, it does not follow that B also likes or loves A. This is particularly clear in the case of 'resemble,' e.g.

(5) a. Tade che hen xiang yu.
his car very resemble fish
(His car looks like a fish.)
b. *Yu hen xiang tade che.
fish very resemble his car
(*A fish looks like his car.)

Even in extremely restricted contexts when (5.b) can be grammatical, its meaning departs from what is intended in (a).

When Process verbs take Goal, it always specifies the State a Patient changes into (indicated by nouns in 2.a-c and State verb in d). Unlike most Goal State verbs, which obligatorily take Goal, Goal Process verbs, as seen in (2), may occur without Goal, as shown below,

(6) a. Zhang Xiaojie bian le.
Zhang Miss chang asp
(Miss Zhang changed.)
b. Bing dou hua le.
ice all melt asp
(Ice all melted.)

Furthermore, note that the verbs in (2.a) to (c) are morphologically complex – containing simple Process verbs and 'cheng' – 'become' or 'wei' – 'as.' However, for some verbs at least, this is not a necessary condition, e.g.

c. Kedou hui bian qingwa.
tadpole will change frog
(Tadpoles will change into frogs.)

This is also true if Goal is specified by State verbs, as seen in (2.d). We may formulate the situation as in Diagram M.

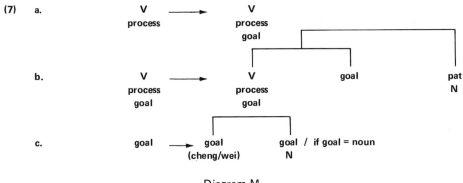

Diagram M

In the area of Action verbs, Goal specifies the "location" whereupon an activity is, in a loose sense, executed. For example, in (3.a) the object specifies the place (hence also "Locative") upon which the action of 'hitting' falls. Thus it qualifies as a recipient.

"Recipient" in the sense that it receives the action, not a Patient, which is the definition of our Circumstantial Goal, as will be discussed below. The Goal of an Action verb is specified in Diagram N.

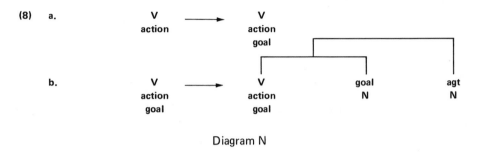

Diagram N

The contrast between the Patient and the Goal of Action verbs is an important one and will be examined in detail immediately below.

3.   Transitivity Goal and Patient Compared

In our framework, within the Transitivity system, the object of an Action verb is defined in terms of the opposition among Patient, Range, and Goal, as illustrated below, in that order,

(1) a.   Ta mài-le shu le.
          he sell-asp book asp
          (He sold the book.)
     b.   Ta chang-le ge le.
          he sing-asp song asp
          (He sang a song.)
     c.   Ta mǎi-le shu le.
          he buy-asp book asp
          (He bought a book.)

In (a) the Patient is disposed of, in (b) the Range is executed (created through performance), and in (c) the Goal is acquired. While Patient and Range are unrestricted as regards the type of noun they take, Range is severely limited to what can be conceived of as an extension of the property of the verb in question.

We noted earlier that Range may not occur in the accusative nor pseudo-cleft constructions. While Patient may occur in both, Goal can only occur in the latter construction. These facts are given below,

(2) a.   Ta ba shu mài le.
          he p.t. book sell asp
          (He sold the book.)
     b.   Ta mài de shi shu.
          he sell m.p. be book
          (What he sold was a book.)
     c.   *Ta ba ge chang le.
          he p.t. song sing asp
          (He sang the song.)

    d.   *Ta chang de shi ge.
        he sing m.p. be song
        (What he sang was a song.)

    e.   *Ta ba shu mǎi le.
        he p.t. book buy asp
        (He bought the book.)

    f.   Ta mǎi de shi shu.
        he buy m.p. be book
        (What he bought was a book.)

In this section, we may add the passive construction to the list of "discovery" constructions. In (1), only Range cannot be passivized, i.e. (Agent is changed in (c) for greater naturalness)

  (3) a.   Shu gei ta mài le.
           book p.p. he sell asp
           (The book was sold by him.)

        b.   *Ge gei ta chang le.
           song p.p. he sing asp
           (The song was sung by him.)

        c.   Shu gei ren-jia mǎi le.
           book p.p. others buy asp
           (The book was bought by other people.)

The constraints are summarized in Table 1.

	Patient	Range	Goal
Accusative	Yes	No	No
Pseudo-cleft	Yes	No	Yes
Passive	Yes	No	Yes

Table 1

In what follows, we shall look more closely at the differences between Patient and Goal, which share identical syntactic environments in many areas.

We define Patient as that which undergoes change-of-state and Goal as a recipient (or locative in some cases). One can do something to or with Patient, but not Goal. This accounts for the non-occurrence of Goal in the accusative construction. Compare the following,

  (4) a.   Zhang San ba Li Si sha le.
           Zhang San p.t. Li Si kill asp
           (Zhang San killed Li Si.)

        b.   *Zhang San ba Li Si da le.
           Zhang San p.t. Li Si hit asp
           (Zhang San hit Li Si.)

'Kill' is a change-of-state verb, while 'hit' is only a "contact" verb, and because 'kill' involves an intrinsic state, viz. 'dead,' it cannot combine with other verbs in causative constructions, e.g.

  (5) a.   Zhang San ba Li Si sha-si le.
           Zhang San p.t. Li Si kill-die asp
           (Zhang San killed Li Si.)

    b.   *Zhang San ba Li Si sha-tong le.
          Zhang San p.t. Li Si kill-painful asp
          (*Zhang San killed Li Si and hurt him.)

    c.   Zhang San ba Li Si da-si le.
          Zhang San p.t. Li Si hit-die asp
          (Zhang San hit Li Si and killed him.)

    d.   Zhang San ba Li Si da-tong le.
          Zhang San p.t. Li Si hit-painful asp
          (Zhang San hit Li Si and hurt him.)

'Hit,' on the other hand, does not imply any state, and one can cause various consequences through such an action, as seen in (c) and (d). (In fact, the verbs in the embedded sentence can be extremely varied, e.g. 'cry,' 'run,' 'sink,' etc.)

A second consequence of this difference is seen in the fact that when a Patient verb (i.e. Process-Action verb) is completed, successfulness of intention is implied, whereas a Goal verb does not have this property, e.g. in

  (6) a.   Ta shao-le shu le.
          he burn-asp book asp
          (He burned the book.)

      b.   Ta zhao-le shu le.
          he look-for-asp book asp
          (He looked for the book.)

the Agent accomplished what he set out to do in (a) but not in (b). The latter only indicates the completion of an attempted act and implies, in fact, a failure in what he set out to do. Observe the following continuations of (6),

  (7) a.   *Keshi mei shao-zhao.
          but Neg burn-s.p.
          (*But didn't manage to burn it.)

      b.   Keshi mei zhao-zhao.
          but Neg look-for-s.p.
          (But didn't manage to find it.)

'Zhao' is a "successful"-marker. ('Dao' is another.) Thus it is obligatory for Goal verbs to combine with a "successful"-marker when "success" is intended. Examples are

  (8) a.   Ta zhao-dao shu le.
          he look-for-s.p. book asp
          (He found the book.)

      b.   Ta deng-dao pengyou le.
          he wait-s.p. friend asp
          (He waited and met his friend.)

      c.   Ta na-dao shu le.
          he take-s.p. book asp
          (He got the book.)

      d.   Ta zu-dao fangzi le.
          he rent-s.p. house asp
          (He managed to rent a house.)

As we shall observe later, 'dao' also functions as "Goal"-marker. Even there, "successfulness" in obtaining the Goal is also anticipated. The "successful"-marker is specified in the following manner.

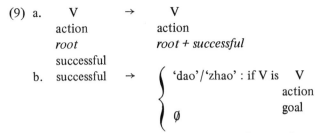

(9) a.   V   →   V
           action   action
           root   *root + successful*
           successful
     b.   successful   →   { 'dao'/'zhao' : if V is   V
                                                          action
                                 ∅   goal

The feature "successful" is introduced as an inflectional unit, similar to "perfective," "progressive," "non-volitional'" etc. (cf. Chafe 1970, Chapter 13).

On the other hand, when 'dao' occurs, although restrictedly, with Patient (but never interchangeable with 'zhao' in this context) it indicates 'non-volitional" (accidental), e.g.

(10) a.   Ta ge-dao tade shou-zhi.
           he cut-reach his finger
           (He cut his finger.)
     b.   Wo chi-dao yi-ge yingyingde dongxi.
           I eat-reach one-AN hard-x-m.p. thing
           (I bit on something hard.)
     c.   Bie shao-dao wode yifu.
           don't burn-reach my clothes
           (Don't burn my clothes.)

The occurrence of this "accidental"-marker is not allowed with verbs which are purely "volitional," such as 'zhu' — 'cook,' 'ba' — 'pull up,' and 'mo' — 'sharpen,' as seen in the following unacceptable sentences,

(11) a.   *Ta zhu-dao ren-jiade fan.
           he cook-reach others' rice
           (He accidentally cooked someone else's rice.)
     b.   *Ta mo-dao wode dao.
           he sharpen-reach my knife
           (He accidentally sharpened my knife.)

These two different 'daos' are subject to different constraints. In the first place, they occur with different types of adverbs, e.g.

(12) a.   Ta hao bu rongyi cai zhao-dao shu.
           he very Neg easy only-then look-for-reach book
           (He found his book with great difficulties.)
     b.   *Ta bu xiaoxin zhao-dao shu.
           he Neg careful look-for-reach book
           (*He carelessly found his book.)
     c.   *Ta hao bu rongyi cai ge-dao shou.
           he very Neg easy only-then cut-reach hand
           (*He cut his hand with great difficulties.)
     d.   Ta bu xiaoxin ge-dao shou.
           he Neg careful cut-reach hand
           (He carelessly cut his hand.)

The adverb in (a) and (c) refers to "effort" put into an attempt, hence compatible with "successful" but not "accidental," and the adverb in (b) and (d) refers to inattention, hence compatible with "accidental" but not "successful." Secondly, only "accidental" may occur in the imperative construction, e.g. (for examples of "accidental" occurring in imperative, refer to 10.c and d).

(13) a. *Bie deng-dao pengyou.
          don't wait-reach friend
          (*Don't manage to meet your friend.)
     b. *Bie na-dao shu.
          don't take-reach book
          (*Don't manage to get a book.)

Thirdly, only "successful" 'dao' may occur in the accusative construction, e.g. (detailed constraints ignored here)

(14) a. Ta ba shu zhao-dao le.
          he p.t. book look-for-reach asp
          (He found his book.)
     b. *Ta ba yingyingde dongxi chi-dao le
          he p.t. hard-x-m.p. thing eat-reach asp
          (He bit on something hard.)

Notice that the fact here seems to contradict our observation about the constraints on the accusative construction (cf. table 1). However, the constraints stated there are applicable only to simple verb constructions. Sentences in (14) involve verb complex. We have stated that the verb 'buy' does not occur in this construction but compare the pairs of sentences below,

(15) a. *Wo ba shu mai le.
          I p.t. book buy asp
          (I bought the book.)
     b. Wo ba shu mai-hui-lai le.
          I p.t. book buy-back-come asp
          (I bought the book back.)
     c. *Wo ba pengyou jie le.
          I p.t. friend meet asp
          (I met my friend.)
     d. Wo ba pengyou jie-hui-lai le.
          I p.t. friend meet-back-come asp
          (I met my friend and brought him back.)

In (a) and (c), the verbs are simple Goal Action verbs, and the objects play the role of Goal. They do not undergo any change-of-state, and thus do not occur in the accusative. In (b) and (d), an additional element, viz. 'back,' is added to the Goal verb, and 'back' involves "locational displacement," which is a type of change-of-state. Accusativization in these cases is in reference to 'back,' not 'buy' or 'meet.' Sentences in (14) should be understood in the same way.

The last difference to be discussed here has to do with a construction, in which activity and result are stated separately, not within the verb-compound itself. This is an extremely productive construction, comprising resultative and extent manner adverbs of various kinds, e.g.

(16) a. Ta zuotian kai che kai de hen kuai.
          he yesterday drive car drive extent very fast
          (He drove his car very fast yesterday.)

b. Ta zuotian kai che kai de hen lei.
    he yesterday drive car drive extent very tired
    (He drove yesterday so that he was tired.)
c. Ta zuotian kai che kai lei le.
    he yesterday drive car drive tired asp
    (Yesterday he was tired from driving.)

In (c), for instance, 'kai che' — 'drive car' refers to activity and 'kai-lei' — 'drive-tired' refers to result. Similarly, "successful," but not "accidental," may occur in this construction,

(17) a. Ta zhao shu zhao-dao le.
         he look-for book look-for-reach asp
         (He looked for his book and found it.)
     b. *Ta ge shou ge-dao le.
         he cut hand cut-reach asp
         (*He was cutting his hand and cut it.)

This may be due to the fact that the activity phrase has to refer to "intentional" activities, and in "non-violitional" or "accidental" events there is no activity involved as far as the Agent is concerned. "Accidental" events are always reported as resultative sentences.

What we have seen in connection with 'dao' is that it can only refer to "accidental" when occurring with Patient. We have also seen that it can refer to "successful" with Goal. However, "accidental" 'dao' is also compatible with Goal, provided that the verb in question is not restricted to "intentional" activities. In the following sentences with Goal, 'dao' specifies "accidental,"

(18) a. Ta bu xiaoxin da-dao wode tou.
         he Neg careful hit-reach my head
         (He hit my head by accident.)
     b. Ta bu xiaoxin cai-dao wode jiao.
         he Neg careful tread-reach my foot
         (He trod on my foot by accident.)

Range does not occur with either "successful" or "accidental" 'dao,' e.g.

(19) a. *Ta chang-dao ge le.
         he sing-reach song asp
         (*He sang a song by accident.)
     b. *Ta zuo-dao meng le.
         he make-reach dream asp
         (*He managed to dream.)

Thus the feature "accidental" is specified as below, (accidental = non-volitional)

(20) a.   V   →   V   / if V ≠ V
         action   action   action
         root   *root + accidental*   range
         accidental
     b. accidental →   'dao'

As remarked above (cf. 4), Patient is in all cases defined in terms of change-of-state, while Goal in some cases (with such verbs as 'hit,' 'feel,' 'kick,' etc.) is defined in terms of "contact." Because of this nature of Goal, it is often difficult to distinguish it from real Locative, especially when the latter is "objectivized." First, compare the difference between Patient and Goal in this respect. In

(21) a.   Ta da Li Side tou.
          he hit Li Si's head
          (He hit Li Si's head.)
     b.   Ta yi-quan da-zai Li Side tou-shang.
          he one-fist hit-l.v. Li Si's head-top
          (He hit Li Si's head with his fist.)
     c.   Ta ti Li Side tou.
          he kick Li Si's head
          (He kicked Li Si's head.)
     d.   Ta yi-jiao ti-zai Li Side tou-shang.
          he one-foot kick-l.v. Li Si's head-top
          (He kicked Li Si's head with his foot.)

(22) a.   Ta sha-le Li Si.
          he kill-asp Li Si.
          (He killed Li Si.)
     b.   *Ta yi-dao sha-zai Li Side xong-shang.
          he one-knife kill-l.v. Li Si's chest-top
          (*He killed Li Si on his chest with a knife.)
     c.   Ta qie-le yude weiba.
          he cut-asp fish's tail
          (He cut the fish's tail.)
     d.   *Ta yi-dao qie-zai yude weiba-shang.
          he one-knife cut-l.v. fish's tail-top
          (*He cut the fish on the tail with a knife.)

The objects in (21.a) and (c) are Goal, which in turn have Locative counterparts, as given in (b) and (d). The objects in (22) are Patient, which lack Locative counterparts. (21.b) and (d) can be understood in two ways: 'fist' and 'foot' can be conceived of as either Instrument or Patient. In the latter interpretation, they undergo locational displacement and terminate at Li Si's head. These two interpretations are not mutually exclusive. In fact, these two nouns play double-roles. We can understand Li Si's head as the location where 'fist' and 'foot' fall, and at the same time as the recipient of the activities executed with these Instruments.

We may specify the property of these Goal verbs as this: 'hit' means 'apply the fist (or other items) at' and 'kick' 'apply the foot (necessarily so) at.' Then the question whether the object of these verbs is Goal or Locative becomes immaterial, since "recipient" and "location" in this case converge in meaning.[1]

Objectivized Locatives as exemplified in (23) do not specify any Patient which undergoes locational displacement and which is relatable to a recipient. At the most, we can only conceive of the Agents as such Patients.

_____

[1] A possible candidate as the Cognate Instrument of 'sit' is seen in
(i)   Ta yi-pigu zuo-zai shafa-shang.
      he one-bottom sit-l.v. sofa-top
      (He sat on the sofa.)
Can we define 'sit' as 'apply the bottom to?' However, it seems that 'yi-pigu' here can also be understood as a manner adverb.

(23) a. Ta shui da chuang.
      he sleep big bed
      (He'll sleep on the big bed.)
   b. Wo zuo shafa.
      I sit sofa
      (I'll sit on the sofa.)

There is a significant difference between Goal and Objectivized Locative. While Goal cannot be locativized without the occurrence of Patient (i.e. Cognate Instrument. cf. Chapter 6, Section 4), objectivized Locative cannot occur with one, e.g. (no deletion should be assumed.)

(24) a. *Ta da-zai Li Side tou-shang.
      he hit-l.v. Li Si's head-top
      (He hit on Li Si's head.)
   b. *Ta yi-shen shui-zai da chuang-shang.
      he one-body sleep-l.v. big bed-top
      (*He is sleeping on the big bed with his body.)

Our discussion in this section is to contrast Transitivity Goal of Action verbs with other roles, especially Patient. They have been shown to reflect different semantic as well as syntactic characteristics.

4. Goal and Causer

All the objects in the following sentences may qualify as Transitivity Goal, according to our definition given so far,

(1) a. Ta hen teng xiaohar.
      he very fond-of child
      (He is very fond of children.)
   b. Ta hen xihuan pao-che.
      he very like sportscar
      (He likes sportscar very much.)
   c. Ta hen pa mingtiande kaoshi.
      he very afraid-of tomorrow's exam
      (He is scared of tomorrow's exam.)
   d. Wo hen houhui zhe-jian shi.
      I very regret this-AN thing
      (I regret this.)

Patients above are all in some kind of emotional state, and such emotions are defined in relation to another party, i.e. Goal in our framework. However, there are differences among the State verbs given in (1). Let us refer to the verbs in (a) and (b) as "active State" and those in (c) and (d) as "passive State." "Passive" in the sense that the emotions are formed within the Patient due to external causation. "Active" States, on the other hand, specify voluntary involvement of the Patient. Observe the difference in the following sentences,

(2) a. *Xiaohar jiao ta hen teng.
      children make he very fond
      (*Children make him very fond.)

b.   *Pao-che jiao ta hen xihuan.
sportscar make he very like
(*Sportscars make him very like.)

c.   Mintiande kaoshi jiao ta hen haipa.
tomorrow's exam make he very afraid
(Tomorrow's exam makes him very scared.)

d.   Zhe-jian shi jiao wo hen houhui.
this-AN thing make I very regret
(This makes me regret.)

The Goal of "active" States cannot function as Causer (cf. Chapter 4, Section 4), while that of "passive" States can.

This indicates that Goal in (1.c) and (d) also plays the role of Causer. More examples are given below.

(3) a.   Ta hen peifu Li Xiansheng.
he very admire Li Mr.
(He admires Mr. Li.)

b.   Li Xiansheng jiao ta hen peifu.
Li Mr. Make he very admire
(Mr. Li makes him admire.)

In addition to 'jiao,' 'ling' and 'shi' may also function as Causer verbs. In many cases, Goal and Causer are not identified, as seen below,

(4) a.   Ta hen chongbai Ma Ke Si.
he very worship Marx
(He workships Marx.)

b.   Gemingde chenggong shi ta hen chongbai Ma Ke Si.
revolution's success cause he very worship Marx.
(The successfulness of the revolution makes him worship Marx.)

c.   *Ta hen chongbai gemingde chenggong.
he very worship revolution's success
(He worships successfulness of revolutions.)

In (b), Causer co-occurs with Goal, and when they are not identified, Causer may not occur as Goal, as indicated by (c).

Furthermore, for some verbs, only Causer is allowed, e.g.

(5) a.   Wode chengji jiao ta hen shiwang.
my grades make he very disappointed
(My grades made him disappointed.)

b.   *Ta hen shiwang wode chengji.
he very disappointed my grades
(He is very disappointed with my grades.)

c.   *Ta hen jiaoao tade chengjiu.
he very proud his achievement
(He is proud of his achievements.)

This observation, however, has to be modified if we bring Circumstantial Goal into the picture, since precisely what cannot occur as Transitivity Goal (b and c) occurs as Circumstantial Goal, i.e.

(6) a. Ta dui wode chengji hen shiwang.
   he to my grades very disappointed
   (He is very disappointed with my grades.)

   b. Ta dui tade chengjiu hen jiaoao.
   he to his achievement very proud
   (He is very proud of his achievements.)

This casts doubt on the validity of differentiating Circumstantial and Transitivity Goals in these cases. Note further that what we referred to earlier as Transitivity Goal in (1.c) and (d) can also occur in prepositional phrases,

(7) a. Ta dui mingtiande kaoshi (juede) hen haipa.
   he to tomorrow's exam (feel) very afraid
   (He is scared of tomorrow's exam.)

   b. Wo dui zhe-jian shi (juede) hen houhui.
   I to this-AN thing (feel) very regret
   (I regret this.)

(1.a) and (b), on the other hand, lack prepositional conterparts,

(8) a. *Ta dui xiaohar hen teng.
   he to child very fond
   (*He is very fond of children.)

   b. *Ta dui pao-che hen xihuan.
   he to sportscar very like.
   (*He likes sportscar very much.)

Thus the Goal in (1.a) and (b) is fundamentally quite different from that in (c) and (d). The former is closely related to Causer.

We shall, therefore, postulate that the objects in (1.a) and (b) play the role of Transitivity Goal and those in (c) and (d) objectivized Circumstantial Goal. The latter is related to (i.e. sometimes playing the role of) Causer on the one hand and may be realized as Circumstantial Goal (i.e. governed by prepositions) on the other.

In Chapter 2, Section 5, we have observed that Transitivity relations are obligatorily specified by verbs while Circumstantial relations are in general optionally specified. This is true with State verbs taking Transitivity and Circumstantial Goals. Thus most verbs taking the latter may occur "intransitively," e.g. (cf. 1)

(9) a. *Ta hen teng.
   he very fond
   (*He is fond.)

   b. Wo hen houhui.
   I very regret
   (I am remorseful.)

Furthermore, while most verbs taking Circumstantial Goal may be embedded under 'feel,' none taking Transitivity Goal is observed to occur in this environment,

(10) a. *Ta juede hen teng.
   he feel very fond
   (*He feels fond.)

   b. Ta juede hen houhui.
   he feel very regret
   (He feels remorseful.)

Under discussion in this section are only State verbs. State verbs are found to occur with Goal, Transitivity or Circumstantial, but Source seems to be absent from the system of relations here, as indicated by the ungrammatical (11.b), (see next section for one rare case of Source with State verbs)

(11) a.   Zhang San gen Li Si shengqi.
          Zhang San with Li Si angry
          (Zhang San is angry with Li Si.)
     b.   *Zhang San cong Li Si shengqi.
          Zhang San from Li Si angry
          (*Zhang San is angry from Li Si.)

(a) above indicates that Zhang San is the Patient of anger and Li Si is the recipient of Zhang San's anger. What is intended in (b) is that Zhang San is the recipient of Li Si's anger (i.e. suffering Li Si's anger). This contrast is available with Action verbs. Compare (11) with (12) below,

(12) a.   Zhang San mài-gei Li Si yi-ben shu.
          Zhang San sell-give Li Si one-AN book
          (Zhang San sold a book to Li Si.)
     b.   Zhang San gen Li Si mǎi-le yi-ben shu.
          Zhang San with Li Si buy-asp one-AN book
          (Zhang San bought a book from Li Si.)

Put roughly, Zhang San in (a) gives a book to Li Si, while in (b) he receives a book from Li Si. Thus Action verbs can be either "outward" or "inward," as will be discussed in detail later. State verbs, on the other hand, are always "outward," i.e. never taking a Source.

Causer of State verbs comes closest to Source of Action verbs, in that it specifies the origin which initiates (or stimulates) a Patient's mental condition. Observe that in the sentences below,

(13) a.   Ta hen ke pa.
          he very-able afraid
          (He is frightening.)
     b.   Ta hen ke ai.
          he very-able love
          (He is lovable.)
     c.   Zhe hen ke xi.
          this very-able pleased
          (This is pleasing.)

the subjects are not Patient but Causer-Goal (e.g. in (a) he arouses fear in others towards him, i.e. he makes people afraid of him). They are not conceived of as in any state, but rather they are the cause for other's mental states. To draw an analogy again from Action verbs, if A sells something to B, we can, for the same event, claim that B buys something from A. A in both cases defines Source and B Goal. Similarly, with State verbs, if A likes B, B is pleasing to A. A in both cases defines Patient and B Causer-Goal. The only difference in (13) is that Patient is not specified. Unspecified Patient is also seen below,

(14) a.   Tade lian zhen pa ren.
          his face real afraid person
          (His face is really frightening.)

b. Zhe-jian shi zhen qi ren.
    this-AN thing real angry person
    (This thing is really annoying.)

"Unspecified" in this particular instance refers to "virtual." "Actual" Patient is not allowed in this construction, e.g.

(15) a. *Ta hen ke pa wo.
          he very-able afraid I
          (*He is frightening to me.)
     b. *Tade lian zhen pa wo.
          his face real afraid I
          (*His face really frightens me.)

We can account for this by stating that if Patient is present, it must be realized as subject, i.e.

(15) c. Wo hen pa ta.
          I very afraid he
          (I am afraid of him.)
     d. Wo zhen pa tade lian.
          I real afraid his face
          (I am really scared of his face.)

What is shown in (13) and (15) is that in Causative-State constructions, Causer and Patient do not co-occur. Interesting cases, however, are exemplified by the following two sentences,

(16) a. Wo hen tao yan ta.
          I very-able disgust he
          (I find him disgusting.)
     b. Wo hen ke lian ta.
          I very-able pity he
          (I pity him.)

As pointed out above, most State verbs taking Circumstantial Goal may occur intransitively, and, in that case, verbs may occur with Patient only, e.g.

(17) a. Wo hen manyi zhe-jian shi.
          I very satisfied this-AN thing
          (I am satisfied with this.)
     b. Wo hen manyi.
          I very satisfied
          (I am satisfied.)
     c. *Zhe-jian shi hen manyi.
          this-AN thing very satisfied
          (*This is satisfied.)

Now, if sentences in (16) are analyzed identically with (17.a), that is, the subject specifies Patient and Object Goal, we cannot account for the peculiarity below,

(18) a. *Wo hen tao yan. (as related to 16.a)
          I very-able disgust
          (I am disgusting.)

    b.   Ta hen tao yan.
         he very-able disgust
         (He is disgusting.)
    c.   *Wo hen ke lian. (as related to 16.b)
         I very-able pity
         (*I am pitiful.)
    d.   Ta hen ke lian.
         he very-able pity
         (He is pitiful.)

Moreover, the objects in (16) occur as Causer below

(19) a.   Ta zhen ling ren tao yan.
         he real make person-able disgust
         (He is really disgusting.)
     b.   Ta zhen ling ren ke lian.
         he real make person-able pity
         (He is really pitiful.)

This is again unique. 'Ke' or 'tao' governing a state has the property of arousing a state within a Patient directed back at the Causer. Since they express causative already, they are not further embedded in a causative construction, as evidenced below, (cf. 13)

(20) a.   *Ta zhen ling ren ke pa.
         he real make person -able afraid
         (*He is really frightening.)
     b.   *Ta zhen ling ren ke ai.
         he real make person -able love
         (*He is really lovable.)

We may postulate the basic meaning of 'tao-yan' and 'ke-lian' as follows,

(21) a.   tao-yan: A has a quality such that A arouses 'loathing' in B for A.
     b.   ke-lian: A has a quality such that A arouses 'pity' in B for A.

The second and third occurrences of A here are necessary specifications of such constructions. The second A defines the Causer and the third defines the Goal, since A plays a double-role. This double-role property is absent in purely causative constructions, such as seen in (14).

In most cases, e.g. in (13), A is present and B absent (implying a general reference), and, furthermore, it is obligatory for A to be realized as the surface subject. However, in (16), both A and B are present, and B is realized as the subject. Instead of postulating a Psyche movement (cf. Postal 1968) which inverts the order of A and B, we may simply account for the fact by adopting Fillmore's hierarchy of subjectivization (1968). Patient is ranked higher than Goal in the subject selection, and just in case Patient is absent Goal can be made the subject.

Viewed from the historical angle, 'ke-pa' — 'fear-arousing' represents an older stage, while 'ke-lian' — 'pity-arousing' represents a change. Verbs such as 'fear' and 'hate' preserve the opposition 'pa vs. ke-pa,' etc., but 'lian' alone to mean 'pity' has ceased to be productive.

5. Circumstantial Goal and Source

The role Circumstantial Goal defines the italicized items below,

(1) *State verbs*:
    a. Ta chang gen *Li Si* shengqi.
        he often with Li Si angry
        (He is often angry with Li Si.)
    b. Ta dui *lishi* you xingqu.
        he to history have interest
        (He is interested in history.)
    c. Ta qian *wo* qian.
        he owe I money
        (He owes me money.)

(2) *Process verbs*:
    a. Wo shu (gei) *ta* san-kuai qian.
        I lost (give) he three-AN money
        (I lost three dollars to him.)
    b. Wo-guo you bai-gei *Riben* le.
        we-country again defeat-give Japan asp
        (Our country lost to Japan again.)
    c. Chuan chen-dao *hai-li*-gu le.
        ship sink-reach sea-inside-go asp
        (The ship sank to the bottom of the sea.)

(3) *Action verbs*:
    a. Wo gen *ta* shuo le.
        I with he speak asp
        (I talked to him.)
    b. Wo bu jie *ta* qian.
        I Neg loan he money
        (I won't lend him money.)
    c. Niao wang *shu-shang* fei.
        bird towards tree-top fly
        (The bird flew towards the tree.)
    d. Niao fei-dao *shu-shang*.
        bird fly-reach tree-top
        (The bird flew to the tree.)

And the role Source defines the italicized items below,

(4) *State verbs*: (rare)
    a. Zhe-jian shi, ni shi cong *shei-nar* zhidao de?
        this-AN thing, you be from who-there know m.p.
        (Where did you learn this from?)

(5) *Process verbs*:
    a. Qingwa shi cong *kedou* bian-lai de.
        frog be from tadpole change-come m.p.
        (Frogs come from tadpoles.)
    b. Wo cong *ta-nar* ying-le san-kuai qian.
        I from he-there win-asp three-AN money
        (I won three dollars from him.)

c.   Ta cong *Li Si-nar* chuanran-dao zhe-ge bing.
     (He caught this illness from Li Si.)

(6) *Action verbs*:

a.   Ta xiang gen *Li Si* jie qian.
     he think with Li Si loan money
     (He would like to borrow money from Li Si.)

b.   Ta cong *jiangtai* tiao-dao di-shang.
     he from platform jump-reach floor-top
     (He jumped down to the floor from the platform.)

c.   Women dei xiang *ta* xuexi.
     we have-to towards he learn
     (We must learn from him.)

One of the characteristics of Circumstantial relations is that they are in general governed by prepositions (relational markers) although they may be occasionally objectivized. They are specified in the Diagram O (the procedure for Source largely omitted).

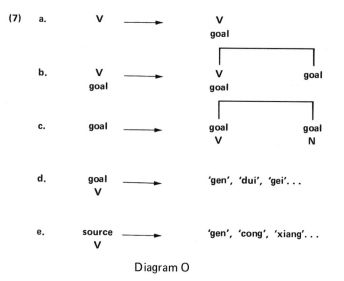

Diagram O

The selection of Goal-verb or Source-verb (i.e. prepositions) is largely lexically determined and sometimes free (i.e. some prepositions are interchangeable), though some generalizations are possible. For example, 'gen' and 'dui' can both take concrete nouns but only 'dui' can take abstract nouns, e.g. (cf. 1.a-c)

(8) a.   Ta dui xuesheng hen yan.
         he to student very strict
         (He is strict to students.)

b.   Ta dui kaoshi hen yan.
     he to exam very strict
     (He is strict in exams.)

c.   Ta gen xuesheng hen yan.
     he with student very strict
     (He is strict to students.)

    d.   *Ta gen kaoshi hen yan.
        he with exam very strict
        (*He is strict to exams.)

'cong' in general takes place or time nouns only (5.a is a rare exception), and 'gen' to mean roughly the same thing cannot take place nouns, e.g.

  (9) a.   Wo cong ta-nar (*ta) na-le san-ben shu.
           I from he-there (*he) take-asp three-AN book
           (I got three books from him.)
      b.   Wo gen ta (*ta-nar) yao-le san-ben shu.
           I with he (*he-there) want-asp three-AN book
           (I got three books from him.)

Important, however, is the opposition between 'wang' — 'towards' and 'dao' — 'to, reach' (cf. 3.d and e). Both indicate the terminal point of a locational displacement, but while the former refers to "intended" or "projected" Goal, the latter refers to "reached" Goal. Thus in the sentences

  (10) a.   Wo yao wang Niuyue kai.
           I want towards New York drive
           (I want to drive towards New York.)
      b.   Wo yao kai-dao Niuyue.
           I want drive-reach New York
           (I want to drive to New York.)

the agent in (b) has New York as the destination, while the Agent is non-committal in (a), that is, New York may be the destination, or else the intended destination is somewhere along the general direction of New York. Differences are also clear in various environments. When 'le' is present, e.g.

  (11) a.   Ta wang Niuyue kai le.
           he towards New York drive asp
           (He drove towards New York.)
      b.   Ta kai-dao Niuyue le.
           he drive-reach New York asp
           (He already drove to New York.)

the intended journey is started in (a) but is completed in (b), and when time-reference is present, e.g.

  (12) a.   Wo jin-wan dei wang Niuyue kai.
           I tonight must towards New York drive
           (I must drive towards New York tonight.)
      b.   Wo jin-wan dei kai-dao Niuyue.
           I tonight must drive-reach New York
           (I must drive to New York tonight.)

the Agent has to arrive at New York in (b) by the time indicated, but no such necessity is implied in (a).

Examples above illustrate the "projected" meanings of 'wang.' The property of "intended" as opposed to "reached" is shown below,

(13) a.   Ta wang qiang-shang yi-tiao.
           he towards wall-top one-jump
           (He jumped up at the wall.)
      b.   Ta tiao-dao qiang-shang.
           he jump-reach wall-top
           (He jumped to the top of the wall.)

(a) reports an attempted activity and (b) the result of an activity. These two aspects are not incompatible, thus the utterance of (a) can be directly followed by (b). Moreover, "intention" and "result" do not have to coincide, as illustrated by the sentence

(13) c.   Ta xiang ju-rende yao yi-dao kan-guo-qu, keshi zhi kan-dao tade jiao.
           he towards giant's waist one knife slash-over-go, but only slash-reach his leg
           (He slashed at the giant's waist, but only got his leg.)

Source and Goal are conjunctively specified; thus they may co-occur more often with Action verbs than with Process verbs and never, it seems, with State verbs. Examples are given below,

(14) a.   Niao cong shu-shang fei-dao di-shang (agt-pat)
           bird from tree-top fly-reach floor-top
           (The bird flew to the ground from the tree.)
      b.   Qiu cong zhuo-shang diao-dao di-shang (pat)
           ball from table-top fall-reach floor-top
           (The ball fell down to the floor from the table.)
      c.   *Ta cong Zhang San-nar dui zhe-jian shi hen manyi.
           he from Zhang San-there to this-AN thing very satisfied
           (*He is very satisfied with this from Zhang San.)

Source and Goal here are specified on the spatial dimension. They can also be specified on the temporal dimension, but only in the context of Action verbs, e.g.

(15) a.   Niao cong zaoshang fei-dao wanshang.
           bird from morning fly-reach evening
           (The bird flew from morning to evening.)
      b.   *Qiu cong zaoshang diao-dao wanshang.
           ball from morning fall-reach evening
           (*The ball fell from morning to evening.)

However, this constraint can be re-stated as follows. Temporal Source and Goal may only modify "durative" verbs (Jespersen's "non-conclusive" 1924), not "terminative" verbs (Jespersen's "conclusive"). While Process verbs are necessarily "terminative," Action verbs are sub-categorized into "durative" (e.g. 'fly,' 'cry,' and 'sing') and "terminative" (e.g. 'give,' 'touch,' and 'return'). The example below shows that "terminative" Action verbs may not co-occur with temporal Source and Goal,

(15) c.   *Wo song ta shu, cong shangwu song-dao xiawu.
           I give he book, from morning give-reach afternoon
           (*I gave him a book from the morning till the afternoon.)

Duration references fall within the same constraint, e.g.

(16) a. Niao fei-le san-ge zhong-tou le.
      bird fly-asp three-AN hour asp
      (The bird has been flying for three hours.)

    b. *Qiu diao-le san-ge zhong-tou le.
      ball fall-asp three-AN hour asp
      (*The ball has been falling down for three hours.)

When time references do occur with "terminative" verbs, they do not refer to the duration (or progression) of the events, but the lapse of time since the events have been terminated,

(17) a. Ta si-le liang-ge yue le.
      he die-asp two-AN month asp
      (He has been dead for two months.)

    b. Ta hui-lai liang-ge yue le.
      he back-come two-AN month asp
      (He has been back for two months.)

To capture these similar constraints as seen in (15) and (16) in a more systematic way, we may postulate that the time references in (15) are not Source and Goal but a sub-type of "duration" which specifies both the initial and terminal points. When this type of "duration" co-occurs with "duration" proper, it seems to stand in an "apposition" relation with the latter, e.g.

(18) a. Niao cong jiu-dian dao shi-dian fei-le yi-ge zhong-tou.
      bird from 9-o'clock reach 10-o'clock fly-asp one-AN hour
      (The bird flew for one hour from 9 o'clock to 10 o'clock.)

Furthermore, it also co-occurs with spatial Source and Goal,

    b. Niao cong jiu-dian dao shi-dian zhi fei-dao Zhijiage.
      bird from 9 o'clock reach 10 o'clock only fly-reach Chicago
      (The bird flew as far as Chicago only, from 9 o'clock to 10 o'clock.)

    c. Wo cong jiu-dian dao shi-dian zhi cong di-yi ye kan-dao wu-shi ye.
      I from 9 o'clock reach 10 o'clock only from first page read-reach fiftieth page
      (I read only from page 1 to page 50, from 9 o'clock to 10 o'clock.)

Unless the alternative analysis is adopted, we would have to specify Source and Goal twice in the underlying structure, in order to account for (18.b) and (c).

6. Goal and Benefactive

The italicized items in the following sentences

(1) a. Ta xiang song *Zhang San* yi-ben shu.
      he think give Zhang San one-AN book
      (He would like to give Zhang San a book.)

    b. Ta mai-le yi-ben shu gei *Zhang San*.
      he buy-asp one-AN book give Zhang San
      (He bought a book for Zhang San.)

    c.   Ta gei *Zhang San* da-le yi-ge dianhua.
        he give Zhang San hit-asp one-AN telephone
        (He telephoned Zhang San.)

are designated as Beneficiary (Halliday 1967a and Chafe 1970) or Dative (Fillmore 1968 and Y.C. Li 1971). These nouns play the role of Beneficiary in the sense that they "benefit from the process expressed in the clause" (Halliday 1967a:53). Whether Beneficiary nouns always "benefit" (positively or negatively) is open to question. It seems that the Beneficiary noun in (c) is quite neutral to this property. Even if we extend the definition of Beneficiary to designate "recipient," we still confront problems. Note that (1.a) is a case of Beneficiary which occurs as "indirect object," and (b) as well as (c) are cases of "adjunct" Beneficiary. In English at least, "indirect object" and "adjunct" are in many cases transformationally relatable. Details aside, what is claimed is that a surface-structure "indirect object" usually defines Beneficiary (cf. Halliday 1967a:58 for a statement similar to this). However, while the Beneficiary in (1.a) and (b) can be said to be "recipient," the following indirect objects are not to be analogously characterized

    (2) a.   Wo xiang qiu ni yi-jian shi.
             I think beg you one-AN thing
             (I would like to beg a favour of you.)
        b.   Ta na-le ni ji-ben shu?
             he take-asp you how-many-AN book
             (How many books did he take from you?)

But rather, they define Source, from which objects are removed. It is inadequate to characterize these two opposing properties by means of a single notion of Beneficiary.

    Indirect objects, then, are characterizable as either Goal, the recipient, or Source, the giver (only very loosely). In many cases, they find adjunct counterparts, e.g.

    (3) a.   Wo jie ta qian. (goal)
             I loan he money
             (I lent him money.)
        b.   Wo jie qian gei ta.
             I loan money give he
             (I lent money to him.)
        c.   Bie shou ta qian. (source)
             don't receive he money
             (Don't receive money from him.)
        d.   Bie gen ta shou qian.
             don't with he receive money
             (Don't receive money from him.)

Goal has additional properties. It may, as adjunct, occur either pre-verbally (1.c) or post-verbally (1.b). It may also be genitivized, when occurring as indirect object, e.g.

    (4) a.   Ta sheng Zhang Sande qi.
             he form Zhang San's angry
             (He is angry with Zhang San.)
        b.   Wo kai tade wanxiao.
             I open his joke
             (I played a joke on him.)

So far, we have presented 'gei' – 'give' as a Goal marker. In fact, it has another quite distinct property. The following sentences are ambiguous,

(5) a.   Wo gei ta xie-le yi-feng xin.
         I give he write-asp one-AN letter
         (I wrote a letter to/for him.)
    b.   Wo gei ta kai-le yi-zhang zhipiao.
         I give he open-asp one-AN check
         (I wrote a check for him.)

'He' in both cases can refer either to the recipient or to the person on behalf of whom an act has been executed. Although in both interpretations 'I' is the Agent, it acts as a "substitute" in the latter. We shall refer to 'he' in this function as Benefactive. Our Benefactive corresponds to Fillmore's Benefactive.

In addition to 'on behalf of," Benefactive also characterizes 'for the benefit of,' as seen in the following sentences which cannot have the Goal interpretation,

(6) a.   Laoshi gei xuesheng jieshi.
         teacher give student explain
         (The teacher is explaining to students.)
    b.   Yisheng gei bing-ren kan bing.
         doctor give patient look illness
         (Doctors treat patients.)

Here the Agent does not do something in place of the Benefactive noun due to the inability of the latter (for whatever cause), but rather he is engaged in an activity such that the Benefactive noun may benefit from the process involved. As is obvious from (6), the activities in question are not usually conceived of as within the capacity of the Benefactive nouns.

While 'gei' as 'on behalf of' can be replaced by 'ti' – 'substitute,' 'gei' as 'for the benefit of' cannot, e.g.

(7) a.   Wo ti ta xie xin.
         I substitute he write letter
         (I'll write a letter for him.)
    b.   *Laoshi ti xuesheng jieshi. (as related to 6.a)
         teacher substitute student explain
         (*The teacher is explaining for students.)

On the other hand, 'wei' – 'for the sake of' occurs in many cases of 'for the benefit of' but not 'on behalf of'

(8) a.   *Wo wei ta xie xin. (as related to 7.a)
         I for he write letter
         (*I am writing for him.)
    b.   Zhengfu wei ren-min fuwu.
         government for people serve
         (The government serves people.)

(a) here may mean 'I'm writing a letter concerning his interest,' which is quite distinct from (7.a). A Sub-type of 'for the benefit of' is seen below,

(9) a. Wo gei ni kan ge dongxi.
I give you look AN thing
(I'll show you something.)

b. Ta zai gei gou xi-zao.
he p.v. give dog bath
(He is bathing a dog.)

c. Wo gei ni chuan yifu.
I give you put-on clothes
(I'll dress you.)

A major difference between this type and the other types of Benefactive is that the Agent in (9) is not directly involved in the activities concerned. While if (6.a) and (7.a) are true, then (10.a) and (10.b) must necessarily be true, the same cannot be said between (9.b) and (10.c),

(10) a. Laoshi zai jieshi.
teacher p.v. explain
(The teacher is explaining.)

b. Wo zai xie xin.
I p.v. write letter
(I'm writing a letter.)

c. Ta zai xi-zao.
he p.v. bath
(He is taking a bath.)

Rather, when (9.b) is true, (d) below is also true,

d. Gou zai xi-zao.
dog p.v. bath
(The dog is having a bath.)

Nonetheless, while (11.a) is true, (b) is ungrammatical,

(11) a. Ta gei gou xi erduo.
he give dog wash ear
(He is washing the dog's ears.)

b. *Gou xi erduo.
dog wash ear
(*The dog is washing its ears.)

This peculiarity may be attributed to the particular type of objects which 'wash' takes. In (9.b), 'bath' plays the role of Range, whereas 'ear' in (11.a) plays the role of Patient. As we have observed in Chapter 6, Verb-Range compounds often constitute closed units (i.e. not subject to various types of transposition). This may mean that while 'wash' is a two-place predicate, Range, being an extension of the verb property, does not qualify as an argument. Thus the compound 'xi-zao' — 'lit. wash-bath' requires the specification of another argument in addition to Agent, namely Patient. This is quite plausible, since we understand in (10.c) that the Agent is washing himself. (Note that it can be translated in English also as 'He is washing himself.') I shall leave it open whether the Benefactive nouns in (9.b) and possibly (11.a) are more feasibly analyzed as Patient.

Let us now look at the syntactic differences between Goal and Benefactive. Firstly, as we have noted in (1.b) and (c), Goal may occur either pre-verbally or post-verbally, in many cases at least, but Benefactive occurs only pre-verbally. Thus while sentences in (5) are ambiguous, their post-verbal counterparts are unambiguous, only meaning Goal, i.e.

(12) a. Wo xie-le yi-feng xin gei ta.
         I write-asp one-AN letter give he
         (I wrote him a letter.)
     b. Wo kai-le yi-zhang zhipiao gei ta.
         I open-asp one-AN check give he
         (I wrote him a check.)

Therefore, since (13.a) can only refer to Benefactive, (b) is ungrammatical,

(13) a. Qing ni gei ta kai men.
         please you give he open door
         (Please open the door for him.)
     b. *Qing ni kai men gei ta.
         please you open door give he
         (*Please open the door for him.)

On the other hand, when alternative positioning is not available for Goal in a particular instance, it can only occur post-verbally, e.g.

(14) a. Ta song gei Zhang San yi-ben shu.
         he give give Zhang San one-AN book
         (He gave Zhang San a book.)
     b. *Ta gei zhang San song yi-ben shu.
         he give Zhang San give one-AN book
         (*He gave Zhang San a book.)

We can account for these facts by the following postulation. In the transformational component of the grammar, unmarked linearization process positions Goal post-verbally and Benefactive pre-verbally, but there is an optional transformation available to Goal in some cases which pre-poses Goal. (Source only occurs pre-verbally.)

This difference between Benefactive and Goal corresponds exactly to that between outer Locative and inner Locative, in that outer Locative occurs only pre-verbally while inner Locative occurs in most cases post-verbally and, in some cases, pre-verbally, as shown below,

(15) a. Ta zai wu-li xiuxi. (outer)
         he l.v. house-inside rest
         (He is resting in his room.)
     b. *Ta xiuxi zai wu-li.
         he rest l.v. house-inside
         (He is resting in his room.)
     c. Shu dao-zai di-shang. (inner)
         tree fall-l.v. floor-top
         (A tree fell on the ground.)
     d. *Shu zai di-shang dao.
         tree l.v. floor-top fall
         (*A tree fell on the ground.)

Secondly, while Goal may occur in the accusative construction, Benefactive is not observed in this context, e.g.

(16) a. Ta ba qian jie gei Zhang San.
          he p.t. money loan give Zhang San
          (He lent money to Zhang San.)
      b. *Ta ba men kai gei Zhang San.
          he p.t. door open give Zhang San
          (*He opened the door for Zhang San.)

We may also account for the ungrammaticality of (b) in terms of the general property of Benefactive that it could not occur post-verbally.

The same principle explains the difference below,

(17) a. Ta song gei Zhang San de shi shu.
          he give give Zhang San m.p. be book
          (What he gave Zhang San was a book.)
      b. *Ta kai gei Zhang San de shi men.
          he open give Zhang San m.p. be door
          (*What he opened for Zhang San was a door.)

In this section, we have discussed the various properties of nouns governed by 'gei' — 'give.' Primarily, they are characterizable as either Goal or Benefactive. Ambiguity between them, though not frequent, can be resolved by various tests.

7. "Outward" and "Inward" Verbs

There are two groups of verbs which exhibit opposing selections of Source and Goal as well as directional references. First, observe that in the following sentences, 'learn' can only take Source and 'teach' only Goal,

(1) a. Ta gen Zhang San xue Yingwen.
         he with Zhang San learn English
         (He is learning English with Zhang San.)
     b. *Ta xue Zhang San Yingwen.
         he learn Zhang San English
         (*He learns English from Zhang San.)
     c. Zhang San jiao ta Yingwen.
         Zhang San teach he English
         (Zhang San is teaching him English.)
     d. *Zhang San gen ta jiao Yingwen.
         Zhang San with he teach English
         (*Zhang San teaches English from him.)

We shall say 'learn' is an "inward" verb and 'teach' an "outward" verb. Next, 'buy' is compatible with the directional reference 'lai' — 'come' but incompatible with 'qu' — 'go,' whereas 'sell' is just the opposite, as seen below,

(2) a. Zhe jiu shi wo mǎi-hui-lai de che.
         this just be I buy-back-come m.p. car
         (This is the car I bought.)
     b. *Nei-ge jiu shi wo mǎi-hui-qu de che.
         that-AN just be I buy-back-go m.p. car
         (*That is the car I bought.)

   c.   Wo xiang ba che mài-chu-qu.
        I think p.t. car sell-out-go
        (I would like to sell my car.)
   d.   *Wo xiang ba che mài-jin-lai.
        I think p.t. car sell-in-come
        (*I would like to sell my car.)

The object of 'buy' must be directed "inward" towards the Agent, while that of 'sell' must be directed "outward" away from the Agent. Again, we shall refer to the former as an "inward" verb and the latter an "outward" verb. A sample of each category is given below,

   (3) a.   *inward*:   b. *outward*:
          mǎi — buy   mài — sell
          wen — ask   gaosu — tell
          yao — request   gei — give
          xue — learn   jiao — teach
          qu — fetch   song — deliver
          ying — win   shu — lose

On the other hand, verbs such as 'jie' — 'borrow/lend,' 'zu' — 'rent/let,' and 'na' — 'bring/take' are direction-free and thus take Goal or Source freely,

   (4) a   Ta gen Zhang San jie qian.
         he with Zhang San loan money
         (He borrowed money from Zhang San.)
     b.   Zhang San jie qian gei ta.
         Zhang San loan money give he
         (Zhang San lent him money.)

    Let us next examine whether the opposition of "inward" and "outward" is semantically primitive or is reducible into such relations as Goal and Source. Can we hypothesize that when the identity of Agent and Goal occurs, "inward" verbs are realized, whereas "outward" verbs obtain when the identity of Agent and Source occurs?

    For example, in this alternative postulation, 'buy' and 'sell' will be collapsed into just one verb of monetary transaction, so that the sentences

   (5) a.   Zhang San gen Li Si mai che.
         Zhang San with Li Si buy car
         (Zhang San bought a car from Li Si.)
     b.   Li Si ba che mai gei Zhang San.
         Li Si p.t. car sell give Zhang San
         (Li Si sold a car to Zhang San.)

share the same underlying structure as given in Figure 25.

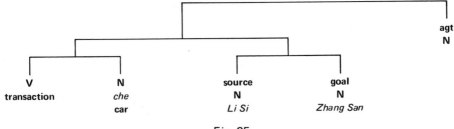

Fig. 25

If Agent in Figure 25 is specified as Zhang San, (5.a) results, but if it is specified as Li Si, (b) results.

In addition to accounting for the features "inward" and "outward," this approach has the advantage of capturing the tendency in Chinese that "inward" and "outward" interpretations of verbs are in many cases largely situational, rather than inherent as given in (3), in that many verbs are "direction-free," e.g. 'jie' — 'loan,' 'zu' — 'rent,' 'na' — 'transport,' 'shu' — 'import/export,' and 'dai' — 'lead.' To say that 'jie' — 'loan' is ambiguous in Chinese between "inward" — 'borrow' and "outward" — 'lend' is intuitively unsatisfactory.

Nonetheless, the following observations point to the infeasibility of this alternative and strongly support the postulation of "inward" and "outward" as primitive features. Firstly, many "inward" verbs may further accept a separate Goal, not identified with the Agent himself,

(6) a. Wo gen ta jie yidiar qian gei ni.
        I with he loan little money give you
        (I'll borrow some money from him to give you.)
    b. Ni qu gen taitai yao yidiar fan gei ta.
        you go with mistress want little rice give he
        (Go and get some rice from the mistress to give him.)

This means that verbs in (3.a) are not necessarily Agent=Goal verbs. Other verbs such as 'learn' have to specify Agent as Goal,

(7) a. *Wo qu gen ta xue Yingwen gei ni.
        I go with he learn English give you
        (*I'll go and learn English from him for you.)
    b. *Wo qu wen ta yi-ge wenti gei ni.
        I go ask he one-AN question give you.
        (*I'll go and ask him a question to give you.)

Therefore, if "inward" verbs are redefined as Agent=Goal verbs, sentences in (6) cannot be accounted for. On the other hand, if "inward" is postulated as a feature of these verbs, we have available a mechanism to specify that some 'inward' verbs require Agent=Goal.

The same is true with "outward" verbs,

(8) a. *Wo gen ta mài yi-ben shu gei ni.
        I with he sell one-AN book give you
        (*I'll sell you a car from him.)
    b. *Wo gen ta shu gei ni yi-kuai qian.
        I with he lose give you one-AN money
        (*I lost one dollar to you from him.)
(9) a. Ta ba Zhang San cong zhuozi-shang yi-tui.
        he p.t. Zhang San from table-top one-push
        (He pushed Zhang San from the table.)
    b. Ta cong Zhongguo ba shu ji-dao Meiguo.
        he from China p.t. book mail-reach U.S.
        (He mailed a book to the U.S. from China.)

Secondly, note that 'car' in Figure 25 is intentionally left unspecified as regards semantic roles. In fact, it cannot be specified in that postulation, since it is Transitivity

Goal in (5.a) but Patient in (b). It is entirely ad hoc attempting to derive nouns of two different semantic roles from one and the same element in the underlying structure.

It may be argued that the objects of "inward" and "outward" verbs should receive identical relations, and the differences between them (cf. Section 3 of this chapter) can be accounted for by Source and Goal. For example, in

(10) a. Wo ba yaoshi gei-le ta le.
  I p.t. key give-asp he asp
  (I gave the key to him.)
  b. *Wo ba yaoshi gen ta yao le.
  I p.t. key with he want asp
  (I asked him for the key.)

the non-occurrence of 'key' in the accusative construction (b) is not due to its being Transitivity Goal but because the Agent is Goal. Again, this is not workable. Note that the verb in (4.c) is "inward" (in that context) and that in (4.d) is "outward," but the object in both sentences occurs in the accusative construction, since 'book' is Patient in both, in our framework. The same situation is seen below,

(11) a. Ta ba yizi yi-la. (inward)
  he p.t. chair one-pull
  (He gave the chair a pull.)
  b. Ta ba yizi yi-tui. (outward)
  he p.t. chair one-push
  (He gave the chair a push.)

The difference between Transitivity Goal and Patient is independent of Goal and Source, but is lexically determined. The difference between "inward" and "outward" is also defined in the same way.

For these reasons, we postulate "inward" and "outward" as selectional features of verbs. The requirement of identity between Agent and either Source or Goal further sub-categorizes these verbs, as given below, (the arrow specifies "require" and slashed arrows "not require")

(12) *"Inward" verbs*:
  a. Agent → Source: xue-'learn,' wen-'ask,' qiu-'beg'.
  b. Agent ↛ Source: mǎi-'buy,' yao-'want, ask for,' ying-'win,' la-'pull.'
(13) *"Outward" verbs*:
  a. Agent → Goal: mài-'sell,' shu-'lose,' jie-'lend,' jiao-'teach.'
  b. Agent ↛ Goal: ji-'mail,' tui-'push,' ti-'kick,' gan-'chase out.'

8. Three Dimensions of Directional Reference

In the last section, we have remarked that "inward" and "outward" verbs require opposing sets of directional reference. More examples are given below for easy reference,

(1) a. Wo ba ni tui-xia-qu, hao bu hao?
  I p.t. you push-down-go, good Neg good
  (Shall I push you down?)
  b. *Wo ba ni tui-xia-lai, hao bu hao?
  I p.t. you push-down-come, good Neg good
  (*Shall I push you towards me?)

    c.   Wo ba ni la-xia-lai, hao bu hao?
        I p.t. you pull-down-come, good Neg good
        (Shall I pull you down?)
    d.   *Wo ba ni la-xia-qu, hao bu hao?
        I p.t. you pull-down-go, good Neg good
        (*Shall I pull you (away from me)?)

'Push' is an "outward" verb and is compatible only with 'qu' — 'go,' while 'pull' is "inward" and requires 'lai' — 'come.' However, this selection is very often violated, as seen in the sentences

    (2) a.   Ta ba shitou tui-xia-qu le.
             he p.t. rock push-down-go asp
             (He pushed the rock down.)
      b.   Ta ba shitou tui-xia-lai le.
             he p.t. rock push-down-come asp
             (He pushed the rock down.)
      c.   Ta ba Li Si la-xia-lai le.
             he p.t. Li Si pull-down-come asp
             (He pulled Li Si down.)
      d.   Ta ba Li Si la-xia-qu le.
             he p.t. Li Si pull-down-go asp
             (He pulled Li Si down.)

In this section, we shall develop a set of three dimensions to account for the differences between (1) and (2). These three dimensions are given in (3),

    (3) a.   Dimension of Agent.
        b.   Dimension of speaker.
        c.   Dimension of addressee.

    Firstly, when an Agent is engaged in such activities as 'push,' 'pull,' 'buy' and 'sell,' he can only push something outward, pull something inward, etc. Let us say that in 'push,' the Agent "identifies" himself with Source (but is not necessarily Source), whereas he "identifies" himself with Goal in 'pull.' Now when such activities are viewed from the point of view of another party, what is "outward", e.g. for the Agent, may be "inward" or "outward" for the other party, depending on where he is and to whom he is reporting the activities.

    In (1), the Agent and Patient are intentionally specified as the first person and the second person respectively. This arrangement has the effect of forcing the identity between the Agent and the speaker as well as between the Patient and the addressee. In this way, 'push' and 'pull' are reported from the point of view of the Agent himself. The ungrammaticality of (b) and (d) indicate that 'push' is "outward" for the Agent and 'pull' "inward."

    In (2), the Agent is the third person, so that the speaker cannot be the Agent, and moreover, there is a separate addressee. Whereas 'come' and 'go' in (1) are Agent-oriented, they are speaker-oriented in (2). In (2.a), the rock must be pushed away not only from the Agent but from the speaker also, and in (2.b) the rock is pushed away from the Agent but towards the speaker. The same difference holds for (c) and (d),

Next, in the sentences

(4) a. Wo ba shitou tui-xia-qu, hao bu hao?
        I p.t. rock push-down-go, good Neg good
        (Shall I push the rock down?)
    b. Wo ba shitou tui-xia-lai, hao bu hao?
        I p.t. rock push-down-come, good Neg good
        (Shall I push the rock down?)

the Agent is also the speaker (the first person), but 'push' may take either 'come' or 'go,' contradicting the case in (1). The difference lies in the addressee. He is "identified" (i.e. speaker's Goal is the addressee's Goal, etc.) with the speaker in (1) but is not necessarily identified in (4). (b) unambiguously means that the addressee is away from the speaker but the rock will be pushed towards the addressee. Thus 'come' here is addressee-oriented. (a) is ambiguous, with 'go' either speaker-oriented or addressee-oriented.[2]

Even when Agent is in the third person, reference can still be made in the dimension of the addressee. This is demonstrated below,

(5) a. Zhang San ba shitou tui-xia-qu, hao bu hao?
        Zhang San p.t. rock push-down-go, good Neg good
        (May Zhang San push the rock down?)
    b. Zhang San ba shitou tui-xia-lai, hao bu hao?
        Xhang San p.t. rock push-down-come, good Neg good
        (May Zhang San push the rock down?)

Thus either of the following two sentences

(6) a. Xiaoxin, shitou diao-xia-gu le.
        careful, rock fall-down-go asp
        (Careful, the rock is falling down.)
    b. Xiaoxin, shitou diao-xia-lai le.
        careful, rock fall-down-come asp
        (Careful, the rock is falling down.)

---

[2] This sentence is subject to different interpretations with different speakers. To some, (a) can only refer to the rock being pushed away from the direction of the addressee. To these speakers, then, both (a) and (b) are necessarily addressee-oriented. To others, (a) is either addressee- or speaker-oriented. That 'go' as in (a) may be addressee-oriented or speaker-oriented is proved by the pair of sentences (talking to someone downstairs)
  (i) Wo mashang ba shu na-xia-lai gei ni.
       I immediately p.t. book take-down-come give you
       (I'll bring the book down immediately to you.)
  (ii) Wo mashang ba shu na-xia-qu gei ni.
       I immediately p.t. book take-down-go give you
       (*I'll take the book down immediately to you.)

can be uttered in one and the same event, depending on whether the motion of the rock is viewed as speaker-oriented (a) or addressee-oriented (b). This freedom of dimension-shifting is particularly great in telephone conversations, such as

> (7) a.   Ni yao wo mashang dao ni-nar qu/lai a?
>   you want I immediately reach you-there go/come particle
>   (You want me to come to you right now?)
>   b.   Haode, wo mashang jiu lai.
>   good-m.p., I immediately just come
>   (Yes, I'll be coming.)

although the addressee-dimension may be preferred in (a).

Sentences are not often uttered in the Agent's dimension, since linguistic communication usually takes place between the speaker and the hearer. Moreover, we can say that unmarked communication is conducted in the speaker's dimension. This unmarked dimension overrides that of the Agent's (2.b) and the addressee's (6.a).

It is clear from our brief discussion that grammaticality of sentences is correlative to contexts of communication. A sentence may be grammatical in one dimension, ungrammatical in another, and even ambiguous in yet another.

The specification of 'go' and 'come' (as verb suffixes in the surface structure) in each dimension may be formulated as in Diagram P (e.g. for the same event concerning 'pull').

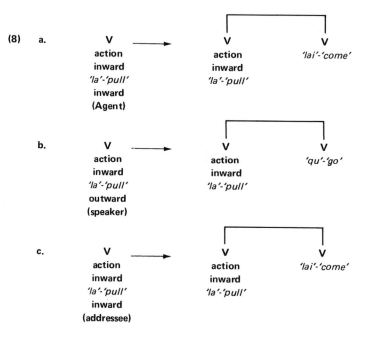

Diagram P

Note that we are postulating two sets of "inward" and "outward," one (above the lexical item) as intrinsic selectional feature, (this is what differentiates 'push' from 'pull'), and the other (below the lexical item) as inflectional feature (not of the verb as such, but referring to the movement of whatever undergoes "locational displacement"). One set is lexically, the other contextually determined. The only constraint which holds between the two is between the selectional features and inflectional features in the Agent's dimension. They have to agree in all cases. Thus, for example, if a verb is inherently "inward," it can only be inflected as "inward" in the Agent's dimension, but may be "inward" or "outward" in the other two dimensions.

APPENDIX

Verb Classification

In the preceding chapters, we have postulated three major classes of verbs, viz. Action, State, and Process (see Chapter 4, Section 1 for a complete discussion of these), as well as a set of Transitivity relations (see Chapter 3, Section 3 for a summary of these relations). The various configurations of these verb features and noun relations further sub-classify these three major classes. We shall now give a representative list of verb classification. Comparisons with Chao's (1968) and W. Wang's (1964) classifications will also be briefly presented.

Here is a summary of what has been discussed in various places throughout the preceding chapters. Readers are referred to relevant sections for fuller discussions.

1. SAMPLE CLASSIFICATION

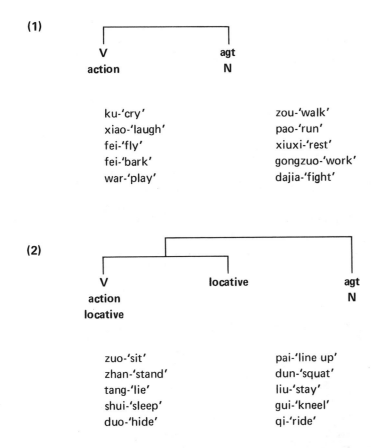

(1)

V	agt
action	N

ku-'cry'	zou-'walk'
xiao-'laugh'	pao-'run'
fei-'fly'	xiuxi-'rest'
fei-'bark'	gongzuo-'work'
war-'play'	dajia-'fight'

(2)

	locative	agt
V		N
action		
locative		

zuo-'sit'	pai-'line up'
zhan-'stand'	dun-'squat'
tang-'lie'	liu-'stay'
shui-'sleep'	gui-'kneel'
duo-'hide'	qi-'ride'

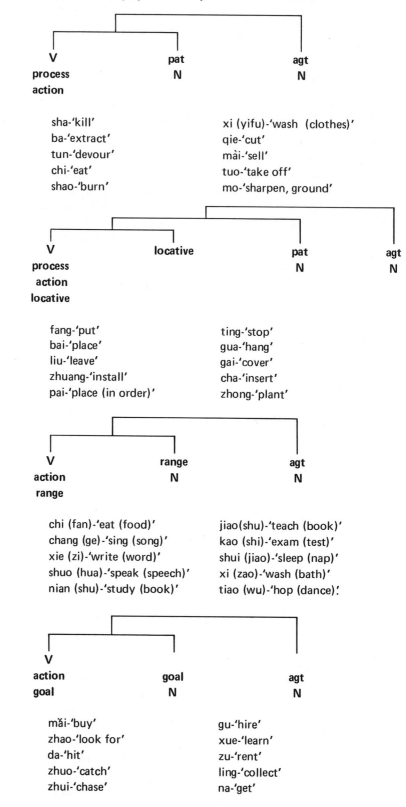

(3)

V   pat   agt
process   N   N
action

    sha-'kill'   xi (yifu)-'wash (clothes)'
    ba-'extract'   qie-'cut'
    tun-'devour'   mài-'sell'
    chi-'eat'   tuo-'take off'
    shao-'burn'   mo-'sharpen, ground'

(4)

V   locative   pat   agt
process   N   N
 action
locative

    fang-'put'   ting-'stop'
    bai-'place'   gua-'hang'
    liu-'leave'   gai-'cover'
    zhuang-'install'   cha-'insert'
    pai-'place (in order)' zhong-'plant'

(5)

V   range   agt
action   N   N
range

    chi (fan)-'eat (food)'   jiao(shu)-'teach (book)'
    chang (ge)-'sing (song)' kao (shi)-'exam (test)'
    xie (zi)-'write (word)'   shui (jiao)-'sleep (nap)'
    shuo (hua)-'speak (speech)' xi (zao)-'wash (bath)'
    nian (shu)-'study (book)' tiao (wu)-'hop (dance)'.'

(6)

V   goal   agt
action   N   N
goal

    mǎi-'buy'   gu-'hire'
    zhao-'look for'   xue-'learn'
    da-'hit'   zu-'rent'
    zhuo-'catch'   ling-'collect'
    zhui-'chase'   na-'get'

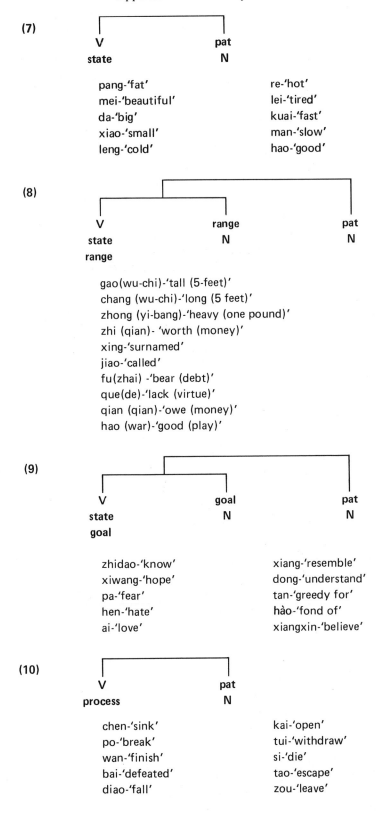

(7)

V — pat
state — N

pang-'fat'   re-'hot'
mei-'beautiful'   lei-'tired'
da-'big'   kuai-'fast'
xiao-'small'   man-'slow'
leng-'cold'   hao-'good'

(8)

V — range — pat
state — N — N
range

gao(wu-chi)-'tall (5-feet)'
chang (wu-chi)-'long (5 feet)'
zhong (yi-bang)-'heavy (one pound)'
zhi (qian)- 'worth (money)'
xing-'surnamed'
jiao-'called'
fu(zhai) -'bear (debt)'
que(de)-'lack (virtue)'
qian (qian)-'owe (money)'
hao (war)-'good (play)'

(9)

V — goal — pat
state — N — N
goal

zhidao-'know'   xiang-'resemble'
xiwang-'hope'   dong-'understand'
pa-'fear'   tan-'greedy for'
hen-'hate'   hào-'fond of'
ai-'love'   xiangxin-'believe'

(10)

V — pat
process — N

chen-'sink'   kai-'open'
po-'break'   tui-'withdraw'
wan-'finish'   si-'die'
bai-'defeated'   tao-'escape'
diao-'fall'   zou-'leave'

(11)

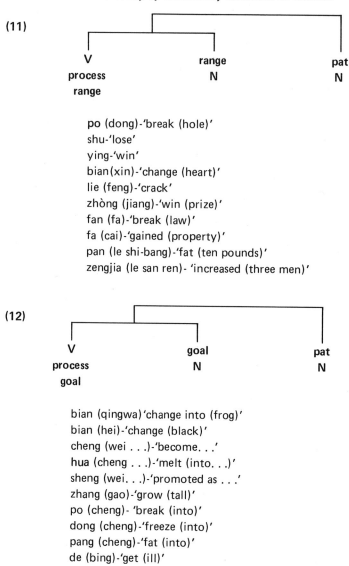

po (dong)-'break (hole)'
shu-'lose'
ying-'win'
bian(xin)-'change (heart)'
lie (feng)-'crack'
zhòng (jiang)-'win (prize)'
fan (fa)-'break (law)'
fa (cai)-'gained (property)'
pan (le shi-bang)-'fat (ten pounds)'
zengjia (le san ren)- 'increased (three men)'

(12)

bian (qingwa) 'change into (frog)'
bian (hei)-'change (black)'
cheng (wei . . .)-'become. . .'
hua (cheng . . .)-'melt (into. . .)'
sheng (wei. . .)-'promoted as . . .'
zhang (gao)-'grow (tall)'
po (cheng)- 'break (into)'
dong (cheng)-'freeze (into)'
pang (cheng)-'fat (into)'
de (bing)-'get (ill)'

The twelve categories above are inherent features of verbs given. Class-overlap (i.e. verb derivations) will be outlined in the next section.

2. Verb Derivations

(1)   V   V
     action   →   process
     root   action
                      root + causative

pao-'run' → pao(ma)-'run(horse)'
yao-'wave' → yao(tou)-'shake(head)'
dou-'fight' → dou(ji)-'fight(chickens)'

(2)   V   V
   state   →   process
   root   *root + inchoative*

      pang-'fat' → pang(le)-'gained'
      shou-'thin' → shou(le)-'lose'
      gao-'tall' → gao(le)-'grow'
      hao-'good' → hao(le)-'improved'
      liang-'cool' → liang(le)-'become cool'

(3)   V   V
   state   →   process
   root   action
                    root + inchoative + causative

      re-'hot' → re(fan)-'heat(rice)'
      e-'hungry' → e(ta)-'starve(him)'
      tang-'hot' → tang(yifu)-'iron(clothes)'

(4)   V   V
   process   →   process
   root   action
                    root + causative

      lai-'come' → lai(wan tang)-'bring(soup)'
      ting-'stop' → ting(che)-'stop(car)'
      tui-'withdraw' → tui(piao)-'return(ticket)'
      sheng-'lift' → sheng(qi)-'raise(flag)'
      kai-'open' → kai(men)-'open(door)'

The derived verbs given above are "incorporated" verbs. "Analytic" forms are more productive, as exemplified below ('nong' — 'causative marker'),

(5) a.   (=1)(rare)
      ku-'cry' → nong ku-'make cry'
      lai-'come' → nong lai-'make come'
      pao-'run' → nong pao-'make run'
   b.   (= 3)
      re-'hot' → nong re-'make hot'
      chang-'long' → nong chang-'make long'
      shou-'cooked' → nong shou-'make cooked'
   c.   (= 4)
      po-'break' → nong po-'make break'
      si-'die' → nong si-'make die'
      huai-'out of order' → nong huai-'make out of order'

The above derivations are across major verb classes. The derivations below remain in the same class but import additional semantic properties.

(6) "Non-volitional":
     V   V
     action   →   action
     root   *root + non-volitional*
     non-volitional

non-volitional
  qie-'cut' → qie-dao-'cut-reach'
  ge-'cut' → ge-dao-'cut-reach'
  shao-'burn' → shao-dao-'burn-reach'
  da-'hit' → da-dao-'hit-reach'
  cai-'tread' → cai-dao-'tread-reach'

(7) "Successful":

  V   V
  action   →   action
  root   *root + successful*
  successful
    mai-'buy' → mai-dao-'buy-reach'
    zhao-'look for' → zhao-dao-'find'
    deng-'wait' → deng-dao-'wait-reach'
    zu-'rent' → zu-dao-'rent-reach'
    kan-'look' → kan-dao-'look-reach, see'

These derivational features are postulated as inflections of verbs.

3. Other Semantic Categories

(1) "Affective" (disposal):

shao-'burn'	si-'tear'
mài-'sell'	tun-'swallow'
ban-'move'	chai-'dismantle'
bang-'tie, bind'	dao-'pour out'
qie-'cut'	he-'drink'

(2) "Effective" (creation):

gai-'build'	chao-'duplicate'
zao-'build'	xie-'write out'
zuo-'make'	pao(cha)-'make(tea)'

  feng(yifu)-'make(dress)'
  bao(jiaozi)-'wrap (chiaotsu)'
  zhe(zhi feiji)-'fold(paper airplane)'
  da(maoyi)-'knit(sweater)'

(3) "Inward":

mai-'buy'	tao-'beg'
xue-'learn'	la-'pull'
wen-'ask'	qu-(opposite of)'marry off'
qu-'collect'	jie-'meet and bring back'
ling-'collect'	yao-'request'

(4) "outward":

mai-'sell'	shang-'reward'
shuo-'tell'	jia-'marry off'
gei-'give'	tui-'push'
jiao-'teach'	gan-'drive off'
fa-'hand out'	tou-'throw'

4. Chao's Classification

The classification of verbs as presented in Chao (1968:665) is given below.

A. Intransitive.
1. Action: lai-'come'
2. Quality: da-'big'
3. Status: bing-'ill'
B. Transitive.
4. Action: chi-'eat'
5. Quality: ai-'love'
6. Classificatory: xing-'surnamed'
7. BE (shi)
8. HAVE (you)
9. Auxiliary: hui-'can'

5. Wang's Classification

Wang's classification (1964) is given below (re-organized for easy comparison and reference).

A. Vi.
1. Action: lai-'come'
2. Status: bing-'ill'
B. Vt.
3. Action: da-'hit'
4. Quality: pa-'afraid'
5. Classificatory: shi-'be', xing-'surnamed'
6. Perceptual: kan-'look'
7. Quotative: shuo-'say'
8. Telescoping: qing-'ask'
9. d-o-1 (double object): gaosu-'tell'
10. d-o-2: jiao-'call'
11. d-o-3: dang-'regard'
C. Adjectives: gao-'tall'
D. Auxiliary: hui-'can'

BIBLIOGRAPHY

(*)   — Distributed by the Indiana University Linguistics Club.
(**)   — In Chinese.
NSF   — National Science Foundation reports, Harvard University.
POLA — Project on Linguistic Analysis reports. First Series, University of Ohio, Columbus; Second Series, University of California, Berkeley.

Allan, Keith. 1971. A note on the source of 'there' in existential sentences. Foundations of Language 7:1-18.

Bach, Emmon, and Robert Harms (eds). 1968. Universals in linguistic theory. Holt, Rinehart, and Winston.

Boyd, Julian, and J.P. Thorne. 1969. The semantics of modal verbs. Journal of Linguistics 5:57-74.

Chafe, Wallace. 1967. Language as symbolization. Language 43:57-91.

——. 1968. Idiomaticity as an anomaly in the Chomskyan paradigm. Foundations of Language 4:109-127.

——. 1970. Meaning and the structure of language. University of Chicago Press.

——. 1971. Directionality and paraphrase. Language 47:1-26.

Chang, Kun. 1961. A grammatical sketch of late archaic Chinese. Journal of the American Oriental Society 81.3:299-308.

——. 1967a. Descriptive linguistics. In Sebeok (ed) 1967, 59-90.

——. 1967b. National languages. In Sebeok (ed) 1967, 151-176.

Chao, Yuen Ren. 1968. A grammar of spoken Chinese. University of California Press, Berkeley and Los Angeles.

Cheung, Hung-nin. 1973. A comparative study in Chinese grammars: the ba-construction. Journal of Chinese Linguistics 1.3:343-382.

Chomsky, Noam. 1965. Aspects of the theory of syntax. MIT Press

——. 1969. Deep structure, surface structure, and semantic interpretation. (*)

——. 1970. Remarks on nominalization. In Jacobs and Rosenbaum (eds) 1970, 184-221.

Chu, Chauncey C. 1973. The passive construction: Chinese and English. Journal of Chinese Linguistics 1.3:437-470.

Dean, Janet. 1968. Non-specific noun phrases in English. NSF-20.

Dragunov, A.A. 1952. Grammatical studies of modern Chinese. Chinese translation by Zheng Zu-qing. Peking: Kexue Chuban She. 1958.

Fillmore, Charles. 1968. The case for case. In Bach and Harms (eds) 1968, 1-88.

——. 1970. The grammar of Hitting and Breaking. In Jacobs and Rosenbaum (eds) 1970, 120-133.

——. 1971. Some problems for case grammar. Presented at the 1971 Georgetown Roundtable on Linguistics, Georgetown University, March 11, 1971.

Fodor, J.A. 1970. Three reasons for not deriving 'kill' from 'cause to die.' Linguistic Inquiry 1.4:429-438.

Fraser, Bruce. 1970. Idioms within a transformational grammar. Foundations of Language 6:22-42.

Frei, Henri. 1956. The ergative construction in Chinese: theory of Pekinese PA. Gengo Kenkyu 31:22-50 (Pt. 1), 32:83-115 (Pt. 2).

Gruber, Jeffrey. 1965. Studies in lexical relations. MIT Ph.D. dissertation.

_____. 1967. Look and see. Language 43.4:937-947.

Hall [Partee], Barbara. 1965. Subject and object in modern English. MIT Ph.D. dissertation.

Halliday, M.A.K. 1967a. Notes on transitivity and theme in English (Pt.1). Journal of Linguistics 3.1:37-81.

_____. 1967b. (Pt.2). Journal of Linguistics 3.2:199-244.

_____. 1968. (Pt.3). Journal of Linguistics 4.2:179-215.

Hashimoto, Anne. 1966. Embedding structures in Mandarin. POLA 1.12.

_____. 1969a. The verb 'to be' in modern Chinese. Foundations of Language supplementary series. Vol.9, Pt.4, 72-111.

_____. 1969b. The imperative in Chinese. Gengo Kenkyu 56:35-62.

_____. 1971a. Descriptive adverbials and the passive construction. Unicorn 7:84-93. (Princeton)

_____. 1971b. Mandarin syntactic structures. Unicorn 8.

Huddleston, Rodney. 1969. Some observations on tense and deixis in English. Language 45.4:777-806.

_____. 1970. Some remarks on case grammar. Linguistic Inquiry 1.4:501-511.

Huang, Shuan-fan. 1966. Subject and object in Chinese. POLA 1.13:25-103.

Jacobs, Roderick, and Peter Rosenbaum (eds). 1970. Readings in English transformational grammar. Ginn.

Jespersen, Otto. 1924. The philosophy of grammar. New York: Norton. 1965 edition.

Joos, Martin. 1964. The English verb. University of Wisconsin Press.

Karttunen, Lauri. 1968. What do referential indices refer to? (*)

_____. 1970. The logic of English predicate complement constructions. (*)

_____. 1971. Implicative verbs. Language 47.2:340-358.

Kiparsky, Paul, and Carol Kiparsky. 1970. Fact. In Progress in linguistics, Bierwisch and Heidolph (eds). 143-173. The Hague: Mouton.

Kuno, Susumu. 1970. Some properties of non-referential noun phrases. In Studies in general and Oriental linguistics (presented to Shiro Hattori), 348-373. Tokyo: TEC Co.

Lakoff, George. 1965. On the nature of syntactic irregularity. NSF-16.

_____. 1966. Stative adjectives and verbs in English. NSF-17.

_____. 1968a. Instrumental adverbs and the concept of deep structure. Foundations of Language 4.1:4-29.

_____. 1968b. Pronominalization and the analysis of adverbs. NSF-20.

_____. 1970. Linguistics and natural logic. Synthese 22:151-271.

Lakoff, George, and S. Peters. 1969. Phrasal conjunction and symmetric predicates. In Reibel and Schane (eds). 1969, 113-141.

Lee, Gregory. 1969. Subjects and agents. Working papers in linguistics 3:37-113.

Li, Charles. 1969. Semantics and three syntactic constructions in Chinese. Unpublished paper, UC Berkeley. (A portion of this paper was read at the Linguistic Society of America meeting, December, 1969, under the title "The semantics of the Passive (Bei) and Executive (Ba) constructions in Mandarin Chinese).

_____. 1971. Semantics and the structure of compounds in Chinese. Ph.D. dissertation, University of California, Berkeley.

Li, Ying-che. 1971. An investigation of case in Chinese grammar. South Orange: Seton Hall University Press.

_____. 1972. Sentences with BE, EXIST, and HAVE in Chinese. Language 48.3:573-583.

Lü, Shu-hsiang. 1942. Aspects of Chinese grammar. Shanghai: Commercial Press. (**)

_____. 1945. The scope of the usage of 'ge,' with notes on the deletion of 'yi' before classifiers. In Lü 1955, 69-94. (**)

_____. 1946. On the analysis of Chinese sentences viewed from the differences between subject and object. In Lü 1955, 95-124. (**)

_____. 1948. A study of the usage of Ba. In Lü 1955, 125-144. (**)

_____. 1955. Papers on Chinese grammar. Peking: Kexue Chuban She. (**)

Lyons, John. 1966. Towards a "notional" theory of the "parts of speech." Journal of Linguistics 2.2:209-236.

_____. 1967. A note on possessive, existential, and locative sentences. Foundations of Language 3:390-396.

McCawley, James. 1968. Lexical insertion in a transformational grammar without deep structure. In Papers from the Fourth Regional Meeting of Chicago Linguistic Society, 71-80.

Mullie, Joseph. 1932. The structural principles of the Chinese language. English translation by A.C. Versichel. Peking.

Palmer, F.R. 1968. A linguistic study of the English verb. University of Miami Press.

Perlmutter, David. 1968. Deep and surface structure constraints in syntax. MIT Ph.D. dissertation.

_____. 1970. The two verbs begin. In Jacobs and Rosenbaum (eds) 1970, 107-119.

Peters, Stanley, and Emmon Bach. 1968. Pseudo-cleft sentences. Unpublished paper, Texas.

Postal, Paul. 1968. Cross-over phenomena: a study in the grammar of coreference. Unpublished paper, IBM.

Reibel, David, and Sanford Schane (eds). 1969. Modern studies in English: readings in English transformational grammar. Prentice-Hall.

Rosenbaum, Peter. 1967. The grammar of English predicate complement constructions. Cambridge: MIT Press.

Ross, John. 1967. Auxiliaries as main verbs. Unpublished paper, MIT.

_____. 1970. On declarative sentences. In Jacobs and Rosenbaum (eds). 1970, 222-272.

Sebeok, Thomas (ed). 1966. Current trends in linguistics, Vol.III, Theoretical foundations. The Hague: Mouton.

_____. 1967. Current trends in linguistics, Vol.II, Linguistics in East Asia and South East Asia. The Hague: Mouton.

Tai, James H-Y. 1970. Coordination reduction. Ph.D. dissertation, Indiana University. (*)

_____. 1973a. Chinese as an SOV language. Papers from the Ninth Regional Meeting of Chicago Linguistic Society, 659-671.

_____. 1973b. A derivational constraint on adverbial placement in Mandarin Chinese. Journal of Chinese Linguistics 1.3:397-413.

Teng, Shou-hsin. 1969. Verb inflection constraints in complementation. Dec. Monthly Internal Memorandum, POLA, UC Berkeley.

_____. 1970. Comitative vs. phrasal conjunction. Papers in Linguistics 2.2:314-358.

_____. 1971a. On the relatedness of existential and locative sentences. First Annual California Linguistics Conference, Berkeley.

_____. 1971b. Some remarks on aspects in Mandarin. POLA 2.15.

_____. 1972a. An analysis of definite and indefinite. Summer Meeting of the Linguistic Society of America, Chapel Hill.

_____. 1972b. Direct discourse complementation and the imperative in Chinese. Mimeographed, University of Massachusetts, Amherst.

_____. 1972c. Possessive structures and evidence for predicative sentences in Mandarin. Fifth International Conference on Sino-Tibetan Language and Linguistics, Ann Arbor.

_____. 1973a. Negation and aspects in Chinese. Journal of Chinese Linguistics 1.1:14-37.

_____. 1973b. A constraint on comparative in Chinese. Sept. Monthly Internal Memorandum, POLA, UC Berkeley.

_____. 1973c. Negation in Chinese. Sixth International Conference on Sino-Tibetan Language and Linguistics, San Diego.

_____. 1973d. Verb classification and its pedagogical extensions. Annual Meeting of the Chinese Language Teachers Association, Boston.

_____. 1973e. Scope of negation. Journal of Chinese Linguistics 1.3.

_____. 1974a. Predicate movements in Chinese. Linguistic Society of America Summer Meeting, Amherst, July, 1974.

_____. 1974b. Double nominatives in Chinese: a case for sentence predicate. Language 50.4.

Thompson, Sandra. 1971. More on the imperative in Chinese. Mimeographed, UCLA.

_____. 1973a. Resultative verb compounds in Mandarin Chinese. Language 49.2:361-379.

_____. 1973b. Transitivity and the *ba* construction in Mandarin Chinese. Journal of Chinese Linguistics 1.2:208-221.

Thompson, Sandra and Charles Li. 1973. Co-verbs in Mandarin Chinese: verbs or prepositions? Sixth International Conference on Sino-Tibetan Language and Linguistics, San Diego.

T'sou, Benjamin. 1971. Studies in the phylogenesis of questions and diachronic syntax. Ph.D. dissertation, University of California, Berkeley.

_____. 1972. Morphophonemics vs. syntax: diachronic development in Chinese causatives. Fifth International Conference on Sino-Tibetan Language and Linguistics, Ann Arbor.

_____. 1973. The structure of nominal classifier systems. First International Conference on Austroasiatic Linguistics, Honolulu.

Wang, Huan. 1959. Ba-sentences and Bei-sentences. English translation in POLA 1.4:61-102.

Wang, Li. 1944. Theory of Chinese grammar. Shanghai: Commercial Press. (**)

_____. 1956. A definition of subject and its application in Chinese. In Yu Wen Hui Bian, Vol. 9:169-180. (**)

_____. 1957. Essentials of Chinese grammar. Shanghai. (**)

_____. 1958. Hanyu Shigao. Peking: Kexue Chuban She. (**)

Wang, Peter C-T. 1970. A transformational approach to Chinese ba and bei. Ph.D. dissertation, University of Texas, Austin.

_____. 1972. Additional support for the transformational approach to Mandarin ba and bei. Papers in Linguistics 5:422-433.

Wang, William S-Y. 1964. Some syntactic rules for Mandarin. Proceedings of the Ninth International Congress of Linguists, 191-202. Mouton.

_____. 1965. Two aspect markers in Mandarin. Language 41.3:457-470.

_____. 1967. Conjoining and deletion in Mandarin syntax. Monumenta Serica 26:224-236.

Weinreich, Uriel. 1966. Explorations in semantic theory. In Sebeok (ed). 1966.

Zhang, Xiu. 1956. On the system of tense and aspect of Chinese verbs. In Yu Fa Lun Ji, Vol. 1:154-174. (**)

Zimmer, Karl. 1964. Affixal negation in English and other languages. Word monograph 5.

INDEX

Romanization is in the Pin Yin system except where conventional form is called for.